FOR PUBLIC BENEFIT
Churches cared for by Trusts

FOR PUBLIC BENEFIT
Churches cared for by Trusts

Edited by Trevor Cooper

Ecclesiology Today · Issues 49 & 50 · 2014

ISSN: 1460-4213
ISBN: 978-0-946823-25-3

Published 2014 by the Ecclesiological Society
c/o The Society of Antiquaries of London
Burlington House
Piccadilly
London
WIV 0HS

The Ecclesiological Society is a registered charity.
Charity No. 210501.

www.ecclsoc.org

Ecclesiology Today

Journal of the
Ecclesiological Society

Contents

Issues 49 & 50 for
December 2013 & July 2014
published September 2014

Chairman's letter

Dear Fellow Member

Here is a jumbo volume of *Ecclesiology Today*, being the joint edition for December 2013 and July 2014. With this publication we have virtually caught up with our production cycle. The next edition will be dated December 2014, and we will do our best to keep to tempo and mail it to you in December or January.

This volume is devoted to church buildings owned or otherwise cared for by Trusts. It concentrates on churches which have not been converted for an alternative full-time use. Instead, these buildings have their interiors kept more or less intact, because someone, somewhere thinks they are worth keeping as they are, for public benefit.

There are a good number of such buildings: at least 435 Church of England churches alone are looked after in this way, and an unknown number of churches and chapels of other denominations and countries – an estimated 80 or more Church of Scotland churches, for example are cared for by single-building Trusts.

So these Trusts are looking after a significant proportion of our ecclesiastical heritage, and that proportion will grow in future.

There is enormous variety in this volume, both as regards the church buildings, and the groups looking after them, and we are grateful to the more than twenty authors who have contributed. I hope that you find something here to interest you. Perhaps, like me, you will emerge with a new respect for these Trusts, and the entrepreneurial, dogged and devoted spirit that shines through so many of their stories.

I would be very grateful to be notified of additional single-building church and chapel Trusts in England and Wales, using the contact address at the rear of this volume.

While this volume was in preparation, we heard the sad news of the death of the Revd Dr Michael Peel, the previous but one Chairman of Council. I did not know Michael well, but was always impressed with both his natural courtesy and deep knowledge of matters ecclesiological. I am pleased that Paul Velluet, who followed Michael as Chairman of Council, has been able to write a brief obituary to put on record something of Michael's life and work. Our sympathies go to his wife and family in their loss.

Trevor Cooper
Chairman of Council

Introduction: the what and why of Church Trusts

Trevor Cooper

THIS VOLUME CONCENTRATES on churches cared for by charitable Trusts, where the Trust has full repairing responsibility for the building, and the purpose of the Trust is the long-term preservation of the building for public benefit.

Hundreds of historic church and chapel buildings no longer needed for worship are already cared for by Trusts (see Table 1, overleaf). Over the coming years it is likely that fewer church buildings will be needed for regular worship and Trusts are likely to take over the care of some of the more historic ones. In addition, as discussed later, Trusts may have a role looking after churches which are not being closed.

So we need to ask, how well does the Trust model work? What does it mean for the buildings? Where does the money come from? Are these Trusts sustainable? Is this a model which deserves to be rolled out more widely?

As will become clear, I believe that the answers are broadly positive. The model most certainly can work, and often does. But there are issues, some of them systemic, which need to be borne in mind.

This introduction attempts to pull out some of the themes emerging from the individual chapters in this volume. After a brief survey of the types and numbers of Trusts, I will discuss single-building Trusts looking after closed churches, then look more briefly at multi-building Trusts, and will finally discuss whether Trusts might look after churches which are still open.

A quick word about scope. All specialist multi-building Trusts are included. Amongst the single-building Trusts, I have concentrated on Trusts looking after Church of England buildings in a 'quiet' way, a term explained later. Within these, a few estate churches are included (chapters 10 and 22), though I have not made any particular effort to track them down. I have excluded ruins, and proprietary and private chapels. I have somewhat regretfully excluded buildings owned by the National Trust or English Heritage, and also those which have been physically moved to a museum; regretfully, as they may well have something to teach us about interpreting these buildings to visitors.

Types and numbers

The Trusts fall into two types. The first is multi-building Trusts, each of which cares for a number of closed churches or chapels. They are described in Part 1 of the volume. Between them these multi-building Trusts look after some 455 churches and chapels of all denominations, across Great Britain (Table 1).

The second type is the single-building Trust, a local (often a

Table 1: Number of churches and chapels looked after by charitable Trusts in England and Wales

	England		Wales		Scotland	
	CofE	*Free, RC, etc*	*Anglican*	*Free, RC, etc*	*Anglican*	*Free, RC, etc*
The Churches Conservation Trust	343					
Friends of Friendless Churches	18	5	21			
Ipswich Historic Churches Trust	4					
Norfolk Churches Trust	12	1				
Norwich Historic Churches Trust	18					
Scottish Redundant Churches Trust					1	6
Welsh Religious Buildings Trust				6		
The Historic Chapels Trust		20				
Total	*395*	*26*	*21*	*6*	*1*	*6*
Single-building Trusts ('Quiet' buildings: see note)	40+	5+	5+	2+	?	80–100

CofE = Church of England; Free = Free Churches; RC = Roman Catholic. For the first eight rows, see the relevant chapters in this volume.

Note: The figures for single-building Trusts in England and Wales are of those known to me and are certainly an underestimate. As explained in the text, these are 'quiet' buildings: that is, I have excluded buildings routinely in use. For single-building Trusts in Scotland, see Chapter 7 in this volume, p.87.

community) Trust looking after just one church or chapel. A number of single-building Trusts looking after Church of England (CofE) buildings are described in Part 2 of the volume, along with a few other single-building organisations of interest. There are further examples in the Appendix to this introduction, including a number of non-CofE examples. The figures in the Table for this type of Trust will certainly be an underestimate, as no one holds a reliable master list for England and Wales; the Scottish figures may be more accurate.

Adding up the first column in the Table shows that there are 435 Church of England buildings known (by me) to be looked after by Trusts. To put this in context, this is almost a quarter of the Church of England churches which have been closed since 1969. These Trust churches would form a good-sized diocese.

Single-building Trusts and closed churches

In this section I will discuss single-building Trusts looking after closed CofE churches. Tracking down the various Trusts has been difficult, but I have been in contact with a reasonable number, and some of these conversations led to the chapters in Part 2 of the book, on which this part of the Introduction is based.

Selection of 'quiet' churches

My focus has been those Trusts which are directly responsible for repairs and insurance and all other running costs of the building. Except in a few instances of particular interest, I have not included cases where the Trust is responsible for only part of the building, or has no direct responsibility for it.

For this investigation I have been most interested in cases where the closed church is being looked after for its own sake, in a 'quiet' way, respecting the original use of the building, rather than being converted to provide a new income-generating purpose. So I have for the most part excluded cases where the interiors have been purposefully converted to generate revenue – for example, converted to a theatre, a cafe, an exhibition space, rehearsal studio, concert hall, bookstore, museum, heritage centre, village hall, and so on. Such buildings rely on a quasi-commercial business model for long-term sustainability, and although relatively common and important as a model, the issues are rather different from those which interested me in this study, where I wanted to look at 'quiet' churches with no obvious source of income. Perhaps not surprisingly, the majority of my 'quiet' churches are rural.

These Trusts vary. But they often have points in common. For example, they do not seem very often to be looking after Grade I buildings, perhaps because churches of such importance have tended to go to other caretakers. There are exceptions: Mickfield (chapter 19), is one example. But on the whole these buildings have been saved because they are important to people locally, whatever their grade of listing.

Mostly these Trusts lease their buildings from the diocese at a peppercorn rent, rather than own them freehold. The buildings have usually been freed of the legal effects of consecration, which would otherwise have restricted their use – this is, incidentally, a purely legal move: there is no 'service of deconsecration'. There are, however, different arrangements between the Trusts over graveyards (which can be costly to maintain) and regarding access (see for example Wattisham, chapter 27).

Use of the buildings

Given that I had selected these single-building Trusts because they looked after their buildings in a 'quiet' way, I fully expected their approach to be rather conservative, taking on the building as they found it, and freezing it more or less unchanged.

But I was wrong. I was often told of pew removal, and of kitchenettes, toilets and other facilities being introduced when the Trust took the building over, or of the wish to do this in future. Some, such as Melton Old Church Trust (chapter 18), seem to have introduced facilities well before this became fashionable. Others, such as Sibton (an unusual Friends group, chapter 24) have introduced neat solutions in sensitive spaces. Some, of course, have left the building as it is, for example at Brampton Old Church (chapter 12). On the whole, these 'quiet' Trusts take a pragmatic but cautious approach, avoiding dramatic change, yet often modifying the building to be usable on occasions.

The majority of these single-building Trusts hold a few services per year, at Christmas and other major festivals, the lease usually placing a restriction on how many services are held, presumably to avoid competition with a neighbouring parish.

I have the strong impression that many of those attending these services are not regular churchgoers: these are communal events. Also, of course, they raise funds. One has to ask, over the longer term will this habit of holding services die away as nostalgia for the past use of the building grows more distant? Will these 'quiet' church buildings eventually lose the associations originally attached to them and turn into quasi-concert-halls? My personal view is that this may happen, but only slowly. However I cannot help noticing that Southolt's Summer Service contains hymns, but little else requiring religious affirmation (chapter 25); and No Man's Heath (chapter 20) has found that visitors like simply to sit quietly in the decorated and candlelit church during the Christmas period. Perhaps these are early signs of change.

In some cases, such as Plumpton (chapter 21) the main use of the building seems to be holding services from time to time. But most Trusts use their building for a number of other fund-raising events during the year, such as lectures, music evenings, and film nights, a creative mix of activities designed to attract people and donations. Food and drink frequently make an appearance at these events, and as rapidly disappear.

No doubt there is the same mix of motivations as in most charitable fund raising. I sense that after the initial excitement of restoring the church (many churches are in bad condition when taken over – a subject in itself), the building itself acts as a firm reminder to continue with organising events. Gradually the events take on a life of their own, and seem often to be attended not by a small coterie of staunch 'regulars' but by people often living some distance away, with no deep commitment to the building. One side effect is that although these Trusts may sometimes have no formal local accountability (of the type that is typical of a village hall), most of them seem to be open and porous in their activities, and thus indirectly influenced by a wide group of stakeholders.

In talking to the more long-standing of the single-building Trusts, I sometimes received the impression that their purpose was slowly changing. The Trust may have been set up to block the sale or demolition of the building, or to maintain access to a churchyard. The initial aim, then, was often to keep memory alive by keeping the building available – though there are important exceptions, such as Warter (chapter 26). But as new blood came on board, and as the population turned over, this begun to seem less important and the use of the building for occasional community purposes grew in importance. I cannot prove this is happening and I may be wrong; but the reader may perhaps sense this change in some of the chapters.

The Trusts I spoke to are genuinely proud of their buildings and of their role in maintaining them for public benefit, and most make an effort to keep the buildings open, or name a keyholder. This is easier in those cases where the church is in the grounds of a house converted to a hotel, as at Bramhope (chapter 11), or Babington and Ettington, listed in the Appendix. But most of them are not marketed as 'destination' sites, and there is wide variation in the amount of interpretative material provided, such as guide books

Money

Money does not arrive by magic, and the need for it is clearly a major driving force. Some Trusts have a membership structure, but I was surprised how many do not, and rely instead on donations and people attending events via a mailing list.

The costs of maintaining the building are typically around four or five thousand pounds per year, some higher, some lower. As I have shown elsewhere, most churches only have large repair bills once every few decades, so a relatively low annual budget for repairs is not surprising. For the most part these Trusts are not putting money aside for future very large bills (one exception is Ickworth, chapter 17) and are by default assuming that they will find a way to raise very large sums of money when the need arises.

The cost of insurance was often mentioned. This is to insure for full repair, as (I believe) is often required by the lease from the diocese. It is not clear to me that one would actually want to replicate some of these buildings if they were destroyed, the requirement then perhaps being for a replacement meeting space, not a copy of the destroyed building. Matthew Saunders discusses this in his article on the Friends of Friendless Churches (chapter 3). However, full insurance may possibly be made necessary by the Trust deeds or the requirements of the local planning authority.

As regards public funding, we are grateful to both the Listed Places of Worship Grant Scheme, and the Heritage Lottery Fund for providing notes of clarification about their schemes; these are in Part 3 of this volume.

Sustainability

A small number of single-building Trusts are known to have failed – there are a couple of examples in the Appendix. There are a number of reasons why Trusts might struggle and perhaps fail. One is, of course, the lack of funds, particularly when a large repair bill is faced.

However I believe that the most common pressure is finding new people to take the cause forward, as described at Fordham (chapter 16) and Coombe Keynes (chapter 14). A few single-building Trusts in this volume are certainly facing a shortage of people to do the work. It is interesting that Victoria Collison-Owen has identified the same problem in Scotland (chapter 7).

One wonders whether a tie-up, formal or informal, between the Trust and the Parish Council might be one way of providing some degree of long-term continuity. (It is currently illegal for Parish Councils to make grants to *living* churches, under the Local Government Act 1894: I am not sure whether this prohibition also applies to closed churches.)

Longevity of single-building Trusts

It is important to appreciate that my sample may be biased: there were many Trusts who did not respond to my approach, and I wonder if some of those are facing difficulties which they did not want to publicise. Furthermore very few single-building Trusts have been around long enough for us to understand how stable they are over any significant period of time. So we simply do not have the knowledge to comment with any certainty on the typical longevity or performance of a single-building Trust.

We can say, though, that a significant number do get past their twenty-year mark and are still going strong. My general feeling is that in a very uncertain world, this form of self-help is at least as stable as relying on Local Authority ownership (see for example the case of Ryde, chapter 23), or as relying on the organs of central Government, as we will see in the next section.

Multi-building Trusts and closed churches

So far I have been looking at single-building Trusts. The next, rather briefer, section considers eight multi-building Trusts in Great Britain which look after closed churches and chapels.

The largest such Trust is the Churches Conservation Trust, a veritable giant with more than three hundred and forty buildings. This Trust is exceptional, in that it has a statutory duty to care for certain closed CofE buildings of very high quality, and in recognition of this is more than two-thirds funded by government, and also has a substantial grant from the CofE. Nevertheless, despite its statutory obligations, successive governments have increasingly squeezed it financially. As a result it has actively been seeking to broaden its financial base.

The other multi-building Trusts vary in size from more than forty buildings (the Friends of Friendless Churches) to four, previously five (the Ipswich Historic Churches Trust). None of these other Trusts has a statutory duty, and they have a range of funding relationships with government and other public authorities.

Purposes

One interesting difference between these Trusts lies in how they see their purpose – though I must emphasise that what follows is my personal analysis. It seems to me that there is a spectrum from 'curatorial' – that is, preserving a portfolio of good buildings, passing them on unchanged to future generations; to 'repurposing' – a rather unpleasant neologism conveying the idea that an existing building is converted for a new purpose, perhaps drastically so, whilst trying not to lose what is important about it.

The Trusts can perhaps be split into three groups. The first group is more or less curatorial. In this group are the Friends of Friendless Churches and the Norfolk Churches Trust. At the other end of the spectrum are two groups who actively seek to find new uses for all or most of their buildings – the Ipswich Historic Churches Trust and the Norwich Churches Trust. It is surely no coincidence that the first two Trusts mainly look after rural churches, whereas the second two work in an urban environment, where population density make it more likely that a new use will be found, together with the necessary investment, and that if a new use is not found, there will be vandalism. It *may* be no coincidence that the first two have a strong membership base, the latter two less so; though the direction of causality is not obvious.

The third group is of three Trusts – the Scottish Redundant Churches Trust, the Welsh Religious Buildings Trust and the Historic Chapels Trust. These were founded relatively recently on one tenet (curatorial), and took on expensive long-term commitments on that basis; now the world has changed, funding streams are turning against this principle, and the Trusts are having to move to a different model (repurposing). This is not an easy transition, especially if there is an existing portfolio of buildings in poor condition acquired on the curatorial principle.

The giant, statutory, Churches Conservation Trust is rather different. It was founded in 1969, and in that very different world its mission was explicitly curatorial: looking after important buildings, with no use in mind. Its original name says it all: the Redundant Churches Fund. Since then its approach has changed, and is perhaps best described by saying it treats each of its buildings on their merits (these are my words). Thus, for a small number of its buildings it has worked with a range of partners to invest heavily in the building for brand new uses, though at my request, these are not discussed in their article in this volume (chapter 2), as our focus here is rather different. (Details of these cases can be found on the Trust's website.) So this organisation stretches along the spectrum.

Comparison of multi- and single-building Trusts

The multi-building Trusts have some obvious advantages compared to single-building ones, for example continuity and expertise. On the other hand, a multi-building Trust will tend to lack local knowledge; and it also risks 'freeloading' by individual churches: that is, locals having use of a building free of charge, because it is funded from the centre – explaining why it can be difficult for this form of Trust to hand its buildings back.

Given this, it is not surprising that the multi-building Trusts have attempted to acquire some of the characteristics of a single-building Trust, mainly by encouraging local Friends groups and similar, and giving them a degree of autonomy. This is an area where I suspect the different multi-building Trusts could usefully learn from each other.

What is surprising is that many of the single-building Trusts I have spoken to show little sign of trying to acquire the advantages of a multi-building Trust. They seem to go it alone. For example, few if any of the 'quiet' single-building Trusts have joined the Association of Preservation Trusts (www.ukapt.org.uk), or made use of the extensive help that is available from that body. There is room for improvement here, for existing Trusts, and perhaps as a requirement for new ones.

Trusts looking after open churches
Churches used for special services only
The Trusts described in this volume mostly look after closed churches – closed in the sense that they are no longer used for regular worship.

One idea that seems to have been gaining ground recently is that a church building could stay open, but could cease holding regular services of worship. It would however remain in use for major festivals, and for weddings, funerals and baptisms, for a total of at least six services per year, which is the minimum required by some grant schemes. The choice of services might be in the hands of the local community, and funded by them.

A Trust could be responsible for such a building, as the parish no longer exists; and although the Trust would have an independent legal personality, it would probably fall under the aegis of the diocese or other church authority.

In discussing this idea, such buildings are described variously as 'festival churches' (see chapter 32) , 'pilgrim churches' (chapter 30), 'celebration churches' (by the diocese of Lincoln, not printed in this volume), 'shrine churches' (diocese of Ely) or 'Trust churches' (chapter 31). Richard Halsey's article in *Ecclesiology Today* 45 (2012), explored the idea in some depth.

Thus in rural parishes where attendance is very low a church could be converted to festival/pilgrim/celebration/shrine/Trust status without actually closing it, closure often being the trigger for objections and resistance. Under this arrangement, the church would still be there, still maintained, still within sight of the diocese, and still occasionally holding services.

This of itself would not save much money, probably mainly the variable cost associated with heat and light for services, and a small proportion of a stipendiary priest. So who would pay the ongoing costs? Would it be the existing tiny congregation, despite having no services in their church? Or perhaps those living nearby (if there are any) might contribute - would they be willing? Or there could be a central Trust pot of money, to which people are invited to contribute (though this would mirror the activities of some existing bodies). All in all, this is an interesting idea, and well worth exploring, but I do think that the question of how to widen the pool of supporters is fundamental.

PCC paying for use of church building

There is another model, which might signal the future. In two cases, (Fernham and Yarpole, chapters 15 and 28), the Trust is responsible for a church building which has not been closed, and is still used for regular worship, and the Parochial Church Council (PCC) makes a financial contribution for use of the building.

Under such arrangements, the PCC reduces its cost base and any worries as to future costs, and the Trust has access to the church building for community use.

In physical terms, the building is in much the same state as it would be if the PCC had created and managed a long-term lease to the Trust for part of their building. However in these two examples the PCC is not burdened with the responsibility of managing a lease, and the Trust has greater control. In addition, there are more people concerned over the future of the building, so if it ever needed major repairs, there would probably be increased support for saving it, and an appropriate organisation in place to do the fund-raising. All in all, I expect this model to become more popular.

Imaginary worlds

And now to enter the realm of the imagination.

It is not hard to at least conceive of a different motivation for a Trust, though I know of no actual examples – namely a Trust which had no interest in using a building for community purposes, but simply wanted to preserve an exceptionally important building for the sake of the nation. In such a case, why not release the PCC of any responsibility for the building, put it in the hands of a preservation Trust, and allow the PCC to rent it back, without closing the church?

Some years ago I explored this and other ideas in a series of four imaginary case studies, here printed as chapter 33. Two further thoughts emerged from those musings – first, that ownership by a Trust could make church closure less traumatic; and secondly that perhaps we would benefit from an overarching Trust to provide a backstop for individual single-building Trusts. The list of legal options provided in the CBC's article (chapter 29) might add useful flexibility to some of these early ideas.

Conclusion

It seems to me that the evidence from this volume is that Trusts are capable of looking after closed church buildings in a way that preserves their integrity and is sustainable at least over the medium term. In addition Trusts can have a role in looking after living church buildings. There are just two examples in this volume, but I would expect this model to become more common.

Perhaps surprisingly, the major threat to single-building Trusts is not money, but replacing their people. Conversely, the major threat to multi-building Trusts most certainly is money, as they can be heavily reliant on a small number of public funders whose priorities can and do change.

Perhaps Trusts are best not seen as a solution but as a *mechanism* – a mechanism for thinking about options, raising funds, directing enthusiasm, bringing together expertise, managing projects, keeping things running, and making sure everyone stays on board. They are a mechanism for involving others who share similar values and will support the cause; for maintaining some fixity of purpose beyond the desires of any one individual; for demonstrating the popularity and validity of the cause to funders; for focusing on the longer term; and for seeking public rather than private or commercial benefit.

As a mechanism, Trusts can be flexible and effective; and at a time when church and chapel buildings are under continuing pressure, we should encourage their use and continue to explore what they can do – but we should not expect miracles.

APPENDIX: Single-building Trusts not otherwise described in this volume

This is a list of Trusts (mostly charitable Trusts) looking after single church or chapel buildings which do not have separate chapters in the body of this volume. It is intended to include only buildings which are used occasionally ('quiet' churches). It excludes ruins, buildings moved to a museum location, and those owned by the National Trust or English Heritage. All these Trusts are active to the best of my knowledge, unless I indicate otherwise.

There will be errors. There will also be omissions, probably many of them. I would be very grateful to be notified of either, using the contact address at the rear of this volume.

ENGLAND: CHURCH OF ENGLAND

St Margaret, Babington, Somerset. *In hotel grounds.*

All Saints, Burghclere, Hampshire. *Status not known.*

St Bartholomew's, Covenham, Lincolnshire

Church of the Assumption, East Wittering, Sussex.
   Trust appears to be inactive.

Ellerton Priory (St Mary and St Lawrence), Ellerton,
   East of Yorkshire. www.ellertonpriory.co.uk

Ettington Old Church, Warwickshire. *In hotel grounds.*
   See http://warwickshirechurches.weebly.com/ettington-
   park---holy-trinity.html

St Mary, Iwerne Steepleton

St Andrew, Lilstock, Somerset

Lyscombe Chapel, Dorset.
   Was ruinous, repaired, atmospheric shell; open.

Old Murston Church, Murston, Kent. *Trust appears inactive;
   no further details.* See http://tinyurl.com/oldmurstonchurch

St Mary the Virgin, Perivale, London Borough of Ealing.
   Active, organises concerts.

St Mary, Rimswell, Yorkshire

Rycote Chapel, Rycote, Oxfordshire. *Chapel regularly open.*
   http://rycote.bodleian.ox.ac.uk/visiting

All Saints, Santon, Norfolk

Holy Trinity, Sunk Island, Yorkshire. *Status not known.*

St James, Titsey, Surrey. *Associated with an estate.*

St John, Toller Whelme, Dorset

St Peter and St Paul, Tunstall, Norfolk.
   Nave in ruins, chancel preserved.

St Peter's, Ufton Nervet, Berkshire

St Peter and St Paul, Winderton, Warwickshire

ENGLAND: NONCONFORMIST

Billy Bray's Three Eyes Chapel, Baldhu, Cornwall.
  www.billybray.org.uk/
Clovelly Methodist Chapel, Clovelly, Devon.
  www.methodistheritage.org.uk/clovelly.htm
Gwythian chapel, Cornwall.
  www.gwithianchapel.org.uk
Osmotherly Chapel, Yorkshire. *Restored chapel; used for services.*
  www.methodistheritage.org.uk/osmotherley.htm
Raithby Chapel. *Privately owned; occasional services.*
  www.methodistheritage.org.uk/raithbybyspilsby.htm
Tewkesbury Old Baptist Chapel. www.johnmooremuseum.
  org/our-collections/old-baptist-chapel.html

SCOTLAND

Clachan Church, Applecross, Wester Ross.
  www.visit-applecross.org/pagex.asp?bioid=33640
Crichton Collegiate Church, Midlothian.
  www.crichtonchurch.com/
Edderton Old Kirk, Easter Ross.
  www.spanglefish.com/eddertonoldkirk/
Kineff Old Kirk, Aberdeenshire.
  www.kinneffoldchurch.co.uk/
Kirkaldy Old Kirk, Fife.
  www.kirkcaldyoldkirktrust.org.uk/
Nigg Old Church, Easter Ross.
  www.niggoldtrust.org.uk/
Tealing Kirk Heritage Centre Trust. *Trust failed; building at risk.*
  http://tinyurl.com/tealingchurch

WALES

St Michael's, Betws-y-Coed, Snowdonia.
  www.stmichaelsbyc.org.uk/
Llandegwning church near Botwnnog, Gywnedd.
  ww.tremadog.org.uk/content/projects.php
St Julitta's, Capel Curig, Snowdonia.
  www.stjulittas.org
Carnguwch church near Llithfaen, Gwynedd.
  No further information.
Ceredigion chapel, Machynlleth, Powys.
  Apparently cared for by a museum. No further information.
  www.methodistheritage.org.uk/theoldchapel.htm
Burnett's Hill Chapel, Martletwy, Naberth, Pembrokeshire.
  www.burnettshill.co.uk/
St Mary's, Warren, Pembrokeshire.
  www.warren-church.org.uk/

Part 1

MULTI-BUILDING TRUSTS

Fig. 1: Old Christchurch, Waterloo, Merseyside: taken into the care of the CCT in 1998. There is an active Friends group. The church is used for various events; stacked tables can just be glimpsed in the south aisle.

Saving historic churches strengthens communities: the work of the The Churches Conservation Trust

IN SAVING THEIR HISTORIC BUILDINGS, communities are strengthened and in their turn become better able to protect their environment in the future. Beautiful public spaces make for beautiful communities.

For the last half century, relatively generous state funding has put our historic churches in good condition, but those days look to be numbered and we face a major challenge to secure their future.

History holds the answer: in medieval times the parish church was the centre of all community life. Mixed, secular community, arts and worship use and much wider community engagement will also provide sustainability in the future. There is a widespread consensus on this now in the UK, but a good deal of uncertainty about how you go about it and there have been both successes and failures.

Churches are essentially community buildings and so any solution which is going to last has to be community led. Parish churches in particular have been kept going by local people for a thousand years or more, and it is local people who are going to be the main support for the next thousand. At The Churches Conservation Trust in our own small way, we are striving to develop such solutions.

The CCT

The Churches Conservation Trust (CCT) is the national charity protecting historic churches at risk. We have saved over 340 beautiful buildings which attract almost two million visitors a year. With our help and with support they are kept open and in use – living once again at the heart of their communities (Fig. 1).

The churches in our care are English parish churches of particular historic significance which are no longer needed for regular worship by the Church of England.

The Trust is funded by a wide variety of sources, of which donations and grants are an increasingly important part. Some 50% of its funding comes in a grant from the Government and the Church Commissioners, a proportion which has dropped from 70–80% in recent years. The grant was frozen for a decade and the DCMS contribution has dropped steeply since 2010.

The Trust's £6m annual budget pays for the maintenance and repair of all our churches. A small staff team, based mostly in the regions, provides specialist historic church management and supports 1,500 volunteers who keep CCT's churches open and active.

Crispin Truman

Crispin Truman is Chief Executive of The Churches Conservation Trust.

Description
Cares for more than 340 churches no longer needed for regular worship by the Church of England.

Founded
1969

Location
Owns buildings throughout England.

Access
Varies; many are open during the day.

Website
www.visitchurches.org.uk

The Collection

The Trust owns 345 Grade I and II★ listed Anglican churches, a number which is increasing by two or three a year. Even before a church is placed in our care we start to consider the conservation needs together with the potential of each building in terms of community and other use. Based on location and support within the community and from other local partners we can begin to assess options for opening the church and seeing it in use. With a huge range of churches in our care, from tiny rural gems in parts of the country where the locals moved away centuries ago, to significant small town churches and massive Victorian buildings suffering vandalism and arson in inner urban areas, the considerations can be very different.

With smaller rural churches our priority is to promote the church as a place for visitors to enjoy whilst encouraging local people to hold occasional events and services. With the larger churches we seek partners – including Friends' groups - to work with us to manage and use the church on a regular basis.

Our strategy

A lot of our work involves conserving a very special collection. But there is much more to do if we are to keep these buildings for the future. Faced with reduced funds, an increasing number of churches at risk and several additional churches each year, our strategy has to be about engaging a wider constituency of support and sustaining our buildings through widespread local activity.

Our current strategic aims are shown in the box. In practice that means there are a wide range of small, medium and large projects which are at various stages of development, including:

- Conservation repairs – (there has been no let-up here)
- Tourism and visiting
- Education and learning
- Arts/cultural uses
- Community use
- Volunteering and local management
- Craft skills training

Community solutions

With over 12,000 listed parish churches in England, the answer to the increasing pressure on these buildings is not going to come from the centre in the form of a big Government initiative. The solution has to involve engaging new audiences, broadening uses and trying new forms of community management and ownership. In some cases this means physically adapting buildings, but this is

> **Current strategic aims of the CCT**
>
> **Inspire** people to visit, enjoy, understand and use our churches
>
> **Sustain** our churches: conserve and adapt them for twenty-first century use
>
> **Create** value in our churches: social, environmental and economic

not always necessary and it is often very subtle changes which are needed. As has been said, 'a new use must be in conversation with the original use and not obliterate it'.

The key principles of wider engagement, partnership and locally-led 'visioning' apply across the diverse situations historic church buildings find themselves in. However the practicalities vary hugely and at CCT we approach each church building individually, though we have a number of different models depending on size, context and location.

One way in which we work with the local community is through Friends groups. Many of our churches have groups of individuals who care passionately about the future of their local church and are keen to use the church as their own. These groups are independently constituted and our relationship with them is as partners. We draw up a formal partnership agreement in which we agree a shared vision as to how the church is to be protected and used in the long-term and which places responsibilities on each partner for its management and financing.

In other situations CCT has its own, directly-managed volunteer team who will provide the visitor welcome and run the church for the Trust.

Our churches play host to a wide range of activities from the traditional – carol services, cake sales, art exhibitions, classical concerts and theatre – to the unusual, for example, our new initiative 'champing' which allows camping in church.

Sharing stories

In recent years we have become more focused on telling our story. This can be general PR promoting the CCT and specifics about what we do; working with schools to bring history alive; or through the churches themselves, by interpreting the stories of our churches onsite in an accessible way for visitors.

We aim through PR to promote CCT in various ways such as through fun campaigns like our current 'Great Church Bake Off' competition. This raises awareness amongst those who may not know about CCT already and who may not be aware of the beautiful historic churches on their doorsteps. We also promote

Fig. 2: Interpretation panels at St Michael and All Angels, Princetown, Devon. They tell the story of the building of the church by French and later American prisoners of war.

the more serious side of our work, such as conservation projects and tourism initiatives. The more people who are aware of what we do, the more likely we are to generate support.

At the heart of our National Plan for Learning is the Explorer Church Partnership (ECP) project. This is facilitated by three regional Heritage Learning Officers based in Bristol, Cambridge and Leeds, and it encourages schools to engage with their local CCT church through a bespoke programme of access and activities. In this way the staff, students and wider school communities have the opportunity to develop a greater understanding and sense of pride in these buildings, which stand at the heart of their communities.

The Trust has recently developed an interpretation plan to ensure that the way we tell stories in our churches is engaging for visitors (Fig. 2). We are starting with pilot projects which we will then roll out to more churches. For example, in St Peter's church, Sandwich a recent project, funded by the Heritage Lottery Fund, included the addition of new interpretation panels telling the story of the church through images of key events in the history of the town; the panels engage visitors as soon as they enter the church and allow them to interpret the story in their own way.

Some may ask why provide interpretation when the economic pressures on repairing the estate are so great? As one of the leading operators of heritage attractions, we need to connect people with our heritage so that people keep visiting and coming back to our sites, and are keen to contribute and participate as volunteers, donors and ambassadors: from which our profile and income rise and our estate becomes sustainable. Good – proportionate and relevant – interpretation is a powerful tool for engagement.

We warmly invite people to join one of our annual gift schemes and be kept informed about our work and our plans for the future. Full details of the various schemes are on our website. For example, for as little as £3 a month you can join our Supporters scheme. As well as knowing your gift will make an enormous difference to the work of CCT, you will also enjoy a number of benefits including:

- Priority booking and discounts for our Historic Church Tours, craft skills courses and occasional conferences;
- Special discounts for other heritage attractions;
- A bi-annual newsletter and a bi-annual bulletin giving you an exclusive insight into our work and plans for the future;
- A complimentary copy of our annual review;
- Special discounts on CCT merchandise, such as Christmas Cards.

Supporter gift memberships are available for both individual and joint supporters. For more details, see our website www. visitchurches.org.uk

See the following pages for case studies.

Christchurch, Waterloo, Merseyside

Old Christchurch, Waterloo (Fig. 1) is an imposing church which has for over 100 years served as a landmark building in this once prosperous seaside resort. Known locally as Waterloo Cathedral and the Mariners Church, on a clear day its majestic Old Red Sandstone tower can be seen as far away as Anglesey.

The church was disused for many years and World War II bombing and later vandalism took its toll (Fig. 3). In 1998 the church was vested into CCT's care and in 1999 the Friends of Old Christ Church, Waterloo were formed with the aim of working with and assisting the Trust in the care and preservation of the contents and church. The Friends (www.oldchristchurch. moonfruit.com/) have been so successful at organising events and raising money (Figs 4 & 5) that they are now looking to become a Charitable Incorporated Organisation. However the church currently faces huge repair liabilities and CCT and the Friends are working together to apply for funding to ensure the future of this building.

Fig. 3 (right): Old Christchurch, Waterloo, Merseyside, a photograph taken in 1996 showing the effect of vandalism on the building. The building was taken into the care of the CCT in 1998.

Fig. 4 (opposite top): A farmers' market in Old Christchurch.

Fig. 5 (opposite bottom): An exhibition in Old Christchurch.

St Michael & All Angels, Princetown, Devon

St Michael and All Angels' church at Princetown on Dartmoor (Fig. 6) is the only church in England to have been built by prisoners of war.

In the last year CCT has worked with local volunteers and funders to conserve the east chancel window (Figs 7 & 8) which was donated in 1904 , a group which is still in existence today. The harsh Dartmoor weather had affected the delicate painted detail of the stained glass window and water ingress had caused the internal bars of the window to bow and leak. This has become the first CCT project to be entirely externally funded with a combination of donations and grants (from the Heritage Lottery Fund, the National Society United States Daughters of 1812 and other sources). The conservation project included a range of learning opportunities including a conservation internship and educational workshops with Princetown Primary School.

Funding has allowed us to secure a range of new heritage visitor information (Fig. 2) with the support of the community and volunteers who play such an important role in the church, putting St Michael's firmly on the Dartmoor tourist trail. We have also joined the local tourism initiative, the 'Dartmoor Partnership'.

What was particularly encouraging about this project was how CCT was able to work in a focused way with a small dedicated group of volunteers who all had important roles to play, working to a tight schedule; and how with the help of overseas support the team worked creatively within the conditions imposed by the church.

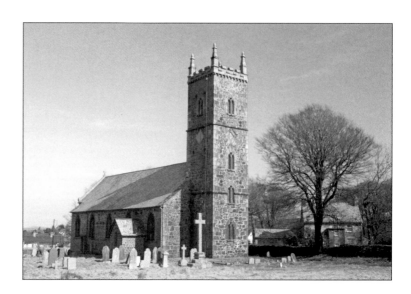

Fig. 6: St Michael and All Angels, Princetown, Devon. Designed by John Walters, built by prisoners of war, completed in 1816. (Jen Bryant)

Fig. 7 (above): The east window of St Michael's, now restored. It was donated by the National Society US Daughters of 1812 in the early years of the twentieth century.

Fig. 8 (left): The interior of St Michael's.

St Peter's, Sudbury, Suffolk

This vast medieval church dominates the town of Sudbury from the top of Market Hill (Fig. 9). In 1976 ownership of the building passed to the CCT and in the same year the Friends of St Peter's, Sudbury was formed with the aim of keeping the building open, in good order and enabling its use for the benefit of the community in partnership with the Trust.

Since then the Friends Group (www.stpetersudbury.co.uk) has developed a programme of events all year round (Figs 10 & 11). There are about 50,000 visitors a year, mostly from people attending these events. Events include the popular Kettle & Fish – a peaceful café / information environment, musical concerts and a farmers' market. The Friends raise income to cover most of the running costs and visitor donations provide CCT with unrestricted income to care for other churches.

Fig. 9 (below): St Peter's, Sudbury, Suffolk, from the market square. (Simon Knott, www.suffolkchurches.co.uk)

Fig. 10 (top right): Christmas 2013 at St Peter's, Sudbury.

Fig. 11 (bottom right): A children's project at St Peter's in early 2014, in collaboration with Gainsborough House.

St Peter's, Preston Park, Brighton, East Sussex

St Peter's is a small medieval church (built in about 1250) which originally served the tiny village of Preston, now part of Brighton (Fig. 13). The Friends of St Peter's group (www.stpeterspreston park.co.uk) was formed in 2007, after the church had been closed for several years, and there are now about seventy members. A committee of eight meets regularly to plan events, working in partnership with the CCT and using the Trust's fundraising events programme for ideas.

The church is important as it contains three medieval wall paintings (Fig. 12), which, although damaged in a fire in 1906, can still be understood with the help of earlier drawings. The group has raised money to have one of these cleaned and conserved, by holding an annual book, cake and plant sale, which this year raised £575.

Seven volunteers each have a key and are responsible for opening and closing the church on the same day each week. The church is open 365 days a year, even on Christmas Day, and people write in the Visitors Book how much they appreciate this (Fig. 14). Many couples return on their wedding anniversaries, as much as sixty years after the event.

St Peter's stands at one end of a large public park, and is next to Preston Manor, which is now a museum. In the summer the museum visitors also come into the church, and this increases donations.

This year St Peter's will hold an exhibition for 'Not Forgotten' (The Great War Centenary) on which they have been working for more than a year.

Fig. 12 (right): Wall painting on the east wall of the nave at St Peter's, showing the martyrdom of St Thomas Becket. To the right is a priest celebrating Mass, and to the left the soldiers hack at St Thomas, who kneels in the centre of the picture. (Budby, www.flickr.com)

Fig. 13 (opposite top): St Peter's, Preston Park, Brighton, Sussex, from the south-west.

Fig. 14 (opposite bottom): The chancel at St Peter's, where even a monochrome photograph gives some idea of the exuberant use of colour and pattern.

List of CCT churches

Abbotsley, Cambridgeshire (St Margaret's Church)
Adderley, Shropshire (St Peter's Church)
Akenham, Suffolk (St Mary's Church)
Albury, Surrey (Church of St Peter & St Paul)
Aldwincle, Northamptonshire (All Saints' Church)
Allerton Mauleverer, North Yorkshire
     (St Martin's Church)
Allexton, Leicestershire (St Peter's Church)
Alton Priors, Wiltshire (All Saints' Church)
Ashley, Hampshire (St Mary's Church)
Avon Dassett, Warwickshire
     (Church of St John the Baptist)
Ayston, Rutland (Church of St Mary the Virgin)
Badley, Suffolk (St Mary's Church)
Barnetby-le-Wold, Lincolnshire (St Mary's Church)
Barton Bendish, Norfolk (St Mary's Church)
Battlefield, Shropshire
     (Church of St Mary Magdalene)
Becconsall, Lancashire (Old Church)
Beeby, Leicestershire (All Saints' Church)
Berechurch, Essex (St Michael's Church)
Berwick Bassett, Wiltshire (St Nicholas' Church)
Berwick, Wiltshire (St Leonard's Church)
Billesley, Warwickshire (All Saints' Church)
Birdforth, North Yorkshire (St Mary's Church)
Blackburn, Lancashire (Holy Trinity Church)
Blatherwycke, Northamptonshire
     (Holy Trinity Church)
Bolton, Lancashire (All Souls' Church)
Booton, Norfolk
     (Church of St Michael the Archangel)
Bothenhampton, Dorset (Holy Trinity Old Church)
Botolphs, West Sussex (St Botolph's Church)
Bradstone, Devon (St Nonna's Church)
Brandiston, Norfolk (St Nicholas' Church)
Brentingby, Leicestershire (St Mary's Church)
Bridgnorth, Shropshire (St Leonard's Church)
Bristol, Bristol (Church of St John the Baptist)
Bristol, Bristol (Church of St Thomas the Martyr)
Bristol, Bristol (St Paul's Church)
Brockley, Somerset (St Nicholas' Church)
Brookthorpe, Gloucestershire (St Swithun's Church)
Brougham, Cumbria (St Ninian's Church)
Broughton, Buckinghamshire (St Lawrence's Church)
Brownsover, Warwickshire
     (Church of St Michael & All Angels)
Buckenham, Norfolk (St Nicholas' Church)
Buckland, Hertfordshire (St Andrew's Church)
Bungay, Suffolk (St Mary's Church)
Burham, Kent (St Mary's Church)
Burley, Rutland (Holy Cross Church)

Burringham, Lincolnshire
     (Church of St John the Baptist)
Burwell, Lincolnshire (St Michael's Church)
Buslingthorpe, Lincolnshire (St Michael's Church)
Bywell, Northumberland (St Andrew's Church)
Cadeby, South Yorkshire
     (Church of St John the Evangelist)
Cambridge, Cambridgeshire (All Saints' Church)
Cambridge, Cambridgeshire (St Peter's Church)
Cameley, Somerset (St James' Church)
Capel, Kent (Church of St Thomas a Becket)
Capel-le-Ferne, Kent (St Mary's Church)
Carrington, Greater Manchester
     (St George's Church)
Catmore, Berkshire (St Margaret's Church)
Chadshunt, Warwickshire (All Saints' Church)
Charfield, Gloucestershire (St James' Church)
Cheam, Surrey (Lumley Chapel (St Dunstan's))
Chichester, West Sussex
     (Chapel of St John the Evangelist)
Chickney, Essex (St Mary's Church)
Chilton, Suffolk (St Mary's Church)
Chiselhampton, Oxfordshire (St Katherine's Church)
Church Norton, West Sussex (St Wilfrid's Church)
Churchill, Worcestershire (St Michael's Church)
Chute Forest, Wiltshire (St Mary's Church)
Clapton-in-Gordano, Somerset (St Michael's Church)
Claydon, Suffolk (St Peter's Church)
Clixby, Lincolnshire (All Hallows' Church)
Colchester, Essex (St Leonard-at-the-Hythe Church)
Colchester, Essex (St Martin's Church)
Colemore, Hampshire
     (Church of St Peter ad Vincula)
Conington, Cambridgeshire (All Saints' Church)
Cooling, Kent (St James' Church)
Copley, West Yorkshire (St Stephen's Church)
Coston, Norfolk (St Michael's Church)
Cotham, Nottinghamshire (St Michael's Church)
Covehithe, Suffolk (St Andrew's Church)
Coverham, North Yorkshire (Holy Trinity Church)
Cowthorpe, North Yorkshire (St Michael's Church)
Cranford, Northamptonshire (St Andrew's Church)
Croome D'Abitot, Worcestershire
     (Church of St Mary Magdelene)
Deene, Northamptonshire (St Peter's Church)
Derby, Derbyshire (St Werburgh's Church)
Draycot Cerne, Wiltshire (St James' Church)
Duxford, Cambridgeshire (St John's Church)
East Bradenham, Norfolk (St Mary's Church)
East Heslerton, North Yorkshire
     (St Andrew's Church)
East Horndon, Essex (All Saints' Church)

East Peckham, Kent (St Michael's Church)
East Ruston, Norfolk (St Mary's Church)
East Shefford, Berkshire (St Thomas' Church)
Eastleach Martin, Gloucestershire
    (St Michael & St Martin's Church)
Edlesborough, Buckinghamshire (St Mary's Church)
Edlington, South Yorkshire (St Peter's Church)
Edmondthorpe, Leicestershire
    (Church of St Michael & All Angels)
Edworth, Bedfordshire (St George's Church)
Ellough, Suffolk (All Saints' Church)
Elston, Nottinghamshire (Elston Chapel)
Elworthy, Somerset (Church of St Martin of Tours)
Emborough, Somerset (
    Church of The Blessed Virgin Mary)
Esher, Surrey (St George's Church)
Everleigh, Wiltshire (St Peter's Church)
Evesham, Worcestershire (St Lawrence's Church)
Exeter, Devon (St Martin's Church)
Falinge, Greater Manchester (Church of St Edmund)
Farndish, Bedfordshire (St Michael's Church)
Feltwell, Norfolk (St Nicholas' Church)
Fisherton Delamere, Wiltshire (St Nicholas' Church)
Fledborough, Nottinghamshire (St Gregory's Church)
Fleet Marston, Buckinghamshire (St Mary's Church)
Fordwich, Kent (Church of St Mary the Virgin)
Freefolk, Hampshire (St Nicholas' Church)
Frenze, Norfolk (St Andrew's Church)
Friarmere, Lancashire (St Thomas' Church)
Furtho, Northamptonshire
    (St Bartholemew's Church)
Fylingdales, North Yorkshire (St Stephen's Church)
Garthorpe, Leicestershire (St Mary's Church)
Gloucester, Gloucestershire (St Nicholas' Church)
Goltho, Lincolnshire (St George's Church)
Goodnestone, Kent (St Bartholomew's Church)
Great Steeping, Lincolnshire (All Saints' Church)
Gunton, Norfolk (St Andrew's Church)
Guyhirn Chapel, Cambridgeshire (Guyhirn Chapel)
Haceby, Lincolnshire (St Barbara's Church)
Hales, Norfolk (St Margaret's Church)
Halifax Haley Hill, West Yorkshire (All Souls' Church)
Halstead, Essex (Holy Trinity Church)
Haltham-on-Bain, Lincolnshire
    (St Benedict's Church)
Hardington Bampfylde, Somerset (St Mary's Church)
Harewood, West Yorkshire (All Saints' Church)
Hartley Wintney, Hampshire (St Mary's Church)
Hartwell, Buckinghamshire
    (Church of The Assumption)
Haugham, Lincolnshire (All Saints' Church)
Heaton Norris, Lancashire (Christ Church)

Heckingham, Norfolk (St Gregory's Church)
Hellington, Norfolk (Church of St John the Baptist)
Higham, Kent (St Mary's Church)
Hockwold, Norfolk (St Peter's Church)
Holcombe, Somerset (St Andrew's Church)
Holdenby, Northamptonshire (All Saints' Church)
Holme Lacy, Herefordshire (St Cuthbert's Church)
Hove, East Sussex (St Andrew's Church)
Icklingham, Suffolk (All Saints' Church)
Idmiston, Wiltshire (All Saints' Church)
Imber, Wiltshire (St Giles' Church)
Inglesham, Wiltshire (Church of St John the Baptist)
Ipswich, Suffolk (Church of St Mary-at-the-Quay)
Ireby, Cumbria (Old Chancel)
Islington, Norfolk (St Mary's Church)
Itchen Stoke, Hampshire (St Mary's Church)
Kedleston, Derbyshire (All Saints' Church)
King's Lynn, Norfolk (St Nicholas' Chapel)
Kingerby, Lincolnshire (St Peter's Church)
Kingsbury, London (St Andrew's Church)
Kingsdown, Kent (St Catherine's Church)
Kirk Sandall, South Yorkshire (St Oswald's Church)
Knotting, Bedfordshire
    (Church of St Margaret of Antioch)
Knowlton, Kent (St Clement's Church)
Lambourn Woodlands, Berkshire (St Mary's Church)
Lancaster, Lancashire
    (Church of St John the Evangelist)
Langport, Somerset (All Saints' Church)
Lassington, Gloucestershire (St Oswald's Tower)
Lead, North Yorkshire (St Mary's Church)
Leeds, West Yorkshire
    (Church of St John the Evangelist)
Leicester, Leicestershire (All Saints' Church)
Leigh Delamere, Wiltshire
    (Church of St Margaret of Antioch)
Leigh, Wiltshire (All Saints' Church)
Linley, Shropshire (St Leonard's Church)
Little Barford, Bedfordshire (St Deny's Church)
Little Bromley, Essex (Church of St Mary the Virgin)
Little Cawthorpe, Lincolnshire (St Helen's Church)
Little Hormead, Hertfordshire
    (Church of St Mary the Virgin)
Little Somborne, Hampshire (All Saints' Church)
Little Stanmore, London (Chandos Mausoleum
    (St Lawrence's Church))
Little Washbourne, Gloucestershire
    (St Mary's Church)
Little Wenham, Suffolk (All Saints' Church)
Little Witchingham, Norfolk (St Faith's Church)
Littleborough, Nottinghamshire
    (St Nicholas' Church)

Llanrothal, Herefordshire
  (Church of St John the Baptist)
Long Stanton, Cambridgeshire (St Michael's Church)
Longford, Shropshire (Talbot Chapel)
Low Elswick, Tyne & Wear (St Stephen's Church)
Low Marnham, Nottinghamshire
  (St Wilfrid's Church)
Lower Basildon, Berkshire
  (St Bartholomew's Church)
Lower Gravenhurst, Bedfordshire (St Mary's Church)
Lower Sapey, Worcestershire
  (St Bartholemew's Church)
Luddenham, Kent (St Mary's Church)
Luffincott, Devon (St James' Church)
Macclesfield, Cheshire (Christ Church)
Maddington, Wiltshire (St Mary's Church)
Markham Clinton, Nottinghamshire
  (Milton Mausoleum)
Michaelchurch, Herefordshire (St Michael's Church)
Mongewell, Oxfordshire
  (Church of St John the Baptist)
Moreton Jeffries , Herefordshire (no dedication)
Moulton, Norfolk (St Mary's Church)
Nether Cerne, Dorset (All Saints' Church)
Newnham Murren, Oxfordshire (St Mary's Church)
Newton Green, Suffolk (All Saints' Church)
Normanby-by-Spital, Lincolnshire (St Peter's Church)
Normanton, Lincolnshire (St Nicholas' Church)
North Barningham, Norfolk (St Peter's Church)
North Cockerington, Lincolnshire
  (St Mary's Church)
North Huish, Devon (St Mary's Church)
North Stoke, West Sussex
  (Church of St Mary the Virgin)
Northampton, Northamptonshire (St Peter's Church)
Northover, Somerset (St Andrew's Church)
Norwich, Norfolk
  (Church of St John Maddermarket)
Norwich, Norfolk (St Augustine's Church)
Norwich, Norfolk (St Laurence's Church)
Nuneham Courtenay, Oxfordshire
  (All Saints' Church)
Oborne, Dorset (St Cuthbert Old Chancel)
Offord D'Arcy, Cambridgeshire (St Peter's Church)
Old Dilton, Wiltshire (St Mary's Church)
Old Langho, Lancashire (St Leonard's Church)
Oldbury-on-the-Hill, Gloucestershire
  (St Arild's Church)
Orcheston, Wiltshire (St George's Church)
Otterhampton, Somerset (All Saints' Church)
Oxhey, Hertfordshire (Oxhey Chapel)

Ozleworth, Gloucestershire
  (Church of St Nicholas of Myra)
Paddlesworth, Kent (St Benedict's Church)
Parracombe, Devon (St Petrock's Church)
Parson Drove, Cambridgeshire
  (Church of St John the Baptist)
Patshull, Staffordshire (St Mary's Church)
Pendock, Worcestershire (no dedication)
Pensford, Somerset (Church of St Thomas a Becket)
Pilling, Lancashire (Church of St John the Baptist)
Pitstone, Buckinghamshire (St Mary's Church)
Portland, Dorset (St George's Church)
Potsgrove, Bedfordshire (St Mary's Church)
Preston Candover, Hampshire
  (St Mary the Virgin Old Church)
Preston Deanery, Northamptonshire
  (Church of St Peter & St Paul)
Preston Gubbals, Shropshire (St Martin's Church)
Preston Park, East Sussex (St Peter's Church)
Princetown, Devon
  (Church of St Michael & All Angels)
Privett, Hampshire (Holy Trinity Church)
Puxton, Somerset (Holy Saviour's Church)
Redbourne, Lincolnshire (St Andrew's Church)
Redgrave, Suffolk (St Mary's Church)
Revelstoke, Devon
  (Church of St Peter the Poor Fisherman)
Richards Castle, Herefordshire
  (St Bartholemew's Church)
Rickinghall Superior, Suffolk (St Mary's Church)
Roecliffe, North Yorkshire (St Mary's Church)
Rollestone, Wiltshire (St Andrew's Church)
Roseland, Cornwall (St Anthony's Church)
Saintbury, Gloucestershire (St Nicholas' Church)
Saltfleetby, Lincolnshire (All Saints' Church)
Sandwich, Kent (St Mary's Church)
Sandwich, Kent (St Peter's Church)
Sapiston, Suffolk (St Andrew's Church)
Satterleigh, Devon (St Peter's Church)
Saundby, Nottinghamshire
  (Church of St Martin of Tours)
Seavington, Somerset (St Mary's Church)
Shimpling, Norfolk (St George's Church)
Shipton Sollars, Gloucestershire (St Mary's Church)
Shirburn, Oxfordshire (All Saints' Church)
Shorncote, Gloucestershire (All Saints' Church)
Shotley, Northumberland (St Andrew's Church)
Shrewsbury, Shropshire
  (Church of St Mary the Virgin)
Skelton-cum-Newby, North Yorkshire
  (Church of Christ the Consoler)

Skelton-in-Cleveland, North Yorkshire
    (All Saints' Church)
Skidbrooke, Lincolnshire (St Botolph's Church)
Snarford, Lincolnshire (St Lawrence's Church)
South Cowton, North Yorkshire (St Mary's Church)
South Elmham, Suffolk (All Saints' Church)
South Somercotes, Lincolnshire (St Peter's Church)
South Tidworth, Wiltshire (St Mary's Church)
Spetchley, Worcestershire (All Saints' Church)
Stainburn, North Yorkshire (St Mary's Church)
Stamford, Lincolnshire (St John's Church)
Stanstead Abbotts, Hertfordshire (St James' Church)
Stansted Mountfitchet, Essex
    (Church of St Mary the Virgin)
Stanton, Suffolk (Church of St John the Baptist)
Stanwick, North Yorkshire
    (Church of St John the Baptist)
Stapleford, Leicestershire
    (Church of St Mary Magdelene)
Steeple Gidding, Cambridgeshire
    (St Andrew's Church)
Stirchley, Shropshire (St James' Church)
Stocklinch Ottersey, Somerset (St Mary's Church)
Stockwood, Dorset (St Edwold's Church)
Stonham Parva, Suffolk
    (Church of St Mary the Virgin)
Stratford Tony, Wiltshire
    (Church of St Mary & St Lawrence)
Strensham, Worcestershire
    (Church of St John the Baptist)
Stretford, Herefordshire
    (Church of St Cosmas & St Damian)
Stretton-en-le-Field, Leicestershire
    (St Michael's Church)
Sudbury, Suffolk (St Peter's Church)
Sunderland, Tyne & Wear (Holy Trinity Church)
Sutton Mallet, Somerset (no dedication)
Sutton Veny, Wiltshire (St Leonard's Church)
Swaffham Prior, Cambridgeshire
    (Church of St Cyriac & St Julitta)
Swingfield, Kent (St Peter's Church)
Tarleton, Lancashire (St Mary's Church)
Tarrant Crawford, Dorset (St Mary's Church)
Tetbury, Gloucestershire (St Saviour's Church)
Theddlethorpe, Lincolnshire (All Saints' Church)
Thornton, Buckinghamshire
    (Church of St Michael & All Angels)
Thornton-le-Moors, Cheshire (St Mary's Church)
Throapham, South Yorkshire (St John's Church)
Thurgarton, Norfolk (All Saints' Church)
Thurlbear, Somerset (St Thomas' Church)

Torbryan, Devon (Holy Trinity Church)
Tortington, West Sussex
    (Church of St Mary Magdalene)
Uphill, Somerset (St Nicholas' Church)
Upper Eldon, Hampshire
    (Church of St John the Baptist)
Upton Cressett, Shropshire (St Michael's Church)
Upton, Northamptonshire (St Michael's Church)
Upton, Somerset (St James' Tower)
Vale of Lune, Cumbria (St Gregory's Church)
Vange, Essex (All Saints' Church)
Waithe, Lincolnshire (St Martin's Church)
Wakerley, Northamptonshire
    (Church of St John the Baptist)
Waldershare, Kent (All Saints' Church)
Wallingford, Oxfordshire (St Peter's Church)
Walpole, Norfolk (St Andrew's Church)
Warburton, Cheshire (St Werburgh's Church)
Warminghurst, West Sussex
    (Church of The Holy Sepulchre)
Washbrook, Suffolk (St Mary's Church)
Waterloo, Merseyside (Christ Church)
Wensley, North Yorkshire (Holy Trinity Church)
Wentworth, South Yorkshire (Holy Trinity Church)
West Bergholt, Essex (St Mary's Church)
West Dean, Wiltshire (Borbach Chantry)
West Harling, Norfolk (All Saints' Church)
West Ogwell, Devon (no dedication)
West Stourmouth, Kent (All Saints' Church)
West Walton, Norfolk (St Mary's Bell Tower)
Whenby, North Yorkshire (St Martin's Church)
Whitcombe, Dorset (no dedication)
Wiggenhall, Norfolk (Church of St Mary the Virgin)
Willingale Spain, Essex (St Andrew's Church)
Wilton, Wiltshire (St Mary's Church)
Winterborne Came, Dorset (St Peter's Church)
Winterborne Tomson, Dorset (St Andrew's Church)
Wintringham, North Yorkshire (St Peter's Church)
Withcote, Leicestershire (Withcote Chapel)
Wolfhamcote, Warwickshire (St Peter's Church)
Worcester, Worcestershire (St Swithun's Church)
Wordwell, Suffolk (All Saints' Church)
Wormsley, Herefordshire (St Mary's Church)
Wroxeter, Shropshire (St Andrew's Church)
Yarburgh, Lincolnshire
    (Church of St John the Baptist)
Yatton, Herefordshire (The Chapel)
Yazor, Herefordshire (Church of St Mary the Virgin)
York, North Yorkshire (Holy Trinity Church)
York, North Yorkshire (St Lawrence's Tower)

Fig. 1: St Mary's, Mundon, Essex. A photograph by the late, great Christopher Dalton, showing the church in its days of abandonment. It narrowly escaped demolition.

The Friends of Friendless churches

Development

THE DATE OF THE FOUNDATION OF THE FRIENDS is critical – 1957. That was a good twelve years before the Redundant Churches Fund (known since 1994 as the Churches Conservation Trust) emerged. They in fact shared a common founder – Ivor Bulmer-Thomas, that romantic, uncompromising Welshman, whose passion drove him to weep publicly at the sight of a church of Saxon origins under demolition in Chichester. In 1957 Ivor and The Friends were virtually alone. There was no nation-wide or formal 'safety net' at all. When churches shut, they came down (Fig. 1). As it was, the reality of the history of The Friends in their first 18 years was that although they could in theory take buildings into care, finances precluded it – the first vesting did not come until 1974, by which time the Redundant Churches Fund (RCF) was up and running (with Ivor as its first Chair) and already had a score of vestings to its own name.

Ivor told the world that he expected The Friends to wither on the vine following the arrival of the RCF, its Big Sister. When he was in charge of both no doubt he must have had a soft spot for an organisation like the Friends where, then as now, the Trustees were largely autonomous in their decision-taking whereas the RCF could not be acquisitive (being instructed on what they could take by the Church Commissioners). In fact The Friends have grown to the extent that we now have 47 vestings – not least because in 1993 The Friends were formally recognised as the equivalent in Wales of the Churches Conservation Trust (CCT), which can only cover England. We now own 20 Welsh churches on the back of an agreement by which Cadw provide 70% and the Church in Wales 30% of the cost of taking redundant Anglican churches in the six Welsh dioceses into care.

We can also take private chapels, where the CCT cannot, and we have two of those. Indeed, until the arrival of the Historic Chapels Trust (HCT), redundant Nonconformist chapels of note either faced the demolition man or the compromises of conversion. Hence the vesting with us in 1986 of the Grade II★ listed Strict and Particular Baptist Chapel of 1792 at Waddesdon, in Bucks. And the much more recent vesting in 2011, of our one and only Catholic church – W. D. Caroe's rather eccentric convent chapel of 1930 to St Mary of the Angels at Brownshill near Chalford, tucked away in the hills of the Stroud Valleys. It came to us because the HCT is not at present in expansive mode. (Both Waddesdon and Brownshill are our only examples of purchase,

Matthew Saunders

Matthew Saunders is Director of the Friends of Friendless Churches, and Secretary of the Ancient Monuments Society.

Description
The Friends look after more than forty former places of worship, half in England, half in Wales. Most are medieval; all are listed.

Established
1957

Location
Owns buildings in England and Wales.

Access
Most are open during the day.

Website
www.friendsoffriendlesschurches.org.uk

and Brownshill was only so indirectly – the villagers were so anxious not to be alienated from a building that meant so much to them that they chipped in to buy the chapel from the Roman Catholic diocese of Clifton and then pass the building to us.) We paid £6,000, after an appeal, for Waddesdon but all other vestings have been passed over gratis – indeed one, Thornton le Beans in Yorkshire, granted to us in 2010, came with a dowry, modest but timely, from the Church Commissioners, and the diocese of York. The figure was commuted from the cost of demolition, an expense the two parties were spared by our willingness to take the building off their hands.

Under the arrangements in Wales, The Friends are now proud owners of buildings of unchallenged national distinction such as Derwen in Clwyd, Llanelieu in the Black Mountains, Llanfaglan, overlooking Caernarfon Bay, Llanfair Kilgeddin in Monmouthshire, Manordeifi, in Pembrokeshire and Ynysynhaearn near Pentrefin in Gwynedd, nearly all of them with that elusive badge of distinction, a plate in the relevant Pevsner. Indeed one of them, Henry Wilson's Brithdir Church, near Dolgellau, has been included among the 30 greatest buildings in the country, given 4 star status in Simon Jenkins' *Wales, Churches, Houses, Castles* of 2008. For a very small organisation, with no full-time exclusive staff, this can seem a daunting responsibility.

Potential for vestings

The potential for vestings from among the stock of non-parochial places of worship is legion, again an area where the CCT is not allowed to step in. As almshouses, hospitals and prisons close, the fate of the attendant chapel can be regarded as peripheral. Some are preserved intact, sometimes on the back of a Section 106 Agreement (where the developer funds some public good) as with Henry Woodyer's fabulous chapel built to serve the Hospital of All Saints at Eastbourne. The developers who converted the main building to flats were obliged to finance an independent trust which now has the chapel in care. Much the same has happened to Pearson's magical chapel to the Middlesex Hospital which was retained when all around it was swept away and which now seems destined to be passed to All Soul's Langham Place, partly as their offices. In theory The Friends, and indeed the HCT, can participate in similar packages. So far we have only taken into care private chapels that were intended to serve the house next door – the Grade I listed fifteenth-century chapel at Ayshford near Burlescombe in Devon, built for their own use, for worship and for burial, by the Sandford family and the Grade II★ listed chapel of St John the Baptist of 1897 clinging onto a cliff face at Matlock

Bath in Derbyshire. This was intended by its founder, Mrs Harris, to be a Treasure House of the Arts and Crafts Movement. Within a markedly picturesque shell by (Sir) Guy Dawber, you will find glass by Louis Davis, little plaster birds flying across a ceiling by George Bankart, and newly-uncovered stencil decoration on the reredos (Fig. 2). This we have just uncovered on the back of a conservation campaign where English Heritage, with its grant of £200,000, was an indispensable partner (English Heritage grants of similar magnitude have been our lifeline too at the Grade I listed vestings at Boveney, on the banks of the Thames near Windsor, and Mundon (Fig. 1) in the flat marshlands of Essex).

And it was undoubtedly the case that in the early days Ivor, unable to persuade the Commissioners to pass a building to the CCT, took it into The Friends rather than be party to an unworthy conversion. This was the reason why Hardmead, near Newport Pagnell, came to us. But those days are over – The Friends Trustees are determined not to be regarded as an alternative to the CCT. The CCT was set up by Parliament to take outstanding Anglican churches into care and we will not be used as a cheaper option. Not that we have anything but friendly relations with our Big Sister – two Friends Trustees are former CCT Directors.

Lessons

What lessons have we learned since 1957, particularly those that might be counter-intuitive ?

Firstly, I would stress the importance of a partnership with local people, one of our strengths. Some 9 of our 47 holdings have

Fig. 2: St John the Baptist, Matlock Bath, Derbyshire. Recently discovered stencils on the reredos.

local groups, some of which are very active – raising money, holding concerts, helping in the churchyard, guiding visitors and good old cleaning. Their ingenuity in fundraising knows no bounds – my favourite was the 'Guess the Weight of the Chairman' (of the local Friends) competition. One group, at Llanfihangel Rogiet, where Newport meets the countryside, has set up a local history exhibition in the north aisle, on the back of a grant from The Big Lottery Fund. And in 2 of the 47 we have an artist tenant - Nick Jones at Spernall in Warwickshire and Benjamin Finn, who has established quite a reputation in stained glass, at Wickham Bishops in Essex. With the other 45, however, they are now described by the church authorities as 'monuments' – preserved for their own sake, without full time use. We are in that sense custodians.

We work at our best where we assume the legal and financial responsibility but the locals resume their natural affection for what is very often the emotional centre of their community. Flowers appear on altars, pews are polished, paths cleared often without any requests by us. No other building type draws such loyalty and feels, whatever the legal realities, to be owned, at least emotionally, by everybody. We do have several model constitutions among the local Friends and there are established Procedures for events, especially to cover the legal formalities for formal events like weddings. And yet I hope that most of our local supporters would categorise our guidance and control as essentially light-touch. We are here to advise and occasionally set parameters, the liaison between our main office being mediated in Wales through the twice-yearly visits to each vesting by our Field Officer, Susan Dalton.

Secondly, we will fight shy of 'All Singing, All Dancing' solutions. They do have their place – the multi-million pound HLF grants to redundant churches like Benington, Lincs or those like All Soul's Bolton owned by the CCT will help to diversify use, and therefore the constituency of supporters for buildings that can find themselves in challenging settings. None of our churches are urban; where they do suffer from any anti-social activity it is miniscule, whereas buildings in the inner cities are easy prey to alienated youth, brick in hand, matches in the pocket, and if they are to avoid attack it needs to be obvious that they are used and appreciated. So our budget, modest as it is (we have had £100,000 or £110,000 each year in Wales since 1999), goes a long way where we concentrate on repairs rather than amenities. Where we have not inherited lighting, heating or loos, we will generally not introduce them. There is after all great charm in the fact that Boveney is still lit by candles.

Thirdly, we take the church only, sometimes literally its footprint and a 12 inches circuit all round to allow scaffolding, reserving rights of access for builders and visitors. We only take churchyards where there is no other option. We will take an interest in how they are cared for and have been known to meet the occasional expense – the trees, monuments and lychgate can be vital partners in the visual pleasure of the ancient church. But churchyards can be very expensive – at one of our holdings, repair of the boundary wall proved as expensive as the works to the church itself. Where churchyards are not closed, decisions on burials need to be taken swiftly and with the local intelligence that we cannot always bring to bear.

Fourthly, do not cripple yourself with insurance costs. Never compromise on trustee or third party liability but think through very carefully what hazards you are protecting yourselves against before spending thousands each year on paying the premium. Where a church is preserved primarily for its historic fabric would you actually replace the fabric concerned once lost by fire ? If an important content fell victim to light fingers, would you replace it ? Probably not. You save surprisingly little by going for 'excess' in the thousands but again insurance is there for protection against the catastrophic, rather than the merely annoying, so if you save something by meeting say the first £4,000 or £5,000 of expenditure, then that may appeal.

See following pages for case studies.

St Mary's, Mundon, Essex

St Mary's was the quintessential Friends vesting – remo
picturesque, feeling ancient even if its pleasures are largely po
medieval. The sort of church that Ivor Bulmer Thomas adored
lies tucked away in the Dengie Peninsula, really arresting at f
sight with its skirt and weatherboarding defining a dram.
double storey timber frame (see rear cover).

Inside, after the eyes have adjusted, you see two defined ro
of eighteenth-century boxpews and beyond, the greatest surp
of the lot, the trompe l'oeil eighteenth-century murals (Figs 3
in the chancel simulating curtains with tassels either side of
east window, and the two Commandment Boards, again
painted flat but as if in three dimensions.

By 1957 St Mary's was abandoned (see Fig. 1) and, hav
narrowly escaped demolition, came to us in 1975. Some four ye
ago it was nearly lost again as the eighteenth-century chan
began to break its back and we had to conserve both the mu
and its backing wall as the two threatened to move differentia
We came through, assisted by a huge £200,000 English Herit.
grant and the undaunted professionalism of our architect, Jul
Limentani and the contractors, Bakers of Danbury.

Fig. 3: (right) A detail of a curtain tassel, showing the three-dimensional effect of the east-end painting.

Fig. 4 (opposite, top): St Mary's, Mundon, Essex. The interior, looking east. (Chris Bright – SparkeyB Photography – www.flickr.com/ SparkeyB)

Fig. 5 (opposite, bottom): The trompe l'oeil eighteenth-century murals in the chancel, simulating curtains with tassels either side of the east window. The colour palette makes it hard to reproduce these paintings in black and white.

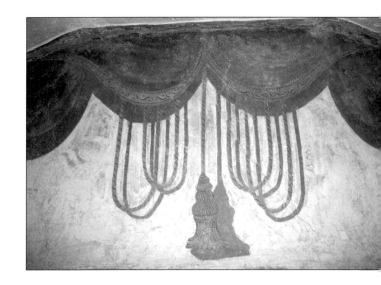

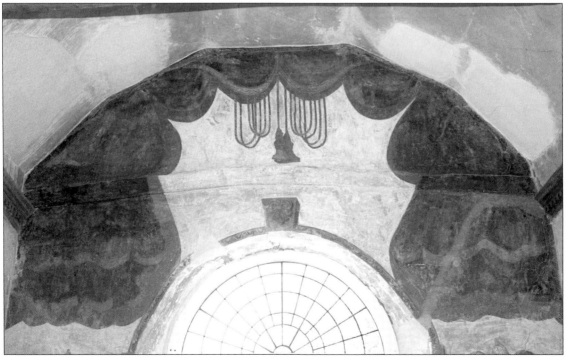

St Mary's, Llanfair Kilgeddin, Monmouthshire

This other St Mary's shares two key characteristics with Mundon (previous page) – it too was an overt candidate for demolition and a modest exterior offers little or no preparation for a heart-stopping interior. Shortly after this medieval church was rebuilt by J. D. Sedding, the internal walls were transformed by a cycle of sgraffiti panels by Heywood Sumner (see Figures 6–8), created over three successive summers – under commission from the aristocratic and artistically well-connected rector, the Revd W. J. Coussmaker Lindsay in memory of his wife, Rosamund, who had died in 1885.

This masterpiece was only saved by us in 1989 after a Battle Royal when the powers-that-be were adamant in their wish to use some localised movement in the building as an excuse for complete destruction.

Fig. 6: The Christ in Majesty, over the chancel arch.

Fig. 7 : (left) St Mary's, Llanfair Kilgeddin, Monmouthshire: the nave looking east, showing some of George Heywood Sumner's sgraffiti panels, painted in the late 1880s.

Fig. 8: (bottom) The sgraffito on the south wall.

45

St Andrew's, Wood Walton, Cambridgeshire

One of our most dynamic local groups is that centred on St Andrew's, which you see fleetingly in its Huntingdonshire field as the railway speeds you on the East Coast mainline (Fig. 10). It sits in the meticulous isolation that was almost its undoing.

The railway cut if off from its village. Abandonment followed and this coupled with severe cracking seemed to be about to seal the fate of what is a substantially medieval Grade II* listed building. But we stepped in and took it into care in 1979. It was then that the heroic local supporters emerged and have since protected the building, raised impressive sums for discrete work, tamed and re-opened the churchyard, opened the church every Christmas Day and issued a regular, highly professional newsletter that binds the whole community together. And all the time, bearing with us as we gradually embark on repairs at what must seem a snail's pace as we wait to check that the movement within the chancel really has ceased.

The internal photo (Fig. 11) shows the displaced plaster in the nave, which has now been replaced. Also shown (Fig. 9) is the Victorian reredos of 1860 that has been partly re-assembled by the local group after heavy-duty vandalism during the years of abandonment.

Fig. 9: The Victorian reredos of 1860, partly re-assembled by the local group of supporters after vandalism during the period when the church was not cared for.

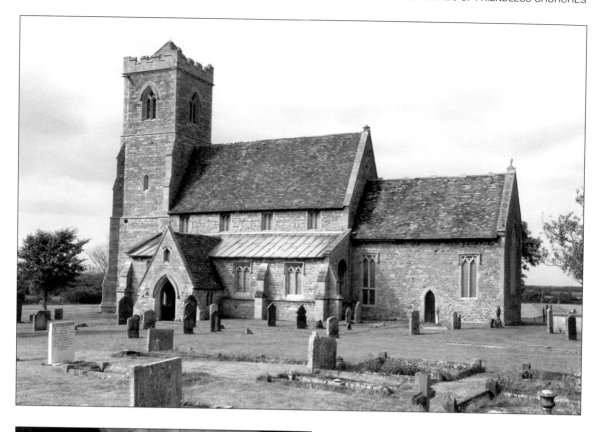

Fig. 10: St Andrew's, Wood Walton, Cambridgeshire, from the south. The church stands alone in its field.

Fig. 11: The nave, showing plaster missing and in a state of disrepair. This has now been put right.

St John the Baptist, Matlock Bath, Derbyshire

One of the strengths of The Friends is that we can take private chapels. One such is this Arts and Crafts Treasure House (Fig. 13) where within an overall design by Guy Dawber, there is glass by Louis Davis (Fig. 12), plasterwork by George Bankart and a partly-concealed richness that it is even now being uncovered. A previous photo (Fig. 2) shows the stencils that were disclosed in the recent round of conservation work to the reredos. We took the building into care in 2002 after the original trust, set up by Mrs Louisa Harris, the founder, had failed. We could not have contemplated the latest round of extensive repairs had not English Heritage been able to find a grant of £200,000.

Fig. 12 (right): Detail of glass by Louis Davis (photo courtesy Peter Cormack).

Fig. 13 (opposite): St John the Baptist, Matlock Bath, Derbyshire. Exterior details. (Paul Heaton, www.flickr.com)

The Friends of Friendless Churches

ENGLAND

Buckinghamshire
　　Boveney St Mary Magdalene, near Eton
　　Hardmead St Mary, near Newport Pagnell
　　Waddesdon Hill Strict and Particular Baptist Chapel,
　　　　near Aylesbury

Cambridgeshire
　　Papworth St Agnes St John the Baptist, near Huntingdon
　　Wood Walton St Andrew, near Huntingdon

Derbyshire
　　Matlock Bath, former chapel of St John the Baptist

Devon
　　Ayshford Chapel, near Tiverton
　　South Huish St Andrew, near Kingsbridge

Essex
　　Mundon St Mary, near Maldon
　　Wickham Bishops St Peter, near Maldon

Gloucestershire
　　Brownshill St Mary of the Angels, near Chalford

Herefordshire
　　Llancillo, near Abergavenny / Hereford
　　Urishay, near Peterchurch

Hertfordshire
　　Caldecote St Mary Magdalene, near Baldock

Kent
　　Eastwell St Mary, near Ashford

Lincolnshire
　　Saltfleetby Old St Peter, near Louth
　　Sutterby St John the Baptist, near Horncastle

Norfolk
　　Fordham St Mary, near Needham Market

Sussex
　　Milland Old St Luke, near Liphook (also known as Tuxlith)

Warwickshire
　　Spernall, St Leonards

Wiltshire
　　Allington St John the Baptist, near Salisbury

Yorkshire
　　Lightcliffe Old St Matthew, near Halifax
　　Thornton le Beans, North Yorks

WALES

Anglesey
　　Llanbeulan, St Peulan
　　Llanfigael, St Migel
　　Llantrisant SSS Afran, Ieuan and Sannan, near Holyhead
　　Tal-y-llyn, St Mary

Camarthenshire
Llandawke St Odoceus, near Laugharne
Denbighshire
Derwen St Mary
Gwynedd
Brithdir, St Marks, near Dolgellau
Llanfaglan St Baglan, near Caernarfon
Llanfrothen, St Brothen, near Penrhyndeudraeth
Penllech St Mary, on the Lleyn Peninsula
Penmorfa, St Beuno
Ynyscynhaearn, St Cynhaearn, Pentrefelin
Monmouthshire
Llanfair Kilgeddin St Mary, near Usk
Llanfihangel Rogiet, near Caldicot
Llangeview St David
Llangwm Uchaf St Jerome
Pembrokeshire
Bayvil St Andrew the Apostle, near Nevern
Hodgeston, near Lamphey
Llandeloy, St Eloi
Manordeifi, St David
Powys
Llanelieu, St Ellyw

The list does not include three vestings agreed but not yet actioned

Membership

The Friends warmly invite members. Ever since 1993 we have been offering a joint membership, for a single subscription (£30 full, £20 reduced) with the Ancient Monuments Society. We now have 2,200 members. As a member you will receive three 60-page newsletters a year, covering all aspects of architectural history and conservation – events, new books, new knowledge and alas new threats. Simon Jenkins has been kind enough to call it the best architectural magazine on offer. And you will also be entitled to the annual AMS *Transactions*, access to Autumn Activities and a reduced purchase price for *Saving Churches*, the account of our first Fifty Years.

You can join directly from our website or by writing to:
The Friends of Friendless Churches
St Ann's Vestry Hall, 2 Church Entry
London, EC4V 5HB
020 7236 3934
office@friendsoffriendlesschurches.org.uk
www.friendsoffriendlesschurches.org.uk

Fig. 1: The interior of St Lawrence, Ipswich, looking west, a church cared for by the Ipswich Historic Churches Trust. The photograph is taken from the mezzanine office inserted where the organ used to stand.

Ipswich Historic Churches Trust: a personal view

In May this year I spent a pleasant day visiting the five medieval churches now or at one time cared for by the Ipswich Historic Churches Trust.

All of them have interpretative displays, and there is a great deal of historic interest. My focus, however, is on their current use, and I will say little about the architecture, and will only glancingly describe a selection of the fittings.

What follows are my personal views.

Trevor Cooper

Background

IPSWICH NOW HAS TWELVE MEDIEVAL CHURCHES, one of which was closed after being bombed during the war. In the 1970s, a tough period if you were a Suffolk church, it became clear that another four of these churches were to be closed for regular worship – to be made redundant, as we used to say. They were all in the town centre where there had been drastic depopulation.

In response to local concerns about what would happen to these buildings – and, it is has been suggested, in the expectation that profitable uses would easily be found – Ipswich Borough Council bought these four churches from the Church Commissioners for the sum of one pound sterling each (Fig. 1). To look after the buildings, the Council set up the Ipswich Historic Churches Trust (IHCT), and in 1981 they were passed to the Trust on a 99-year fully repairing lease (though the Borough pays the insurance premiums, and on occasions assists with major or urgent repairs). Another church closed and was passed to the Trust in 1985. All of these buildings are listed Grade II★.

The aims of the Trust for these building are their 'preservation and maintenance for the public benefit', but it was never intended that the buildings should remain unused – rather that they should remain preserved through occupation by long-term tenants, preferably for cultural, educational or community purposes. Given the care taken today to check the viability of proposed new uses for closed Church of England churches, it is astonishing to learn that there was no firm use in mind for any of these buildings when they were acquired by the town.

The IHCT has an interesting structure. Up to twelve Trustees may be appointed by Ipswich Borough Council and up to six are elected by people who are members of the Trust (of whom there are something under one hundred). Among the Trustees are a number who bring extensive professional expertise relating to historic buildings and their management, and this is provided to the Trust *pro bono*.

Description

Cares for four (previously five) medieval churches in Ipswich, used for a variety of purposes.

Founded
1981

Location
Ipswich

Access
Three are open daily.

Website
www.ipswichhistoricchurches trust.org.uk

How the churches are used				
Church	When acquired by IHCT	Current use and date new use started (all are long term)		Is church normally open to public?
		Date	Use	
St Stephen	1979	1994	Tourist Information Centre	Open
St Nicholas	1986	2001	Transferred back to the diocese. Used for meetings etc.	On request
St Lawrence	1979	2008	Modestly-priced café and community venue, providing protected employment via a social enterprise.	Open
St Peter	1979	c.2008	Converted to concert space, home of the (first-class) Ipswich Hospital Band, rented out for other musical use.	Open
St Clement	1979	ongoing	Under discussion	Closed

I will discuss each of the churches in turn, in the order in which they have found long-term uses (see table).

The churches

St Stephen's church was the first to find a long-term use, when the Council took it over as a Tourist Information Office in 1994, as part of the development of the Buttermarket Shopping Centre.

The wooden fittings created for its new function are beautifully made and have weathered the years well (Fig. 2); on the north their design is reminiscent of a college library whilst on the south they respect the articulation of the arcade, and overall they do not clutter up or fight the space, which is light and airy; a very welcoming interior. The chancel has less furniture, and on the day I saw it, less sense of purpose (Fig. 3). Nevertheless, it is easy to read the building as a church, with differentiated spaces, helped by the splendid Charles II Royal Arms hanging in the chancel arch to separate chancel from nave. (On the reverse of these arms are now framed another set of arms from the church, the Prince of Wales feathers, hidden during the Interregnum.) The monuments, Royal Arms and hatchments are all in excellent condition. The Leman monument (1634) is particularly fine.

One surprising decision was to leave the font standing at original floor level, sunk into the new wooden floor. It is made of Coade stone, so is of some interest, but it does look a little sad and puzzled squatting in its hole (Fig. 4). And did it really have to be left at the west end, where it is rather in the way? (There is another example at St Lawrence's.)

St Nicholas was the second church to find a permanent use. It was sold back to the diocese in 2001 (cost: one pound); the diocese had moved its offices into next-door Churchgate House, and saw the church as a useful conference centre and meeting space. The church is now linked to Churchgate House by an

Fig. 4: The Coade stone font at St Stephen's, in its hole near the door.

Fig. 2: (above) St Stephen's, Ipswich, looking east. The church has been used as a Tourist Information Office since 1994.

Fig. 3: (left) St Stephen's, the chancel, used for various purposes.

atrium which is used as a coffee-shop and café, the link taking you into the east end of the south aisle of the church. This now forms the main entrance to the church.

The pews have been removed, and the floor carpeted (Fig. 5). The east end is screened off with mobile screening, and has been left unchanged; I understand it is used by diocesan staff for daily services. It is also used for intermittent storage. The west end of the church is also screened off: when the screens are rolled back, a cheap and cheerful servery is revealed, which seemed to me to bear a slightly risky relationship to the fine medieval font. I cannot help feeling that new fittings of this relatively poor quality would be refused permission in any living church in the diocese, especially in such close relation to the font.

A number of brasses are displayed on the south wall, but the great treasure of the church is the set of Romanesque sculptures, displayed in front of the old organ chamber at the east end of the north aisle. Recent research suggests these lively carvings may have come here in 1538 from the demolished shrine of our Lady of Grace in Ipswich, a famous pilgrimage destination in pre-Reformation England.[1]

The day I was there an exam was taking place. Even with the clutter of screens and other bits of pieces, this seemed a natural place in which to be silent, serious and focused. But breaking up the space with screens has undoubtedly lost the building its sense of purpose. It has become – simply – a spacious hall.

St Lawrence's is a major landmark in the town with its wonderful faux-medieval tower of 1882, alternately visible and hidden as one walks through the narrow streets of the centre (see front cover). In bellringing circles, it is famous as having the earliest set of five pre-Reformation bells in England, dating from the fifteenth century, all in good condition and with their original tuning. They were recently restored, and are now regularly rung. Thomas Wolsey would have heard them as a boy, sounding just as they do today.

But for many years this was the 'problem' church, with no water or electricity, poor access, and a big repair bill. Despite its importance and centrality, by the late 1990s no use for the building had been found, and the building was falling into serious disrepair. The floors had become dangerous and some were taken up; a monument fell off the wall (though was soon repaired); no-one was allowed in. A pub chain which had shown an interest in the building walked away, not least because of the huge sum involved in restoring it.

Between 2006 and 2008 the 'problem' was at last solved. About £1.2m was spent on the building, one third of which came

---

1 John Blatchly and Diarmaid MacCulloch, *Miracles in Lady Lane: the Ipswich Shrine at the Westgate* (Ipswich, 2013), 58ff.

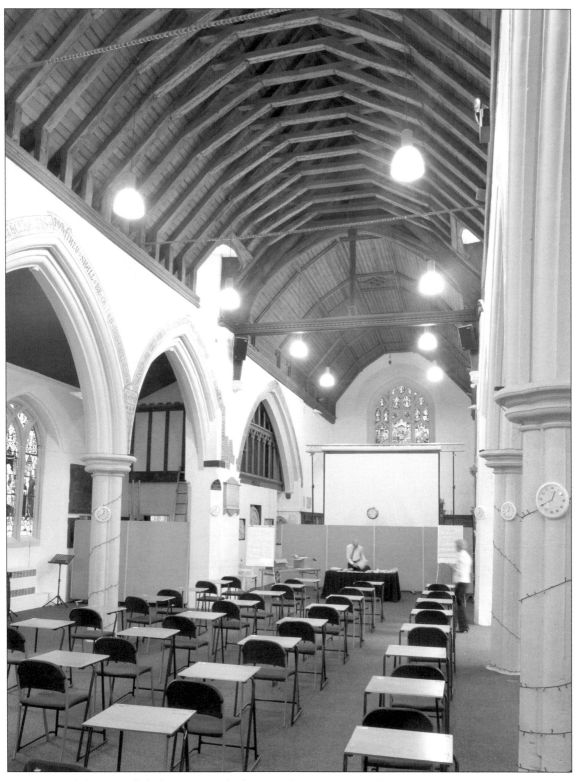

Fig. 5: St Nicholas's, Ipswich, looking east. On the day I visited it was being used for an examination. There is mobile screening at the east end, separating the chancel from nave.

from the Council, the rest from central grants. The interior was converted to a café (Fig. 1), with a thirty-year lease on the building, and it is run by a local social enterprise which provides protected employment.

The interior has been restored, with a new floor and lighting, and an office built in the old organ loft. Tables and chairs are in the nave, the servery is in the chancel, and the altar rails and sanctuary area have been left untouched (Fig. 6). The Victorian stencilling around the walls has been restored, and this, together with the wall panelling, provide an important guiding line for the eye. Overall there is still a strong sense of segregated spaces, and the original purpose of the building is easily understood, helped by a layout of chairs and tables which respects the interior. My only concern was the normal one, that clutter expands to fill the space available, and here the available space is behind the communion rail. The day I was there the church (is it still a church?) was full of noise and joviality, but there was still a real dignity to the space.

There is an informative guide book, which sells steadily, and an interpretative display in the porch. The IHCT has taken particular care with the (very interesting) monuments, recently

Fig. 6: St Lawrence's Ipswich, the east end of the chancel. The servery is in the chancel. The east end arrangements have been retained: as so often, clutter expands to fill the space available, in this case the sanctuary area, though this is hardly noticeable to the ordinary customer or visitor.

replacing a putto stolen in the 1980s, creating a facsimile of a missing brass, and piecing together for the first time a broken brass indent to reveal a previously unsuspected early fourteenth-century military figure with sway. As at St Stephen's, the Coade stone font is centrally placed by the west door, in its very own hole in the ground, nicely positioned for carelessly driven mobility scooters to crash into (Fig. 7). In a church no longer used for worship, how important is it to respect the west-end positioning of these fonts, particularly as many fonts have been moved many times? – I was told that one of the statutory advisory agencies was clear on the point, which decided the matter.

St Peter's is one of three medieval dockside churches, standing relatively close to each other. One of the others is St Clement's (see next entry) and the other is St Mary-at-Quay, bombed during the war, and now cared for by the Churches Conservation Trust. In recent years the dockside area has been undergoing massive development and regeneration, with the dock converted into a marina.

For twenty years the IHCT rented the church to a model railway club, until at about the turn of the century planning permission was given for the building to be converted into offices and a furniture showroom. In the end this commercial use did not materialise, and in 2006 the Ipswich Hospital Band were awarded £772k by the Heritage Lottery Fund (HLF) to convert the interior to a centre for music and the arts. The Council and the IHCT gave further help, and the band did its own fundraising to find the balance. After major refurbishment, the church opened

Fig. 7: The Coade stone font at St Lawrence's, something to swerve around when entering the building.

Fig. 8: St Peter's, looking east. On this occasion a two-man rock band was practising. Behind them is the tiered platform for the resident Ipswich Hospital Band.

for business in May 2008, branded as 'St Peter's by the Waterfront: a great place for music'(www.stpetersbythewaterfront.com). The band is closely linked with Music for Health, a charity which also uses the church, and the space is available for general hire (Fig. 8).

One of the conditions of the HLF grant is that the church should be opened as a Heritage Centre, so it opens five days a week during the summer months, manned by volunteers. The church is closely connected with Cardinal Wolsey (he made it the chapel of the college he created at Ipswich), and at the north-west corner there is an exhibition about the church and Wolsey's connection with it (Fig. 9). The great glory of the church is the huge Tournai marble font of about 1130.

When I arrived to look around, the church-sitters were gathered in the porch. The reason became obvious when I opened the door to find a small rock group practising, quite loudly. Behind them was a raked stage with timpani and music stands; it occupies the east end of the church but is part of the same room as the nave as there is no separate medieval chancel – Wolsey chopped it off. The new floor pattern respects the division of the space into aisles and nave, and thus avoids the airport lounge effect of totally uniform flooring. It is a pleasing space, with the sense of unity just right for a concert hall. I understand it has been a great success.

Fig. 9: St Peter's, looking north-west. The interior has a spacious feel. In the far corner is an exhibition relating to the church and Thomas Wolsey, the local boy made good.

St Clement's is the only IHCT church at present without a settled use. It is tucked away in an enclosed graveyard, and in the 1980s suffered from vandalism. In 1995 there was an arson attack when intruders set fire to theatre costumes kept in the church, and this led to significant roof damage, with almost two-thirds of the roof covering lost, though the Victorian rafter sections only needed cleaning.

The church has been restored to good condition (Fig. 10). It has a fine carved Charles II coat of arms, some interesting monuments and good glass and (for the cognoscenti) Victorian scrolled texts at the east and west end. The pews have been removed, though the pew platforms remain. The chancel has kept all its mid nineteenth-century furniture, none of it (to my eye) particularly distinguished.

The building has no current tenants, but I had the feeling of a well-kept interior waiting for a use. And, walking round the area, it was impossible not to notice the extensive regeneration and banks of new housing and flats, bringing a once blighted area back to life, and surely meaning that a use can be found for this space. At the time of writing a number of enthusiasts, some with personal links with the nearby University Campus Suffolk, are forming themselves into a limited company with a view to using the space for the performing and visual arts.

Fig. 10: St Clement's, looking west. On the far wall are some Victorian scrolled texts and a fine carved Charles II Arms. The pews have been removed, the pew platforms remain.

Final thoughts

So four of these churches have a sustainable use, and the other is in good condition with hope for the future. Thus all have been 'saved', in the important but limited sense of not being demolished and retaining their townscape presence. But it seems to me they have been 'saved' in a much stronger sense than this – they are still owned for public benefit and still operate (to various extents) as public spaces and concourses. Furthermore, none have had their interiors subdivided into offices or dwellings, and their original spatial arrangements can still be read. It is interesting to ask what else one might hope for when 'saving' a church.

Since their transfer to the IHCT, I understand that the desire has always been that these churches should be used for cultural, educational or community purposes, though there was a period when this seemed unlikely to be achieved, and commercial uses were given more consideration. But the large expense involved in bringing the buildings up to scratch, the need (or at least desire) for public access to the interiors, the intermittent planning blight which has arisen as the town has been redeveloped, the difficulties of servicing some of the buildings from narrow streets, the lack of parking in the town centre, the growth of out-of-town facilities over the past thirty years, and raised expectations about the condition in which such buildings should be kept – taken together, these have meant that in the end public and charitable money has been needed to restore the buildings and to convert them for new uses.

But these churches were never commercial buildings, and were largely built through wealthy patronage; perhaps it is not surprising that major capital expenditure today needs to come from equivalent twenty-first-century public and charitable sources, in order to give these buildings a sustainable use providing public benefit.

The subscription for membership of the Trust is £5 a year. Life membership costs £50. You can join via the website www.ipswichhistoricchurchestrust.org.uk or by writing to The Secretary, The Ipswich Historic Churches Trust, 24-26 Museum Street, Ipswich, IP1 1HZ.

Fig. 1: All Saints, Snetterton, Norfolk. View down the north aisle, looking east. The church is from the fourteenth century, and the aisle a century later. The Norfolk Churches Trust took on this church in 1978, some time after it had been closed. (Gary Troughton)

Norfolk Churches Trust

THE NORFOLK CHURCHES TRUST LTD was founded in 1976, a period when many medieval churches in East Anglia were being closed and sometimes demolished. The Trust gives repair grants to churches and chapels of all denominations in Norfolk, typically totalling some £150k per year.

In addition, and as a separate activity, the Trust has responsibility for thirteen churches, none of which is used for regular worship. It is this aspect of the Trust's work which is the focus of this article.

The Trust

The Trust has about 1400 members. It is a very active fund-raiser, to the tune of hundreds of thousands of pounds per year. Some of the fund raising methods are unusual – for example, a Stately Car Boot Sale, a Secret Houses event, an opera staged in a stately home, a classic car run, and a film evening with members of the cast attending.

The fund raising is for the overall purposes of the Trust, and most of the expenditure is on grants, rather than on the thirteen churches looked after by the Trust. Since 1976, more than £5.5m has been awarded in grants, and over £1.25m spent on the Trust's churches, keeping them wind and watertight.

Churches looked after by the Trust

Twelve of the churches which the Trust looks after are medieval Church of England buildings leased from the Anglican diocese of Norwich, mostly on 99-year leases, the majority of which started some twenty or thirty years ago (Figs 1–6). Peppercorn rents are paid. It is only the buildings which are leased: the graveyards, some of which are still open, are not looked after by the Trust.

The Trust also leases one Roman Catholic building, Our Lady of Consolation and St Stephen, Lynford, from the diocese of East Anglia. This is a church of 1878, built for the convenience of the local landowner (and hidden in trees), charming in itself, and with a gilded altar and reredos by Pugin. Its acquisition in 2009 was opportunistic.

All of these churches are closed, in the sense that they are no longer part of the parish system. Thus the twelve medieval Anglican churches have no Parochial Church Council, no routine Sunday services, and no clergy attached to them. However, although closed and removed from parochial life, these twelve buildings have not been through the final stage or stages of the formal Church of England redundancy process.

Description
Cares for twelve medieval churches and one Victorian church in Norfolk.

Founded
1976

Location
Norfolk

Access
By keyholder.

Website
www.norfolkchurchestrust.org.uk

In many cases the churches have little or no population attached to them, as they tend to be in remote and tiny hamlets The churches vary, but the great majority have no electricity or heating. About half of them had their pews removed before the Trust took responsibility for them. There are bats in most of the churches.

The Trust is not seeking new churches to look after, and there has in fact been little need to take on any buildings in recent years, as parish churches have not been closing. The Trust did acquire St Peter's, Corpusty in 2009 from the Friends of Friendless Churches, who had themselves acquired it in 1982, the church having been made redundant in 1965. The Trust has strongly resisted any new church redundancies, and the bishop of Norwich has expressed satisfaction that none has been made redundant in the diocese during his tenure.

Looking after the churches

The leases vary in detail, but all of them make the Trust responsible for keeping the buildings wind and watertight. There is an annual maintenance programme for each church, carried out

Fig. 2: All Saints, Rackheath, Norfolk, which was made redundant in the 1970s and has been in the care of the Trust since 1981. The village is some distance away, and the church feels remote, despite being only a few miles from Norwich. The church and churchyard have many memorials to the Pettus and Stracey families, who owned Rackheath Hall. (John Jollivet)

Fig. 3: All Saints, Barmer, Norfolk. A view from the north-east. This is a very remote church, 250 yards down a track, hardly visible from the road. There is no village. The church was a ruin by 1602, but was restored by Frederick Preedy in 1885 to act as a mausoleum for the Kerslake family. The church was closed in 1970 and taken over by the Trust in 1978. (Simon Knott, www.norfolkchurches.co.uk)

by contractors under the direction of the Trust's nominated architect, with an average cost of less than five hundred pounds per church. In addition, each church has a quinquennial inspection, leading, if necessary, to a planned programme of works. Except when major works are required, the total cost to the Trust of all thirteen of its churches is very approximately £25,000 per year, of which roughly £10,000 is the cost of insurance.

Two of the churches are officially 'at risk', and will require significant works at some stage. Major expenditure is usually supported both by the Trust's own funds and specific fund-raising, together with grants from the County Council (recently ceased), some District Councils, WREN (now ceased), and national sources such as English Heritage (before it ceased to make grants). The investigative phase of a grant application to the Heritage Lottery Fund is currently underway for major repairs to the nave and chancel of Cockthorpe church.

Using the churches

The Trust is allowed to run a limited number of services each year, typically six or fewer in each church, with the permission of the bishop. The aim of the Trust is to preserve these as buildings with a religious purpose, and hold occasional services in them, rather than to find new uses for them (which anyway, might conflict with the terms of the various leases).

Each church has one or more nominated keyholders, all of them volunteers. Most of the keyholders live close to the church, and some of them have done the job for many years. A list of these is published, but there is no attempt to publicise the churches as a

Fig. 4: St Margaret's, Morton-on-the-Hill, Norfolk. The church tower collapsed in 1959, destroying the nave, and the church was abandoned for twenty years. With the support of the Trust, in the late 1970s the owner of Morton Hall organised a sensitive restoration of part of the nave and chancel to create a light-filled space. Although the building is now a private chapel, regular services are held. (Simon Knott, www.norfolkchurches.co.uk)

separate group: to the passer by or visitor, there is nothing to make the churches stand out – for example, there is no sign in the churchyard, though the church itself has a sign mentioning the Trust.

For the most part there is no active policy of encouraging Friends groups, not least because of the low levels of population around most of the churches.

Thus, no attempt is made to find new community uses for these buildings – a long-term sustainable community use might be difficult anyway, given their remoteness and distance from any substantial settlement. Broadly speaking, it is the Trust's current

Fig. 5: The interior of St Margaret's, looking west into the ruined nave. The tower can just be glimpsed, looming over the old west wall of the nave. (Simon Knott, www.norfolkchurches.co.uk)

Fig. 6: St Peter's, Dunton, Norfolk. After at least forty years of neglect, this church came into the care of the Trust in 1978. It probably has Norman origins, but the majority of the fabric is fourteenth- and fifteenth-century. (Simon Knott, www.norfolkchurches.co.uk)

policy to regard these buildings as churches without a current regular congregation rather than spaces available for new purposes.

So the churches are used occasionally for services but otherwise serve no great instrumental purpose. In essence, the Trust – via the generosity of its members and donors – is repairing, maintaining and preserving these beautiful and historic buildings simply because they have value in themselves, and are loved.

Annex: Churches leased to the Trust

St Mary, Bagthorpe
All Saints, Barmer
All Saints, Cockthorpe
St Peter, Corpusty
St Peter, Dunton
All Saints, Hargham
St Andrew, Illington
Our Lady of Consolation and St Stephen
    (Roman Catholic), Lynford
St Margaret, Morton-on-the-Hill
All Saints, Rackheath
All Saints, Snetterton
St Cecilia, West Bilney
St Peter, West Rudham

Fig 1: St Etheldreda, a view from the mezzanine floor inserted in 1995 with help from European funding. Each side of the staircase can be seen stored materials; the artists in residence include painters and printers as well as sculptors.

The Norwich Historic Churches Trust

THE PROBLEM OF REDUNDANT CHURCHES is one which affects all towns with more church buildings than it needs. In many cases (Lincoln, Thetford) those declared redundant have long since vanished, as the concept of 'heritage' had not been invented when they became redundant, usually in the later Middle Ages or the sixteenth century – though of course London shamefully sold a significant proportion of its stock for development in the nineteenth century.

Churches in Norwich

Norwich had (depending on how one counts) about sixty-two churches: ranging from some Anglo-Saxon ones which vanished so long ago that they had been forgotten until unearthed by archaeologists, to the enormous high-gothic fanes we still have. About twenty of these were declared redundant in the 1530s, the buildings demolished, and their sites redeveloped. This left thirty-four churches, all of which continued in use until 1884, when St Peter Southgate was closed and demolished; in 1892 St Simon and St Jude was closed, but saved from demolition by being used as a Sunday School, though it later fell into disrepair. A further impetus was given in 1934, when St Peter Hungate was closed: what to do with this building? Despite misgivings in some quarters, it was turned into a museum of church art, but remained a consecrated building. It was the first redundant church in the country to be so used. Other closures were St Edmund Fishergate and St Swithin in the 1950s, and St Etheldreda in 1961; the Luftwaffe had removed four in 1942: St Benedict, St Paul, St Michael-at-Thorn, none of which was rebuilt, and St Julian, which was, owing to the connexion with Dame Julian. So we now have thirty-one surviving medieval churches (and one tower – St Benedict), a higher concentration than any other town north of the Alps.

This is the background against which the formation of the Norwich Historic Churches Trust (NHCT) is to be seen. In 1967, there was a major review of the city centre churches, after which the diocese of Norwich decided that only eight of the thirty-one medieval churches were needed for worship. In the event twelve were left open The remainder were at risk of demolition unless they qualified for financial assistance from what is now the Churches Conservation Trust (CCT), or if no suitable alternative uses could be found. Thus the Norwich Historic Churches Trust (NHCT) was set up in 1973 to care for most of the unneeded ones and to identify alternative uses for them. Of the twelve churches left open in the early 1970s, four have, various reasons,

Nicholas Groves

Dr Nicholas Groves is a church historian, and has been a Trustee of the NHCT since 2004; he also fills the role of Education Officer.

Description
Cares for eighteen medieval churches in Norwich, used for a variety of purposes.

Founded
1973

Location
Norwich

Access
Varies

since been closed; three of those have to come to the NHCT, and one to the CCT (which cares for two other churches in Norwich as well).

The Trust

The detailed early history of the Trust is still to be extracted from the various documents – something which the present author hopes to do before too long – but the initial body set up was the Friends of Norwich Churches. Out of this, the Norwich Historic Churches Trust grew, and was incorporated on 17 September, 1973. The Trust is a 'quango' of the City Council. Since our formation, we have considered a vast number and variety of applications and proposals for our buildings. To be acceptable, proposals need to be both viable and appropriate, and involve tenants raising funds, in order to meet the capital cost of adaptation where needed. We have a responsibility to seek new and suitable uses, in particular those which are for 'civic, public, or educational purposes, or for storage'. However, emphasis in recent years has been on lettings which will allow public access, either on spec or by arrangement, and we have also had a number of very successful commercial uses, such as antique centres and bookshops. Relationships with our tenants are usually good, and each Trustee has a church for which they are responsible. As might be expected with such a large number of properties, there have been occasional problems over the years, including a couple which gained the Trust bad publicity at the time, but most are sorted out amicably.

The Trust comprises a number of Trustees, with a part-time Administrator (officially the Executive Officer and Company Secretary) and a part-time Surveyor of the Fabric. The work of these last two has increased greatly in the last few years, and since 2010, the Trust has had its own office space in one of the churches (the two-storey medieval vestry attached to the east wall of St Peter Parmentergate) from which they work, rather than, as previously, from home. This also gives the Trust a physical presence in the city.

The Trustees are appointed in two ways. A fixed number each year is nominated by the City Council from among its Councillors, who sit on the Trust as they sit on the various other committees (planning, housing, etc) of the Council. Some of these stay on once their term is over to become Trustees in their own right. The majority of the Trustees are of this nature: appointed for the skills they can bring to the Trust's work. They currently include solicitors, architects, and others with relevant professional skills, as well as those who have a general interest. Until about five years ago, all discussions and decisions were taken by the full Trust at a monthly meeting; as this often led to meetings of over two hours, sub-committees dealing with property (lettings) and repairs have been set up, which meet separately and report back to the full Trust, which then endorses (or not!) their proposals.

Care of the churches

In 2009, a new Friends organisation was set up, which gives people with an interest in supporting the churches and the Trust an opportunity to be involved. Events include social occasions as well as visits to the churches, and these give an opportunity to raise funds for the Trust. They are, currently, relatively small amounts, but do help to fund specific projects, such as restoring the important Norman Bros organ in one of the churches. The Friends have been instrumental in widening participation in, and knowledge of, the Trust's work. One Trustee is nominated by the Trust to sit on the Friends' committee, and the Chairman of the Friends attends Trust meetings.

The basis on which the Trust operates is that the buildings have all been deconsecrated so are technically no longer churches. The Diocese has vested the freeholds in the City Council, which leases them to the Trust on ninety-nine-year peppercorn leases – this includes both the buildings and their churchyards. The City has long had the responsibility of maintaining the churchyards, under the Closed Churchyards legislation. The Trust is responsible for the repair, maintenance, and management of the buildings, and has to raise the income to keep them standing and weatherproof. This has, in the past, been done partly by an annual grant from the Council, and by grants from other sources, as well as rental income. (See the Appendix for a summary of uses.)

Many of the churches taken over by the Trust were in a poor state of repair. With limited funding, our main focus has been to ensure that all properties are structurally sound and watertight. The programme has been determined by the availability of funds in any one year, often – in the past – dependent upon grants from either English Heritage or the City Council. Additional income is derived from rents, other grants, and donations. The former cover the Trust's modest management and administrative expenses, the insurance premiums on unlet churches and minor house-keeping repairs. We are wholly dependent upon grants and donations for all significant repair works. In as many cases as possible, we have improved the facilities at the churches, and as will be seen, insertions of mezzanines, galleries, etc., have been made: all these are reversible, and do not impinge physically on the fabric in any way (Fig. 2).

Fig. 2: St Martin-at-Palace, looking down from the three-level structure occupying the nave (the lowest level is below floor level). This is one of the more radical alterations in the NCHT churches.

The future

However, this *modus operandi* has now proved to be inadequate: the annual Council subvention has been withdrawn, and without major improvements to the facilities of several of the buildings (WCs, heat – even running water in three cases) they become ever more difficult to let, as prospective tenants expect adequate facilities. A sub-committee, set up to raise funds for improving four churches (St Margaret-de-Westwick, St Clement-at-Fyebridge, St John-de-Sepulchre, and St Gregory Pottergate) eventually realized that the way forward was to cease piecemeal fundraising, and to apply for a major HLF grant to cover work at all eighteen churches. This has resulted in a major reassessment of the way the Trust functions: effectively unchanged since its inception in 1973. In early 2014, two meetings were held, led by a heritage consultant. One meeting was for the Trustees and members of the committee of the Friends, and the other for the tenants. We are thus currently reassessing the way the Trust itself functions; how Trustees and officers are appointed; relationships with tenants and with the Friends; and the Trust's physical presence in the city. The way the Friends operate may well change as a result of this exercise, too. We now have to decide whether to go for a grant of over or under two million: this is the figure at which decisions cease to be made at regional level, and happen at national level.

Acknowledgements
I am grateful to Michael Wingate (Surveyor) and Stella Eglinton (Administrator) for their comments on an earlier draft of this article.

See following pages for case studies.

St Etheldreda

This is one of our longest-standing tenancies (Fig. 3). Closed in 1961 when its last Vicar died, the church stood empty until, in 1980, two graduate sculptors from the Norwich School of Art saw its potential as studio space for artists starting out on their careers. The artists currently in residence include painters and printers, as well as sculptors.

It is a small nave-and-chancel building, but a mezzanine floor with north-facing skylights was inserted in 1995 (Figs 4 & 5), with help from European funding, increasing the available space, with WCs and kitchen in the round tower. Despite being somewhat off the main tourist routes, it attracts many visitors on both Heritage Open Days and Open Studio days. The tenant would like to make further alteration to provide a dedicated gallery space.

Fig. 3 (below): St Etheldreda, a view from the south.

Fig. 4 (opposite, top): St Etheldreda, looking into the chancel, from which rise the stairs to the mezzanine floor.

Fig. 5 (opposite, bottom): St Etheldreda, looking west. The mezzanine floor is at roof level, above the ceiling.

St Margaret-de-Westwick

Initially used as a gym, St Margaret (nave, chancel, south aisle and chancel chapel) has been an exhibition space for many years (Figs 6 & 7). It is run by an agent of the Trust, who arranges the exhibitions and other events, and hires out the building. This has resulted in a very wide range of uses by all sectors of the community, and as the church stands on a busy shopping street, the footfall is very high – both those coming to see the exhibitions and those who go in to see the building, having passed by and found it open.

We regard this as one of our most successful ventures. It markets itself as 'St Margaret: Church of Art' (www.church-of-art.co.uk).

Fig. 6 (right): St Margaret-de-Westwick, looking west, being used for an exhibition.
(Aidan McRae Thomson)

Fig. 7 (opposite): St Margaret-de-Westwick, the south aisle, looking west.
(Aidan McRae Thomson)

St Martin-at-Oak

This church (nave, chancel, south aisle) suffered substantial damage in the 1942 Blitz, and the tower was reduced to nave height (Fig. 8). It was closed as a church, and became a church hall in the 1950s This use ceased in 1973, and it was leased in 1976 to St Martin's Housing Trust to provide a night shelter for the homeless. The chancel arch had been blocked in the 1950s, so the nave became a dormitory, with the aisle divided into offices, shower rooms, etc. The chancel became a kitchen space and common room.

The Trust moved out in 2006, and the building was briefly occupied by some artists, but since 2012, it has been the home to the Wharf Academy of Contemporary Music. Improvements have included stripping out the very poor conversion work in the aisle, and replacing it with soundproof pods for teaching and rehearsal. The nave remains as a large performance space (Figs 9 & 10).

Fig. 8: St Martin-at-Oak, a view from the south-west.

Fig. 9 (above): St Martin-at-Oak, the performance space in the nave. (Gary Troughton)

Fig. 10 (left): St Martin-at-Oak, a view of the south aisle, used as teaching and rehearsal space.

Appendix: Uses to which the churches have been put

This is a list of uses to which the redundant churches looked after by the NHCT have been put. The first date is that of closure and/or redundancy; the second is the date the church passed to the NHCT. Where appropriate, the websites of the various tenants have been included.

All Saints (1973; 1973)
Ecumenical Multi-purpose Centre; until July 2014, a place offering hospitality, with a focus on the less-privileged; now newly vacant. Also Mothers' Union office housed here 1989-2003.

St Clement-at-Fyebridge (1971; 1973)
Rented by a Methodist minister and kept open as place of prayer and meditation. There was then a short occupation by the Romanian Orthodox congregation. Now used by a master mason as a city base for eight apprentices with an emphasis on teaching and attracting other young people into the craft.

St Edmund Fishergate (1950; 1973)
Store for cardboard box factory next door. Since NHCT: Scenery store for Puppet Theatre; a community church; pregnancy crisis centre; Call to Prayer. Website: www.call2prayer.co.uk

St Etheldreda (1961; 1973)
Artists' studios since 1980, providing affordable studio space.

St Gregory Pottergate (1971; 1973)
Community arts centre; events centre administered for NHCT by an agent; antique and collectors' centre.

St James Pockthorpe (1971; 1973)
Original home of the Night Shelter – see St Martin-at-Oak; Puppet Theatre. Website: www.puppettheatre.co.uk

St John-de-Sepulchre (1984; 1984)
Used by a Russian Orthodox congregation. Currently vacant, but under consideration by a high school across the street for use as a multi-purpose space.

St Margaret-de-Westwick (1974; 1974)
Gymnasium; now exhibition space administered for NHCT by an agent. Website: www.church-of-art.co.uk

St Martin-at-Oak (1976; 1976)
Night shelter for homeless; briefly artists' studio; now Wharf Music Academy. Website: www.thewharfacademy.co.uk

St Martin-at-Palace (1971; 1973)
Store for furnishings for Diocesan Furnishings Officer; Probation service and successors; Recently vacated.

St Mary Coslany (1971;1973)
HQ of Friends of Norwich Churches; craft and design centre; publishing services company office; internet book business.

St Miles Coslany (1971; 1973)
Scenery store for Puppet Theatre; martial arts gym, attached to nearby sports centre; 'Inspire' Science Centre; currently vacant.

St Michael-at-Plea (1971; 1973)
Antique/collectibles centre; SPCK bookshop; independent Christian bookshop. In all cases with café in chancel. Website: www.norwichcrc.co.uk

St Peter Hungate (1936; 1995)
Museum of church art under Council control 1936–95. Since 2008, Hungate Medieval Art, housing exhibitions of medieval art. Website: www.hungate.org.uk

St Peter Parmentergate (1981; 1980)
Martial arts gym. Website: www.nama4kicks.co.uk

St Saviour (1971;1973)
Parish hall; badminton court; then evangelical youth club; now Thalia Theatre Company. Website: www.thaliatheatre.co.uk

St Simon & St Jude (1892; 1973)
Sunday school 1913–20. Boy Scouts shop and centre 1952–97. Briefly a boxing gym. Now Anglia Academy of Dance.

St Swithin (1951; 1973)
Furniture store. Since NHCT: 'Premises'/Norwich Arts Centre, with contemporary music, art, etc. Website: http://norwicharts centre.co.uk

Fig. 1: The interior of St Margaret's Braemar, one of Sir Ninian Comper's most important buildings, completed in 1907. The chancel screen was installed about1910 in memory of Eliza Schofield, principal benefactor of the church, with the rood figures added a decade later. This photo dates from the end of the twentieth century, after the church was closed, and shows the poor condition of the fabric. (© Crown Copyright: RCAHMS. Licensor www.rcahms.gov.uk)

The Scottish Redundant Churches Trust

"The nature, character and extent of Scotland's ecclesiastical heritage is the product of its own particular political and religious history, notably: its Reformation in the 16th century; its turbulent seventeenth century; the splintering of its Presbyterian denominations in the eighteenth and nineteenth centuries; and their partial reunion in the twentieth century. The survival and revival of the Catholic and Episcopalian Churches, and the arrival of other denominations and non-Christian faiths from other countries and cultures, have added to the richness, diversity and complexity of Scotland's ecclesiastical heritage."[1]

Victoria Collison-Owen

Victoria Collison-Owen is Executive Director of the Scottish Redundant Churches Trust.

Church disposals and the foundation of the Trust

RICH, DIVERSE AND COMPLEX it may be, but one of the most notable characteristics of Scotland's ecclesiastical heritage is its sheer scale. Research in 2008 established that there were over 4,000 protected ecclesiastical structures in the country, plus an estimated 6,000–10,000 unprotected ecclesiastical sites.[2]

The historical over-provision of churches by competing Presbyterian denominations has created a legacy for Scotland which, when combined with demographic change, creates a major challenge for those managing the nation's heritage. It is particularly challenging for the Church of Scotland, owners of the greatest number of ecclesiastical buildings, which, the HEACS report noted, 'has responsibility for the most substantial built heritage estate, or portfolio of built heritage assets, in Scotland – more extensive in number than those cared for by Historic Scotland and the National Trust for Scotland combined, and more widely distributed'.

With too many churches, redundancy and loss is inevitable (Fig. 1). This is by no means a new phenomenon. As the Victoria & Albert Museum's 1977 exhibition *Change and Decay – A Future for our Churches* observed: 'in Scotland, since 1900, more churches have been abandoned, closed or demolished than are now in use'.

Although recognised for decades, the problem of redundancy and loss of Scotland's ecclesiastical heritage is not being addressed in any wider strategic fashion, despite clear recommendations outlined in the HEACS report. Currently, the principal means of disposal of redundant places of worship is sale on the open market, where commercial and preservation bidders compete against each other.

---

1 Historic Environment Advisory Council for Scotland, 'Report with recommendations on the long-term conservation of the ecclesiastical heritage in a time of demographic change', September 2009, at www.heacs.org.uk/documents.htm.
2 N. Haynes, 'Research Report on the Extent of the Ecclesiastical Heritage in Scotland', 2008, at www.heacs.org.uk/documents.htm.

Description
Trust which owns seven closed churches.

Trust Founded
1996

Location
Scotland

Access
Varies

Website
www.srct.org.uk

Fig. 2: (top) St Peter's Kirk, formerly Sandwick Parish Church, disused for over twenty years before being taken into the care of the SRCT in 1998. A rare survival of a traditional Scots kirk, little altered from its construction in 1836. Photographed 1999, before restoration.

Fig. 3: (bottom) St Peter's Kirk, repaired and conserved 2002–3, funded by Historic Scotland, the Heritage Lottery Fund, and Orkney Islands Council. Photographed 2003, after restoration

The preservation of redundant churches in Scotland is undertaken almost entirely by single-building trusts and by the Scottish Redundant Churches Trust. The former are generally community-based organisations set up by volunteers for the sole purpose of keeping their local church open. For years, many historic churches have been successfully cared for in this way, with Kineff Old Church Preservation Trust (1979) and Crichton Collegiate Church Trust (1994) being two examples. However, the failure of Tealing Kirk Heritage Centre Trust (1986) after 10 years left the building derelict and in the hands of the Queen and Lord Treasurer's Remembrancer. To sustain a redundant church a trust must itself be sustainable.

There is evidence to suggest that with an increasing number of church disposals, the number of single-building trusts is also rising. Current estimates of the number of churches cared for in this way in Scotland range from 80–100.

Concern about the gradual erosion of Scotland's ecclesiastical heritage grew during the 1980s and, in particular, concern for the rising number of important redundant historic churches which were too significant for conversion to be appropriate. A conference held in 1994 identified the lack of a national organisation dedicated to the care of redundant places of worship and, in 1996, the Scottish Redundant Churches Trust (SRCT) was established by a group of individuals to fulfil that need. Led initially by a Chairman and three Trustees, the Trust's main objectives were defined as: 'To preserve for the benefit of the local community and of the nation at large, redundant churches situated in Scotland . . . of historic architectural or aesthetic interest, to promote and further the study of the same, and to make information obtained thereby available to the general public'.

First two projects: Orkney and Cromarty

The SRCT's initial approach was curatorial – acquiring the most significant examples of redundant places of worship to be conserved intact as museum pieces and 'saved for the nation'. Ambitiously, the Trust aimed to take on and restore one building

Fig. 4: The interior of St Peter's Kirk. (Leslie Burgher)

a year by securing funding from Historic Scotland and the newly-established Heritage Lottery Fund. With only churches of national significance being taken into the Trust's care, it was anticipated that the importance of the buildings would automatically qualify them for grant support and that, once conserved and returned to a plateau of good repair, churches could be maintained on the strength of income from donations and occasional use.

It was on this premise that the SRCT undertook its first projects at St Peter's Kirk in Orkney and the East Church in Cromarty. The initial testing-ground was the A-listed 'at risk' St Peter's in 2002–3: a £250,000 project which saw the derelict kirk of 1836 painstakingly repaired and conserved (Figs 2–4). The building was remarkably intact and the decision was taken not to impose change through the introduction of electric light, running water or heating. In the repair of the building emphasis was placed on traditional skills and materials and the success of this was acknowledged by Orkney Islands Council who described the project as 'an exemplar of conservation work in Orkney [that] has stimulated interest in a wide variety of traditional building skills and in historic buildings generally'. The kirk was provided with minimal interpretation and opened to visitors. Occasional services are held there and the building is used from time-to-time as a venue for the St Magnus International Festival.

Encouraged by its achievements at St Peter's, and with awards from Europa Nostra, the RIBA and the Civic Trust, the Trust turned its attentions to Cromarty's A-listed East Church (www.eastchurchcromarty.co.uk). Already though, the 'one a year' ambition of the Trust was recognised as unattainable, not least because funding constraints restricted the organisation to employing a single member of staff (a situation which remains today). The East Church (Figs 5–8) also proved to be a hugely complex project, taking five years to develop and fund, and requiring a raft of specialist reports and a comprehensive conservation plan.

Knowledge of the East Church was central to the project, both in terms of addressing long-standing fabric problems and in understanding its cultural significance. Since medieval times the building had charted the fortunes of the community and its townsfolk and, in its fabric, expressed periods of prosperity, change, and hardship. Dating principally from the eighteenth century, the church is notable for its fine interior with box pews, hatchments, and elegant Georgian 'laird's loft'. It also has close associations with the writer and stonemason, Hugh Miller, one of the leaders of the movement that created the Free Church in 1843.

Fig. 5: (above) East Church Cromarty, the town's historic place of worship since medieval times. Declared redundant after decades of intermittent use and limited maintenance. Acquired by the SRCT in 1998, photographed 2008.

Fig. 6: (left) East Church, Cromarty, repaired and conserved 2008–11, the SRCT's second project and a very complex one. Alterations in the late eighteenth century 'Georgianised' the building, masking its medieval origins. Photographed 2011.

As with St Peter's, the Trust's approach was 'conserve as found', with only minor adaptations to meet statutory requirements. But whilst the conservation approach remained the same, there was a shift in the Trust's view of the project. It was recognised that there was value in the actual process of undertaking the repair of the church, and that the building had the potential to be an educational tool both during and after work on site. In part this was driven by funders' priorities, particularly those of the Heritage Lottery Fund, but experience drawn from the St Peter's project was also relevant in shaping attitudes.

With a rich social history, a complex architectural development, technically challenging fabric problems, and major archaeological investigations, the East Church offered learning opportunities for a wide range of people. Between 2008 and 2011 the Trust delivered an ambitious education and audience development programme. Importantly, local people were given the opportunity to be a part of the project: visiting the site, meeting contractors, and sharing discoveries. Developing a sense of ownership of the building amongst local people – most of whom had never worshipped in the church – helped the East Church to be seen as part of the town's heritage, not simply as a religious building. Three years after reopening to visitors, the East Church is cared for by a committed group of local Friends, many of whom volunteer as a result of interest kindled during project visits.

Uses for the East Church, like those of St Peter's, are low-key. Interpretation allows an estimated 10,000 visitors per year to learn about the building and the people who worshipped there through the centuries. An integrated approach to interpretation connects the story of the church with that of Cromarty as a whole, encouraging visitors to explore the town further. Occasional services are held, and secular events include annual fixtures such as the Black Isle Fiddle Festival as well as one-off concerts and performances. Lack of heating is a constraint, and although heating options were originally considered these were discounted on conservation grounds. The relative fragility of the building and its contents is also a constraint – the East Church will never lend itself to intensive use and this, in turn, affects its ability to generate income. When grants were awarded in 2007–8 it was accepted that financial viability was marginal but that the project and the building warranted support. In the current climate it is unlikely that the same investment would be made by funders.

Current major project: Braemar
In its latest project, St Margaret's Church Braemar, the Trust faces its greatest challenge yet, not least in the difficulty of balancing the

Fig. 7: (top) The interior of East Church, Cromarty. (Sandy Sutherland, www.flickr.com)

Fig. 8: (bottom) East Church, Cromarty, detail of painted box pew in the north loft dating from 1740. The decoration of pews was a status symbol for those who rented them.

conservation requirements of a nationally important building with the necessity of demonstrating a viable business case to funders (Figs 1, 9 & 10). A Category A-listed Scottish Episcopal church designed by Sir John Ninian Comper, St Margaret's was built between 1899 and 1907 to accommodate the large number of English worshippers who visited Royal Deeside following the fashion of the time set by Queen Victoria. By the time of its completion this substantial church was no longer needed, and was sustained by a tiny local congregation until 1997. Empty and deteriorating, it has been on the Buildings at Risk Register since 2003.

In 2004 the SRCT carried out a feasibility study which looked at repairing and conserving St Margaret's with minimum intervention and the introduction of low-key uses. The financial case was not strong, but more significantly there was a lack of will amongst the community to engage with a problem building to which they felt no allegiance. The project was shelved but the Trust continued to work with the diocese to find a solution and, in 2009, was joined by the Prince's Regeneration Trust (PRT). PRT's intervention brought key stakeholders to the table for the first time. They supported an initiative with the SRCT working in partnership with a small group of local residents keen for St Margaret's to serve a function that would benefit the village and boost the local economy. An initial vision for the building as a centre for arts and crafts developed into a scheme for a creative hub housing a Scottish fiddle school and performance venue. Crucial to the evolution of the scheme was a series of 'proving uses': events that tested the suitability of the building for a variety of purposes together with the associated market demand. These included a recital by the Dutch Youth Symphonic Orchestra; a creative arts fair; and a concert attended by HRH The Prince of Wales with local performers and children sharing the stage with musicians of international repute. These events also had the effect of opening up a building which had long been perceived by local people as being off-limits, allowing them to see its quality and glimpse its potential. New and exciting proving uses continue to emerge, including plans to host a pop-up exhibition in 2015 for the international contemporary art gallery Hauser & Wirth.

An appraisal commissioned by the SRCT investigated the physical and financial viability of reusing St Margaret's as a creative hub and leasing the regenerated building to a specially formed local operating trust. In 2013 the positive findings of the study, coupled with growing community support, gave confidence to the SRCT to acquire the building for a token £1. The decision marks a watershed for the Trust in taking on a redundant church that will be adapted and extended at an estimated cost of £1.5m to fulfil a range of new uses. Although worship will remain part of the use-mix, St Margaret's will follow a very different model from St Peter's and Cromarty East. The project's aims are more than simply the repair of an important historic building and, whilst the Trust must at all times safeguard the cultural value of St Margaret's, there is also an aspiration – and a need – to bring wider benefits for people.

Sustainability and the future landscape
This looks increasingly likely to be the way that the organisation will work from now on. Although the HEACS report states 'there may always be a small number of outstanding places of worship which cannot be retained in ecclesiastical use, but are of such

Fig. 9: St Margaret's Braemar, considered by many to be Comper's 'Scottish masterpiece', disused since 1997 and on the Buildings at Risk Register for more than a decade. Acquired by the SRCT in 2013. This photograph is from 2004.

heritage importance that they should not be altered and converted for any alternative use' the feasibility of such an approach is now in doubt. Philosophically, the 'conserve as found' approach remains desirable and appropriate in some cases, but as an organisation that receives no statutory funding and is dependent on grants and donations, the Trust must take a realistic approach.

The projects for the four other churches currently in SRCT ownership will, most probably, involve a far greater level of intervention than was anticipated when they were taken into care. Pettinain Church, Tibbermore Church, Benholm Kirk and

Fig. 10: St Margaret's, where 'proving uses' have included a performance by the Dutch Youth Symphonic Orchestra, part of the Aberdeen International Youth Festival, here photographed in 2013.

Kildrummy Kirk were acquired for their architectural significance, and because it was believed at the time that conversion and reuse was inappropriate. All are relatively small churches in sparsely populated rural locations. Restricted access, surrounding graveyards, no mains water, and important interiors all impose constraints. Before investing in projects to repair the ageing fabric of these buildings, funders will require evidence of sustainability: will there be the income, the people and the skills to ensure their investment stands the test of time? For the redundant churches of the type that the SRCT has traditionally taken into its care, achieving what is now expected by funders will require new and different approaches. Difficult decisions will have to be taken in the coming years, both by the Trust and by the communities who value these historic churches.

The question of sustainability and, specifically, financial viability, impacts not only on those churches already in SRCT ownership, but also on those being considered for acquisition. In the past, the primary question considered by Trustees was 'how important is this building?' Now this is asked in the same breath as 'will it pay its way?' and 'will we get grants for its repair?' The choice of which churches to take into care is no longer straightforward.

The Trust may be contacted at:

The Scottish Redundant Churches Trust
15 North Bank Street
Edinburgh
EH1 2LP
0131 563 5135
contact@srct.org.uk
www.srct.org.uk

Fig. 1: The interior of Yr Hen Gapel, Llwynrhydowen, the important Unitarian chapel at Rhydowen, near Llandysul, Ceredigion. The present chapel dates from 1834; the architect is unknown. See also Figure 4.

Addoldai Cymru – the Welsh Religious Buildings Trust

ADDOLDAI CYMRU – the Welsh Religious Buildings Trust – was established in 1999 by Cadw (the Welsh Government's built heritage agency) and the Wales Council for Voluntary Action. This resulted from an inquiry into Wales' built heritage undertaken in 1993 by the parliamentary Welsh Affairs Committee which identified the growing problem of redundancy in Wales' rich religious built heritage.

Whereas the Friends of Friendless Churches takes into care notable examples of redundant Church in Wales (Anglican) churches, the Trust does so in respect of all other redundant religious buildings in Wales. Although the Trust has the ability to acquire, for example, Roman Catholic and non-Christian buildings, in practice its focus is upon Nonconformist chapels (Fig. 1).

Nonconformist chapels

Over 6,500 Nonconformist chapels of various denominations have been built in Wales. By the mid nineteenth century Nonconformity could be described as the national religion of Wales and its chapels as Wales' national architecture. They are the physical testimony of the lives of ordinary Welsh people and as such Wales' Nonconformist built heritage is at least as important to Wales' national identity as Edward I's castles. In comparison, chapels receive limited resources and publicity – perhaps their very ubiquity has been to their disadvantage.

However, Wales's chapels are a very important part of our national heritage, and whereas many continue to be sustained by their congregations, a large number are becoming redundant and are at risk. Many are being converted to other uses, with varying degrees of success. The Trust's specific role is to identify and acquire a small, representative selection of buildings of exceptional quality that are of particular architectural or historic significance, and to secure their conservation, repair, maintenance and interpretation to the highest professional quality. Working with the local community, the Trust develops a project which will give each building a sustainable new life that is commensurate with its significance and with the community's specific needs and aspirations.

In short, the Trust is gathering together for posterity a national collection of primarily Nonconformist chapels of exceptional quality. Selection is made on the basis of merit and availability, and with an eye to denominational variety, location, architectural variety, historic interest, and the context of the Trust's existing

by Neil Sumner and Gruff Owen

Neil Sumner and Gruff Owen are respectively Vice Chair and Trust Manager of Addoldai Cymru – the Welsh Religious Buildings Trust.

Description
Cares for six nonconformist chapels in Wales.

Founded
1999

Location
Wales

Access
Varies

Website
www.welshreligiousbuildings.org

portfolio. The Trust benefits from its legal status as a prescribed charity under the Redundant Churches and Other Religious Buildings Act 1969 which allows disposing Trustees to transfer buildings to the Trust at less than market value.

The Trust currently owns six buildings including the Grade I Peniel chapel in Tremadog, Gwynedd whose vestry is now used as the Trust's Office. A seventh acquisition is imminent.

The Trust does not have a specific 'vesting' arrangement with any denomination to transfer buildings to the Trust. Each acquisition to date has been by an ad hoc and often lengthy process, dependent on the administrative structure of the disposing denomination and often on the wishes of the individual congregations. Typically, the redundant chapels that have been offered to the Trust have already overwhelmed their congregations. This has meant that they are generally in poor condition and in urgent need of attention. This is obviously problematic, as the buildings are barely suitable for any kind of use when acquired, and certainly not for general community use.

The Trust would like to be in a position to be able to plan for each acquisition, to have reliable estimates of the development and capital costs involved, and known sources of income to cover them. Ideally, the Trust should only acquire a building once a comprehensive 'care package' has been assembled. But this has proved impossible because buildings are assessed on the merits of the building itself rather on the basis of a business case, and often the exact nature and cost of work required are not known until repairs are commenced.

Funding

However, although the Trust is not a commercial operator, Trustees fully understand that the Trust's buildings each require a sustainable future. The Trustees have taken the view that the Trust acquires a building, and then makes it work, rather than only taking on a particular building when the business case has been made. Buildings are consequently acquired with the attendant risk of being at the mercy of a protracted process of project development.

Cadw's initial focus when establishing the Trust was upon the conservation of the fabric of exceptional architectural assets for the benefit of posterity. However, over the years growing pressures on funding have meant it has become increasingly apparent that each acquired building, once repaired, can only have a sustainable future if it is grounded in the present day in a viable use by the community, whether that is local residents, a wider community of interest, or a visitor community.

Each project requires development work. Most grant applications are not simply applications dealing with the bricks and mortar; rather they require proof of community need and involvement, and for that, suitable community engagement and activity needs to be undertaken. These are essential precursors to successful large-scale funding applications, and require time. This work should be underpinned by core resources, or by additional flexible development funding so that the Trust has the capacity to develop more than one project at a time. Currently the Trust needs to phase and rotate its resources, from project to project, with the result that project development is often intermittent.

The Trust aims to develop a local support group and a cohort of volunteers at each project. Success at this has been varied to date, partly due to a lack of staff capacity to be able to recruit, induct, train and provide momentum to groups of volunteers at each building.

The Trust applies for project development and capital grant aid for each project through normal grant aid processes from various public bodies such as Cadw and other Welsh Government sources including Visit Wales, the Heritage Lottery Fund, local authorities, landfill tax charities, other charitable trusts etc. Funding packages need to be constructed from a range of

Fig. 2: Bethania Baptist chapel at Bethania Street, Maesteg, Bridgend County Borough. Built 1908 by William Beddoe Rees. A large urban chapel and one of the best surviving architectural achievements by a major chapel architect in his powerful Beaux Arts style. (© Crown Copyright: Royal Commission on the Ancient and Historical Monuments of Wales)

different funders whose differing requirements in terms of timing, match funding, and other conditions all need to be satisfied. The Trust benefits from its status as a charity and company limited by guarantee, making it eligible for various funding streams, such as the Listed Places of Worship Grant scheme, and tax exemptions.

Not all grant applications are successful, or rather, most are unsuccessful. For example, over the last eight years five separate applications to the Welsh Government and the HLF for major funding for an ambitious flagship project at the Grade II★ Bethania Chapel in Maesteg, south Wales (Figs 2 & 3) have been unsuccessful. Even potentially successful applications can fall by the wayside if they do not satisfy all the funder's requirements, for example, unrealistic deadlines by which funding needs to be claimed. Funders also have their own problems in terms of take up and draw down of funds.

The Trust has been successful in recently obtaining funding for a major project at the Grade II★ Yr Hen Gapel, in Rhydowen, Ceredigion (Figs 1 & 4). Funding from the HLF, Visit Wales, Cadw, Ceredigion County Council and Llandysul Community

Fig. 3: The interior of Bethania chapel.

Council will enable significant repairs to the building and the creation of a Unitarian Faith Trail linking it to other Unitarian chapels across Wales.

Project development benefits greatly from working with partner organisations. The Trust has been working closely with the Royal Commission on the Ancient and Historical Monuments for Wales to develop the projects at Bethania and Yr Hen Gapel and to enhance the availability of digital web-based information about Wales' Nonconformist heritage. The Trust has worked with both Ceredigion County Council and currently the Faith Tourism Working Group to provide outputs which will assist in delivering

Fig. 4: Yr Hen Gapel, Llwynrhydowen, the Unitarian chapel at Rhydowen, near Llandysul, Ceredigion. See also Figure 1.

the Welsh Government's Faith Tourism Action Plan. At Bethania, the Trust has additionally worked with Menter Bro Ogwr, the Llynfi Valley Historical Society and Capel, the Chapels Heritage Society, to develop key elements of its flagship project.

Whilst the project at Yr Hen Gapel is taking a major step forward, the Trust has found elsewhere that an incremental approach is needed. Two phases of repairs have been undertaken at the historically important Grade II Hen Dŷ Cwrdd in Trecynon near Aberdare, south Wales (Figs 5–7), and two more phases will be needed before the chapel can be re-launched in a secular role as a community cultural and social facility. Similar phased repairs

Fig. 5: Hen Dŷ Cwrdd, located at Trecynon, Aberdare, Rhondda Cynon Tâf. A Unitarian chapel of 1862 by Evan Griffiths of Aberdare. Hen Dŷ Cwrdd has a particularly rich legacy of historical associations, and represents the continuity of nonconformity in Wales.

Fig. 6: Restoration work at Hen Dŷ Cwrdd.

are being undertaken at the Grade II★ Libanus near Llansadwrn, Carmarthenshire, firstly to the roof and more recently to the windows and doors. This, along with the Grade II Beili Du near Sennybridge, Powys, is in a relatively remote rural location and finding a viable use other than as a visitor attraction will be difficult.

Constraints and pressures

In order to take projects forward, the Trust relies on the commitment of experienced conservation architects – four different practices are currently employed. Because of the Trust's lack of suitable income streams and reserves, all practices are sometimes obliged to undertake speculative preparatory work without guarantee of payment. The Trust is hugely grateful for their support and commitment, but it is a far from ideal situation and the Trust needs funding to enable it to take the burden of risk, rather than relying on architects' goodwill.

The Trust is one of a number of organisations which look after redundant places of worship in the UK, and that receive block core funding grants from the relevant governments. Although work undertaken by the Trust has increased consistently, in common with many organisations the Trust has since 2009 received a declining level of core funding from Cadw in real terms.

The Trust's current staff consists of a full-time Manager and a part-time Development Officer. The amount of work required to secure funding, to develop local community participation, to undertake building repairs and maintenance, and to try to secure an active and useful life for each building, as well as to run the

Fig. 7: The restored interior at Hen Dŷ Cwrdd.

Trust day-to-day, is immense. The Trust has learnt to live a frugal existence, and is barely holding its own. Its workload will inevitably increase if more buildings are acquired.

Even during the development phase, buildings need to be managed and maintained within the constraints of their limited functionality and this involves significant on-going costs. Cadw provides limited core funding for buildings' overheads, such as insurance, utility bills, graveyard grass cutting, and some minor maintenance.

The Trust has endeavoured to diversify its income from other sources but it has met with only limited success. When the Trust takes over a redundant building it relieves the denomination and/or congregation of considerable administrative, security, insurance and other financial burdens. However, the various denominations have not supported the Trust's work financially, primarily because the denominations' financial focus is upon supporting the Christian faith rather than upon heritage conservation. The Trust has been successful in obtaining some additional core funding from other charitable trusts such as the Pilgrim Trust, but this has proven increasingly difficult in recent years. Donations from individuals are welcome but sporadic and inevitably modest.

The staff are supported by eight Trustees who are drawn from a variety of backgrounds – architectural, denominational, legal, historical etc. Trustees have quarterly board meetings but also contribute their expertise as appropriate to project development throughout the year. Trustees have taken personal responsibility for redundant buildings in a poor state of repair but which are of national significance and a vital part of our national heritage. They are therefore anxious about the Trust's future – it is a long term property-owning activity, and it requires long term certainty. Although they are protected to some extent by the Trust's status as a company limited by guarantee, the Trustees still believe that they take a significant personal risk in accepting responsibility for at-risk buildings as the Trust has no underpinning financial security. Trustees have been advised not to offer personal guarantees for loans or overdraft facilities. The Trust has no reserves of any significance, nor has it received any endowment accompanying any building acquired, to help offset some of the liability that it is taking on. As more suitable buildings become redundant, the lack of financial security will increasingly dominate the Trust's decision-making.

The Trust also seeks to be a natural focus for those concerned about the future of Wales' religious built heritage, and endeavours to work with others who share that concern. Therefore, in addition to building acquisition, the Trust does have a remit to act as a champion of Wales' Nonconformist heritage, promoting a wider knowledge and understanding of its cultural and social significance, and to offer information and advice to bodies and individuals responsible for caring for the non Church in Wales built heritage. The Trust produces an occasional newsletter which is circulated to its national Friends membership amongst others.

The future

Chapel redundancy is nothing new of course, but all indications are that it will be rapidly increasing during the next ten years or so. This will include the closure and disposal of some of Wales' most cherished high quality and highly listed buildings. If nothing is done, Wales may well be littered with many more boarded up, crumbling and vandalised redundant religious buildings, which ultimately will be demolished. The Trustees firmly believe that as the crisis is happening now, this is the time to try and address it, with whatever resources and tools are to hand, before it is too late.

Fig. 1: The interior of Walpole Old Chapel, Suffolk, from one corner of the gallery, looking across the width of the building to the pulpit and lectern. The chapel was converted from two timber farmhouses in about 1689. As with all the buildings illustrated here, this is now in the care of the Historic Chapels Trust (HCT), acquired by the Trust in 1994.

The Historic Chapels Trust

THE HISTORIC CHAPELS TRUST (HCT) was founded in 1993, to take into ownership significant nonconformist, independent and Roman Catholic places of worship. It has the power to take on places of worship of other religions as well, but in spite of negotiations has not yet been able to do so. It aims to give its buildings a sustainable future.

HCT's buildings

The Trust now has a collection of twenty churches, chapels and meeting houses, all Grade I or II★, scattered across England from Cornwall to Northumberland. They are a diverse collection, all significant in their individual way. They embrace a wide mix of dates and styles – including two poignantly simple Quaker meeting houses, a nineteenth-century Roman Catholic aristocratic mortuary chapel, a large Unitarian Gothic church, several eighteenth- and nineteenth-century Baptist chapels, a tiny Methodist chapel and a 1500-seater of the same denomination, a medieval domestic chapel (relocated to another site by E. W. Pugin), and a mid twentieth-century chapel designed by F. X. Velarde. A full list and some illustrations will be found immediately after this article.

The Historic Chapels Trust sees itself as an 'acquiror of last resort'. So typically the Trust has only taken on buildings when no other appropriate use could be found for them; usually they are 'difficult' buildings and many are in deprived economic areas. At present the Trust has a moratorium on new acquisitions unless they come with an endowment (or funding under a S106 agreement or Community Infrastructure Levy) to maintain the fabric. If current fundraising activities bring the desired result over several years, the Trust hopes to start taking on new buildings again, as it is regularly approached about buildings of real significance that it would like to consider acquiring but cannot for want of funds.

The Charities Act allows denominations and charities to hand unwanted buildings over to HCT at less than full market value. However it is the on-going maintenance that is often the challenge, so the Trust has been highly selective in accepting the buildings it has been offered.

The majority of its buildings were in poor condition when acquired by HCT, sometimes in severe disrepair. The Trust has not only repaired many of them, but also seeks to find ways in which they can be used and appreciated. However some still require further work.

Roland Jeffery

Roland Jeffery is Director of the Historic Chapels Trust.

Description
Cares for twenty non-conformist and Roman Catholic places of worship.

Founded
1983

Location
Owns buildings throughout England.

Access
Varies; typically by arrangement.

Website
www.hct.org.uk

The HCT has no endowment, and (unlike the Churches Conservation Trust, which looks after some closed Church of England buildings) receives no government funding and no income from the denominations from whom it has acquired buildings. Each campaign of work requires fund-raising, from local and national grant-giving trusts and others. English Heritage has been a generous funder of both capital and repairs projects from the start, though its ability to maintain this support at the same levels is currently in doubt. More recently, large grants from the Heritage Lottery Fund have provided major assistance.

Use of the buildings

Where appropriate HCT's places of worship have volunteer committees attached to them, and many of these committees organise events, where the building and its surroundings make this realistic. For example, at Walpole chapel in Suffolk, about a dozen events are taking place in 2014, including services, a shape-note workshop, concerts, an exhibition, a poetry event, and the re-creation of a nineteenth-century harvest tea. Such activities contribute to operational costs, and they represent a substantial input of volunteer time to the running of the chapels. Named keyholders, who are usually members of the local committee, keep an eye on the building and ensure that there is public access outside the hours of particular events. These committees are a distinctive and integral aspect of the Trust's work.

There is also a national Supporters scheme, and Supporters receive a regular newsletter about the work of the Trust. Patrons giving larger sums are invited to invitation-only events.

The Trust's website (www.hct.org.uk) gives details of each building and access arrangements. The buildings can be visited by prior arrangement (unless unsafe from repair work), and many of them have specified opening times. Free two-page guides are available as free downloads for all the buildings, and some have lengthier guide books commissioned by the Trust. Many of the buildings are available for hire for suitable events, and some can host weddings, funerals and memorial services.

The changing landscape

Like many conservation charities HCT is now under some financial pressure. For two decades generous support from English Heritage (EH) has been key. But the Exchequer is cutting its grant to EH by more than a third over the next few years, and this is having a knock-on effect on the grant EH provides to the HCT – and a number of similar organisations.

So earned income will in future be playing a much more significant role at HCT. A new (2014) post (funded by the

Heritage Lottery Fund Transition Grant scheme) over two years aims to generate much more earned income from use of the charity's buildings. This may embrace traditional uses like marriages (several HCT sites are registered for this) baby-naming and funerals. But it will also look to newer directions such as performances, art installations, festivals and business events. More time is also being spent on raising voluntary donations.

In general, non-Anglican buildings are still under-studied, under-listed, and under-appreciated. The Trust continues to play its part in putting this right, by caring for an England-wide collection of significant buildings. Between them they represent important strands in our history. The 'co-op and chapel' culture of many northern working-class areas was its defining character; the Roman Catholic influence was profound in its strongholds. The religious liberties we today take for granted were hard-fought by Quakers in the seventeenth century through to Unitarians and Methodists in the nineteenth.

Some chapels and churches convert well into houses and offices and when this happens at least the outline of the buildings are retained in their landscapes. HCT deals with those that are too important for this – and with those which would otherwise be demolished entirely. As populations change, religious observance evolves, and cultures become more diverse, many non-Anglican places of worship are falling out of use. There is much work still to do.

The Historic Chapels Trust welcomes Supporters. The Trust can be contacted via its website www.hct.org.uk or by writing to St George's German Lutheran Church, 55 Alie Street, London, E1 8EB.

An extensive article by Roland Jeffery about the Trust's buildings, entitled 'Rescuing the built heritage of dissenters, recusants and nonconformists: the Historic Chapels Trust' appeared in the most recent edition of Transactions of the Ancient Monuments Society 58 (2014), 155–69, and anyone wishing to learn more about the Trust is encouraged to read that article.

See the following pages for list of buildings and illustrations.

List of chapels, churches and meeting houses
Full details of each building can be found on the Trust's website.

East of England
Petre Chapel, Thorndon Country Park, off Hartswood Rd, Brentwood, Essex, CM13 3SA. *Roman Catholic private mortuary chapel of the Lords Petre, designed by William Wardell, dedicated 1857, Grade II★.*

Walpole Old Chapel, Halesworth Road, Walpole, Suffolk. IP19 9AZ. *Independent chapel, Grade II★, converted in about 1689 from two timber farmhouses (Fig. 1).*

London
St George's German Lutheran Church, 55 Alie Street, London, E1 8EB. *German Lutheran, built 1762–3, Grade II★, the oldest Lutheran church in the country.*

The Dissenters' Chapel, Kensal Green Cemetery, Harrow Road, Kensal Green, London, W10 4BA. *Designed about 1834 as a chapel for non-Anglican funeral services at Europe's first public cemetery, Grade II★.*

Fig. 2: Biddlestone Roman Catholic chapel, Northumberland, a private chapel built in the 1820s on the undercroft of a medieval pele. Acquired by HCT in 1996.

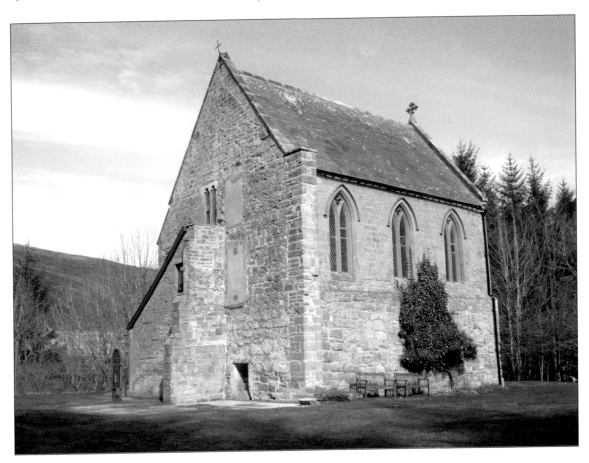

Fig. 3: The interior of the tiny chapel at Penrose, Cornwall, built in 1861. Once Bible Christian, now Methodist. Acquired by HCT in 2000.

North East

Biddlestone RC Chapel, Biddlestone Village, near Netherton, Northumberland, NE65 7DT. *Roman Catholic private chapel (house disappeared), built in the 1820s on an undercroft of a medieval pele tower, Grade II★ (Fig. 2).*

Coanwood Friends Meeting House, Coanwood, near Haltwhistle, Northumberland, NE49 0PU. *Society of Friends (Quakers), constructed 1760 to serve an upland mining area, Grade II★.*

Westgate Methodist Chapel (formerly Primitive Methodist), Bishop Auckland, Co Durham, DL13 1LQ. *Methodist, built 1871, designed by the chapel specialist George Race, Grade II★.*

North West

Shrine of Our Lady of Lourdes, Whinney Heys Road, Blackpool, FY3 8NP. *Built 1955–7 by public subscription to the designs of F. X. Velarde as a thanksgiving for Blackpool's avoidance of bombing in WWII, Grade II*.*

St Benet's RC Chapel, Merseyside, Chapel Lane, Netherton, Merseyside, L30 7PE. *A simple Roman Catholic hall church self-built by a working class community the year Catholic worship was legalised, opened 1793, Grade II*.*

Wallasey Memorial Unitarian Church, Manor Road, Liscard Village, Wallasey, Merseyside, CH44 1DA. *Unitarian, Arts and Crafts furnishings, opened in 1899, Grade II*.*

South West

Grittleton Strict Baptist Chapel, High Street, Grittleton, Wiltshire, SN14 6AP. *Strict Baptist, opened in 1721, Grade II*.*

Penrose Methodist Chapel, Penrose, St Ervan, Cornwall, PL27 7TB. *Tiny Methodist (formerly Bible Christian) chapel, dating from 1861, Grade II* (Fig. 3).*

Salem Chapel, Vicarage Road, East Budleigh, Devon, EX9 7EF. *Dating from 1719, with successive Presbyterian, Congregational, Independent congregations, Grade II*.*

Fig. 4: Cote Baptist Chapel, Oxfordshire, built 1756 partly incorporating an earlier chapel's fabric.

Fig. 5: Umberslade Baptist Church, Hockley Heath, near Solihull. Baptist 'estate' chapel, built in 1877 at the expense of George Muntz, a Birmingham metals magnate whose patent alloys 'copper bottomed' much of the national merchant fleet in the nineteenth century. Acquired by HCT in 1999. (Aidan McRae Thomson)

West Midlands

Bethesda Methodist Chapel, Albion Street, Hanley, Stoke-on-Trent, ST1 1QF. *Methodist, said to have accommodated 2,000, built 1819 and later, Grade II*.*

Cote Baptist Chapel, Shifford Road, Cote, Near Bampton, Oxfordshire, OX18 2EG. *Baptist chapel, built 1756 partly incorporating an earlier chapel's fabric, Grade II* (Fig. 4).*

Longworth RC Chapel, Frome Court, Bartestree, Herefordshire, HR1 4DX. *Medieval private chapel relocated wholesale in 1869–70 for use of Roman Catholic convent, Grade II*.*

Fig. 6: Farfield Friends Meeting House, Farfield, Yorkshire; built 1689 and one of the oldest Friends meeting houses. There are five table tombs to the Myers family, which with their aristocratic and royal associations are 'un-Quakerly' and probably unique for a Friends burial ground. Quakers preferred small, standardised headstones or no burial marker at all. Acquired in 1994 by Historic Chapels Trust after lying empty for several decades, its restoration was the charity's first project. (Gordon Hope)

Umberslade Baptist Church, Spring Lane, Hockley Heath, Near Solihull, B94 6QY. *Baptist, 'estate' chapel, built 1877 at the expense of George Muntz, Birmingham metals magnate, Grade II★ (Fig. 5).*

Yorkshire

Farfield Friends Meeting House, Farfield, Near Addingham, West Yorkshire, LS29 0RQ. *Society of Friends (Quakers), Grade II★, built 1689 and one of the oldest Friends meeting houses (Fig. 6).*

Todmorden Unitarian Church, Honey Hole Road, Todmorden, West Yorkshire, OL14 6LE. *Unitarian, Gothic and spacious, built at the expense of the philanthropic and reforming local MP, 'Honest' John Fielden, 1865–9, Grade I.*

Wainsgate Baptist Church, Wainsgate Lane, Old Town, Hebden Bridge, West Yorkshire, HX7 8SU. *Baptist, built 1859–60 and extended later for the congregation of celebrated preacher and hymnist John Fawcett, Grade II★.*

Part 2

SINGLE-BUILDING TRUSTS, ETC

Fig. 1: Barlaston Old Church (dedicated to St John the Baptist), Barlaston, Staffordshire. The church lies close to the house. The tower is medieval, the body of the church Victorian. (top: Mark Higginson; bottom: Staffordshire Historic Churches Trust)

Barlaston Old Church, Staffordshire

THE VILLAGE OF BARLASTON lies just south of Stoke-on-Trent at the edge of the old Staffordshire coal fields. It is an ancient settlement which developed during the nineteenth century as a commuter village for wealthy pottery owners keen to live away from the smog and grime of the Potteries.

Barlaston Old Church (dedicated to St John the Baptist) sits at what is now the edge of the village in the Wedgwood estate, close to Barlaston Hall, a mid eighteenth-century Palladian villa (Fig. 1). The church consists of a medieval tower and a large Victorian nave. It is listed Grade II.

In the early 1980s, parishioners arrived one day at the church to discover a significant split in the walls of the nave caused by coal-mining underneath. The church was immediately evacuated and propped internally to prevent its immediate collapse. The National Coal Board (NCB) offered to repair the church, with the risk it would split again, or build a new one closer to the village. The latter offer was accepted, with the intention of demolishing the old church except for its medieval tower.

In the same period the fate of Barlaston Hall also hung in the balance. Owned by the Wedgwood company since the 1930s, and empty since the war, vandalism, neglect and mining had taken their toll on the Grade I listed Hall. In 1981 Wedgwood and the NCB jointly applied for permission to demolish the Hall on the grounds that it could not economically be rescued. At the subsequent public enquiry the demolition was opposed by SAVE Britain's Heritage, a newly formed crusading conservation charity for which this was an early test of resolve. After a few days of the enquiry, SAVE were quietly approached by Wedgwood: "If you feel so strongly about this building, you can have it for one pound". The subsequent successful restoration of the Hall is a story for another place, but when it became clear that there was an intention to demolish the old church SAVE stepped in and brought the church with the Hall into the Barlaston Hall Trust, a newly created building preservation trust.

Some ten years later in 1992, Barlaston Hall was sold on to the current owners, Mr and Mrs James Hall who completed the restoration of the Hall and took responsibility for the care of the Old Church. With the threat of further mining finally eliminated in the mid 1990s, it was possible to step in and repair the church. The church currently serves as a storehouse for the Hall. Some of the windows and monuments from the old church were incorporated in the new church, many others remain boxed and protected in the old church.

James Hall

Description
Preserved as part of a much larger restoration campaign by a Building Preservation Trust, the restored building now cared for privately.

Founded
1982

Location
Barlaston, Staffordshire.

Access
Private, no access.

Fig. 1: Bramhope Puritan Chapel, Bramhope, Leeds, the interior looking east. The building dates from 1649, and some of the furnishings are of that period. The steps to the left lead up to a small platform, used as a tiny stage.

The Puritan Chapel, Bramhope, near Leeds

History

BRAMHOPE PURITAN CHAPEL (Figs 1 & 2) was built in 1649, and was in use for worship in Bramhope from 1649–1881 when the new St Giles church was opened. From the time of the Restoration it was a Chapel of ease to Otley parish church, leaving the period of Puritan worship technically confined to the first eleven years of its existence, though the indications are that such worship went on in some form for some time after that.

For most of that time the Chapel remained in the ownership of its Trustees though it was long associated with the Dyneley and Rhodes families, in turn owners of the nearby Bramhope Hall in whose grounds the Chapel was originally built. The hall itself was converted to flats in the last century.

The Chapel remained well maintained until 1927 when the Bramhope Hall estate was sold, and Bramhope Hall itself was eventually purchased by Trust Houses (Trust House Forte) to make way for a new hotel. From 1927, the Chapel remained unused, becoming neglected and eventually falling into disrepair. In the gales of 1962 a large tree fell onto the Chapel seriously damaging its roof. At this point the local community, including the parish council, decided action should be taken for fear of losing the building altogether.

Within a year the then owner transferred the Chapel by deed of gift to the Wharfedale Rural District Council (WRDC) which then took the lead in getting the restoration under way. With the help of some external grants the Chapel underwent a complete restoration and at the time of local government reorganisation in 1973, which saw the end of WRDC, the Chapel became vested in Bramhope parish council.

Visitors

We are fortunate in that the Britannia Hotel, situated next door, has always worked well with us. It keeps the key to the Chapel at Reception which allows visitors access at any time. The hotel also provides a degree of informal security cover – in recent years swift action by their security people prevented the loss of much of the roof, thieves having already stacked a pile of slates ready for transporting from the site.

For many years now the parish council has arranged for the Chapel to be open for visitors on Sunday afternoons during the period Easter to September. It employs someone as part-time curator and guide to be present on those occasions There are a modest number of visitors, mostly local to the area, though they do come from all over the world as evidenced by the visitor book.

Cllr Clive Fox

Until his recent death, Clive Fox was a Bramhope Parish Councillor and a Leeds City Councillor.

Description
Small building of 1649 with early furnishings.

Taken over by local council
1963

Location
Bramhope, about 9 miles north of Leeds.

Access
Key available at all reasonable times.

Website
http://bramhopecarlton.org.uk /puritan-chapel

Fig. 2: Bramhope Puritan Chapel from the south-west.

Fig. 3: The small stone font of 1673.

We have participated in recent years in the Heritage Open Days with a speaker giving a ten minute talk about the Chapel and its history every half hour throughout the afternoon. Though we did not participate last year owing to other commitments, we will consider doing so on future occasions.

So far as marketing the Chapel as a visitor attraction is concerned, very little is done. The absence of marketing arises from the lack of facilities and the limited income stream that increased visitor numbers might generate. For a visitor to get the best out of the experience it really needs someone there to talk about the history and background of the place and we do not have anyone available to do that outside the regular summer Sunday openings, or for occasional group visits. So we recognise our limitations by conducting marketing on a low key basis.

Use of the Chapel

In recent years thought has been given to using the Chapel more frequently and the regular events now include a parish council carol service. Additionally, other services are held from time to time include occasional Christenings (Fig. 3), Marriage Blessings and funerals.

Over the past three years the parish council has run a summer festival of events comprising generally three concerts held at the Puritan Chapel, including jazz evenings, operatic evenings, play reading and other classical music concerts. The Chapel seats about 80 people comfortably but is capable of seating up to about 100.

The greatest single constraint in making better use of the Chapel is the fact it has no facilities – no parking, no water supply and therefore no toilets etc. Further limitations include the hard wooden seats and the box pews which means some people sitting with their backs to the performers. However people readily accept its limitations on account of the Chapel's unique setting.

Marriage Blessings at the Chapel are always held in conjunction with the hotel, which of course does have all the necessary facilities and is where the reception is held. Unfortunately it has not been possible to hold weddings in the Chapel, which limits the income potential somewhat.

Finances

The ongoing costs of operating the Chapel have been relatively modest over the past 50 years. Externally the Chapel has a relatively small grassed area which the parish council maintains but internally little maintenance work has been necessary. The biggest single cost is the heating, though the temperature is kept low simply to air the building. The parish council bears the cost of the part-time curator. Insurance costs are of the order of £2000, heating about £1,200, and other costs, including the seasonal part-time curator, bring the total to perhaps £5,500 per year.

Money is raised by donations received from visitors and half a dozen or so Blessings, Funerals and Christenings a year plus the fees from one or two outside organisations holding their carol services there, and this raises perhaps £500 per year. But the main source of funding is the parish council via the council tax precept. To put this into context the parish precept is £55,000 and cemetery charges bring in a further income.

With the parish council owning and responsible for the Chapel, funding has not been a particular problem and is unlikely to be a problem in the future. We will shortly be coming to the end of a £25,000 refurbishment programme which has involved enhanced lighting and heating (for the benefit of the building as opposed to people). In addition we have worked our way through a schedule of work under the guidance of an ecclesiastical architect and as agreed with English Heritage. This includes improved external drainage to deal with some damp issues and an element of re-plastering and repointing plus other routine maintenance work. That will leave the Chapel in a first class condition, we hope for some years to come. We secured a £7,500 grant from Leeds City Council towards this project.

The future

As for the future, there are good grounds for optimism. There is clearly a commitment from the community to look after the Chapel and when the current refurbishment programme is complete by early summer (2014) we should be up to date in terms of what is necessary to maintain its fabric.

Fig. 1: Brampton Old Church, Cumbria, from the west, showing the west-end porch of 1861, and the chancel of the earlier church, now acting as the nave. The churchyard is no longer used for burials.

Brampton Old Church, Brampton, Cumbria

Introduction

BRAMPTON OLD CHURCH is situated on the banks of the River Irthing, a tributary of the River Eden in north-east Cumbria, ten miles north-east of Carlisle and one mile from the market town of Brampton (population 4,500). It lies within the outer walls of a Roman fort. The fort was located on a late first-century Roman road, the 'Stanegate', which ran between forts at Carlisle and Corbridge, about 30 miles to the east of Brampton. The fort was used prior to the construction of Hadrian's Wall, about a mile further north.

A church on this site was certainly in place in 1169, when it is referred to in the dedication of Lanercost Priory, two miles to the north east. At that time it consisted of a chancel, nave and tower or 'steeple'. The main part of the current building consists of various reconstructions of the original chancel (Fig. 1), the rest of the church having been demolished.

The building was the subject of major works in 1987/88 at which point it became the property of Brampton Preservation Trust.

History as a parish church

The Old Church's history before the late twelfth century is obscure. It has been suggested, as with many of the walls and buildings in the area, that some of the stones in the current church had first been used by the Romans. Documentation from 1603 indicates an oval graveyard, suggesting pre-Norman origins.

After the founding of Lanercost Priory in 1169, a period of relative cross-border harmony ended in 1296, when the accidental death of the Scottish king led to Edward I of England invading Scotland. There followed a period of intense cross-border conflict for nearly 300 years, producing a very uncertain setting for the local population, who developed a lawless, family-based culture of ruthless survival; they are known as the 'border reivers'.

The full church of chancel, nave and tower survived this turmoil, but only to find itself in a period of severe competition between churches in an area of strong non-conformity. In 1662, the rector was ejected and he formed an independent congregation in the town, over a mile away. This situation finally led in 1789, after lack of investment and desertion of the parishioners, to the decision to demolish the building in order to assist the conversion of the Almshouse Chapel in Brampton into a new Parish Church, on the site of the present St Martins' Church in Front Street. In 1878, that eighteenth-century church

Robert Allan

Robert Allan is a Trustee of Brampton Preservation Trust, which owns Brampton Old Church.

Description
A small church on the edge of a market town, used for occasional services, supported by the local Preservation Trust.

Acquired by Trust
1987/88

Location
About a mile north-west of Brampton, Cumbria.

Access
Key from nearby farm.

was replaced by the current building, the only church designed by Pre-Raphaelite architect, Philip Webb, with stained glass windows designed by Edward Burne-Jones and manufactured by Morris and Co.

The demolition of the nave of the Old Church left the chancel for use for funeral services related to the continued use of the churchyard. It remained a mortuary chapel for 190 years. The church has been subject to a succession of repairs and rebuilding, including the addition of the porch at the west end in 1861, and some internal changes including the removal of the ceiling and re-roofing in 1891 (Fig. 2).

Acquisition and use by the Trust

In 1948 the church was listed as an historic monument, and in 1951 it was listed as a Grade II★ listed building. It was declared redundant in 1978. A faculty to demolish was sought and this led to the then Department of the Environment, in 1983, approaching the Brampton Preservation Trust with a view to the Trust accepting ownership of the building following the allocation of a grant to the Trust to carry out stabilisation works in the building to address, in particular, the south wall, which was increasingly leaning outwards.

The Trust accepted the offer of a grant and undertook to take ownership of the building. Works costing £40k were satisfactorily completed during 1987/88. The main stabilisation works involved the insertion of longitudinal and cross steel tie bars to prevent further movement of the walls. Since 1988 the Trust has undertaken quinquennial surveys, and the building remains essentially sound, with occasional minor repairs being undertaken.

Fig. 2: Brampton Old Church, the interior looking east. This was originally the chancel of the parish church.

The churchyard is no longer used for burials and is the responsibility of Carlisle City Council.

In the porch there are several artefacts, including a list of the incumbents, a Victorian bier, the possible base of an Anglian preaching cross used as a Norman font, and some gravestones. A leaflet about the building prepared by the Trust in the late 1990s is available in the building, as are extracts from a learned article on the church.

Since acquisition, the Church has been used on two or three occasions throughout the year by local churches for mainly ecumenical services; otherwise it is open to viewing by visitors obtaining a key from the immediately adjacent Old Church Farm. The walk from the town takes about 25 minutes, or one can drive up a narrow lane, at the end of which there is limited parking. There are no toilets or other facilities in or near the building. The building has lighting, activated by a push-button timer.

The Trust and the future

The Trust was established in 1981, during a period when many of the buildings in central Brampton were threatened with demolition. It acquired and renovated three blocks of property, and was instrumental in averting any widespread loss of buildings. This renovation work provided some financial security for the Trust and apart from a few grants, the Trust continues to exist on the surpluses acquired at that time. The Trust has not undertaken any building works since the 1980s but has continued to seek and support the conservation of the important buildings of the area. Old Church is the only building it currently owns, and the main expense is building insurance. It is currently considering options for protecting the building's future.

Apart from the onerous insurance costs, the Trust has found this small, little-used building inexpensive to keep, and has been able to rely on its accumulated funds to cover any occasional small expenditure, although this cannot continue indefinitely. The Trust has considered establishing it as venue for various kinds of events and raising revenue. It keeps this option under review, but has not so far felt the need to prioritise taking this forward. This will be necessary in the not too distant future, and we are open to suggestions.

Note

The history of the building given here is based on John Robinson, 'Notes on Brampton Old Church', Transactions of the Cumberland and Westmorland Antiquarian & Archaeological Society, *Vol. LXXXII (1982).*

Fig. 1: Two views of the interior of the New Room, Bristol, showing the galleried chapel, lit by an octagon. (Phil Draper)

The Horsefair Project at the New Room, Bristol

Editor's introduction: This article discusses the future of the New Room, Bristol, an important building in the history of Methodism.

Although the scale of the operation is larger than many other Trusts discussed in this volume, the issues are similar – particularly the importance of volunteers in keeping a building alive, the need to arrange events which go with the grain of the building, the difficulties which can arise with the various statutory organisations when there is a change of personnel, and the major effort required to raise large sums of money.

Gary Best

Gary Best is Warden of the New Room, Bristol.

THE NEW ROOM was built by John Wesley in 1739 and extended by him in 1748. It has been described as 'the cradle of Methodism' and is a Grade I listed building. It consists of a galleried chapel, lit by the famous octagon (Fig. 1), with a range of rooms above. It lies between two courtyards.

With the help of six volunteer stewards every day the New Room is open to visitors from 10.00 – 16.00 Monday to Saturday all the year round and is sometimes open at other times for special events. It currently has around 26,000 visitors per year and is the most visited Methodist heritage site in the UK. It is ranked as one of Bristol's five star buildings (alongside places like St Mary Redcliffe, Bristol Cathedral, Clifton Suspension Bridge, and Brunel's Temple Meads Station) and it has not only featured regularly in the local press, radio and television but also in many national TV programmes.

Above Wesley's chapel there are preachers' rooms (Fig. 2), and seven of these house an accredited museum. It has a unique collection of ceramics, portraits, letters, personal effects, and furniture. Two of the other upstairs rooms contain a very significant 5,000 volume library that contains one of the best collections in the country on Methodist history. The New Room has two courtyards and each contains a Grade II listed statue – the main Broadmead Courtyard has an iconic statue of John Wesley on horseback and the rear Horsefair Courtyard has the world's only significant statue of the hymn-writer Charles Wesley. The Trustees also maintain Charles Wesley's House (which is Grade II listed) in Bristol and arrange for group visits to this.

Activities

Every year a programme of regular concerts and occasional special events is devised. Examples include an all-day workshop on the history of hymnody, an eighteenth-century preaching day to contrast Calvinist and Wesleyan preaching, a walking tour of early Wesleyan preaching sites in Bristol, a series of Lenten lectures on environmental issues, a concert of music written by Samuel

Description

The New Room was built by John Wesley, and has been described as 'the cradle of Methodism'.

Location
Bristol

Access
Open daily.

Website
www.newroombristol.org.uk

Fig. 2: Preacher's room, New Room, Bristol. (Wendy Harris)

Wesley (Charles Wesley's son), and hosting (in conjunction with Bristol University) the launch of the new international Dictionary of Hymnody. There is also an educational programme for schools (such as experiencing aspects of life in a Georgian townhouse) and a publishing programme, most recently short biographies of Wesley's mother and sisters.

In addition to maintaining this important heritage site, the New Room fulfils an important outreach role in the centre of Bristol. One of our stewards has written movingly of having met and given support to a wide range of people in difficulties or under pressure, such as a failed asylum seeker, a recovering drug addict, a homeless person, and a young man suffering from depression for seven years. That outreach opportunity is an important factor in helping us recruit volunteers.

We need at least seventy stewards to act as guides and recruiting these is becoming increasingly difficult because traditionally they have been drawn from Methodist churches and the membership of the church is declining. Managing the New Room is further complicated because we lack appropriate facilities – there is no kitchen or dining area to offer refreshments, no adequate toilets, no proper facilities for our archives, etc.

All of this work is dependent on visitor donations and on the money raised by volunteers through coffee mornings and other fund raising events. We currently receive a grant from the Methodist Church that covers the cost of the salary of one full-time employee – the Manager – but we have to raise around £80,000 every year to meet the other maintenance and running costs.

Plans and difficulties

So in 2010 the Trustees embarked on the Horsefair Project – an ambitious scheme to provide much needed facilities and to reorganise our programme and attract a wider range of volunteers.

The main proposal was to erect a three-storey building in the rear courtyard that would provide visitor facilities, a new room for educational purposes, new archives and library facilities, disabled access via a lift, and meeting rooms. Alongside this the Museum would be extended and redeveloped into nine themed rooms with two further rooms for temporary exhibitions.

From the outset there was public support for what we were proposing and no objections from the Georgian Society, but achieving planning permission has proved far more complex and drawn-out than we expected, not least because in the course of the last three years we have had to deal with three different English Heritage Officers and three different Methodist Conservation Officers, and because for a long time the local planning office refused to meet us and insisted on doing everything entirely by correspondence. We eventually had to use local councillors to achieve a face-to-face meeting last year (since when progress has been far greater).

The whole experience has convinced me that planning is very largely a subjective issue, though it pretends otherwise. For example, we wanted to remove an ugly old lean-to building that had been erected on the rear of the New Room in the nineteenth century. The first Bristol case officer insisted that this building had to be retained and the entire scheme had to be redrawn. Then the case officer was changed and the new one immediately decided the scheme made far more sense if the lean-to was removed, especially as it was not historically significant.

From the outset it has been accepted by everyone that development is essential if the long term future of the building is to be assured, but this immense benefit does not – in itself – make for an easy passage. In our experience it is very easy for a single issue to distort perceptions of a scheme's impact and cause problems. For example, the main concern about our proposals from the point of view of the original English Heritage officer was that a new building would impact on the view behind Wesley's pulpit (by preventing the glimpse of blue sky that was possible if one stood in a small area of the chapel). His successor, who refused to hold any meeting with us, then took this a step further, saying the new building would block out light and therefore affect the light levels within the listed building. This was repeatedly said even though we had commissioned a light level report and this showed the difference in light level was so small that it would not be observable to the human eye! It took a change in officer (who did meet us) before this was accepted and we could resolve the issue.

What has also complicated matters is that there is not always joined up thinking at a local level. For example, we have been trying to sort out rights of light issues. The Bristol planners would have liked us to do that in advance of planning permission but the Bristol officer responsible for the buildings next to us (which the city own and lease out) will not make an agreement until planning permission is obtained.

In general, it is not easy to get planning experts to understand the nature of the work a charity undertakes and the particular problems posed by relying on volunteers. No consideration is given for the fact that finances may be tight – we have had to pay for a number of surveys that we know were pointless – such as a coal mining survey and a flood assessment – simply because boxes have to be ticked.

Having said all this, we have now produced an amended scheme that has the support of English Heritage, the Methodist Conservation Officer, and the Bristol planners – and we hope this is going to lead to both planning permission and listed building consent being granted in July (2014).

Money

Raising the money for the Horsefair Project has also involved immense work. We knew we had to raise in the region of £3.6 to £3.75 million. We were fortunate to be offered £1.4 million by the Bristol Methodist District and, with that support, to make a successful first round bid for Heritage Lottery Fund money. It took us two goes, but we were offered £2.3 million in July 2013.

Alongside these two big donors, we have been campaigning for money from Trusts and other sources (in what has proved to be a very tight market) and undertaking a raft of small fund-raising activities (flower festivals, coffee mornings, and the like).

We are currently engaged in preparing for our second round HLF bid and I will not disguise that this has been and is a very time-consuming (and expensive) business. I have found the HLF very helpful and they contribute financially towards the cost of developing the scheme, but they require very detailed reports. In order to produce the Activity and Business Plans they require, and the Museum Interpretation Plan, we have had to employ considerable professional support as well as using volunteer work. We hope that we will be in a position to make our second round bid this October.

Looking ahead

There is still lots to do – the finalisation of the building and museum proposals, the work to recruit more volunteers, the tendering and the building process, etc will take another couple of years. However, four years on I can see that all the effort is likely to result in a wonderful new building that will transform the way we work and what we can offer. It will also put this important and fascinating site on a safer financial footing. It will have been worth it – but there were many times on the way when I doubted that!

Fig. 1: The church of the Holy Rood, Coombe Keynes, Dorset, rebuilt in 1861 by John Hicks. The tower is of the thirteenth century, with a roof of Purbeck stone. The bells are in the County Museum. The churchyard is managed for wild life.

The Coombe Keynes Trust, Coombe Keynes, Dorset

THE CHURCH OF THE HOLY ROOD at Coombe Keynes, Dorset is recorded as existing as far back as the thirteenth century, but was extensively rebuilt in 1861 by John Hicks of Dorchester, to whom Thomas Hardy was at that time articled: only the tower now contains any earlier fabric. It is listed Grade II.

The village and the foundation of the Trust

Coombe Keynes today is a shadow of the village which existed in the medieval period, depopulated by changes in agriculture and/or the Black Death. It now consists of a dozen or so houses round a small green, plus a handful of outlying farms and cottages, and six council houses built after the last war just far enough away from the village centre to make the residents feel like outsiders.

Apart from the council houses, the church and the vicarage, all of the village belonged to the local Estate until the 1970s, when farming on the Estate was reorganised and the two farms in the village, with all the farm buildings and workers cottages, were put up for sale. Only a handful of 'locals' remained in the parish; and attendance at the church was clearly poor. The Diocese took the decision to close it in 1974.

At that time I was working in the County Planning Department, and in 1976 the Historic Buildings Officer mentioned to me that the building was likely to be sold, suggesting that I and my wife might be interested in a conversion project. We came to see it but, overlooked as it was by the vicarage, and with problems relating to the conversion (not least sewerage, parking, use of the churchyard) we decided it was not for us. Fortunately, walking around the village after looking at the church, we saw a sale sign on West Coombe Farmhouse which fitted our specifications very closely; and we purchased that instead.

At this time the village was experiencing a remarkable re-birth, as other young couples purchased the vicarage and several of the barns for conversion, and set about raising families. We considered that it would be regrettable for the one public building in the village to be lost and set about finding a way to keep it for the village. (After all, there could be another great religious revival!) There had been no meeting of the Parish Council for several years, so we revived it as a Parish Meeting and suggested to the parishioners that we might take the church on as a village hall. I was the first Chairman of the revived Parish Meeting, and soon discovered that it was a hopeless mechanism for taking such decisions: one meeting would agree to go ahead, and the next

Peter Brachi

The Coombe Keynes Trust, Coombe Keynes, Dorset

Description
The Trust keeps the church at the small village of Coombe Keynes for use as a local meeting place.

Founded
1980

Location
Coombe Keynes, Dorset (five miles south-west of Wareham).

Access
By named keyholder.

Website
www.coombekeynes.com/church-history/

Fig. 2: The interior of the church, looking east. The ancient font was first removed to Wool church, but is now back on loan, and placed in the sanctuary. The Trust was permitted to sell the pews, a few of which are retained against the walls.

would back-pedal! Accepting that the Parish would never take on this responsibility, the sub-committee who had taken on the task divorced itself from the Parish Meeting and set about the business of setting up a charitable trust to take on the building. In 1981, the Coombe Keynes Trust's constitution was approved and the Diocese handed the building over into our care. (Having initially insisted that we must raise an endowment of £10,000 to cover the care of the building - which we started trying to do – the eventual price was £10.)

Use of the building

The Trust now owns the building (lodged with the Public Trustee) but not the churchyard, which is still in use. The vicar of Wool is responsible for this. However, Wool has been happy to leave the management and maintenance of the churchyard to the Trust, contributing the occasional burial fee toward our costs.

Having been substantially rebuilt in 1861, and with (fairly) sound Purbeck stone roofs, the burden of keeping the building in reasonably good repair has not been too onerous so far. However, the Trust has made no attempt to adapt the building by adding kitchen or toilet facilities, and accepts the restrictions on its use that this brings. In any case, there is little or no car parking in the vicinity of the building, so use by persons outside the community is not really practical. We have been advised that with only one entrance, we should not hold events involving more than 50 people; and this limits the potential income of an event (such as for example a barn dance, if a band has to be paid).

The building is available for Parish Meetings, and small private functions for residents and/or members of the Trust; and the Trust organises a handful of events each year (for example, our Harvest Supper) which aim to provide social interaction for residents, and some educational input (a talk, quiz, or music) and raise small sums for our funds. For thirty years (I think) our big annual fund-raiser was the Village Fete held in the adjacent Vicarage garden, with cream teas being served in the church. We have built up a fund (never quite the £10k first mentioned) which covers occasional repair works and improvements – and most critically, our biggest annual expense, the insurance.

The future

We have kept individual (or family) contributions by members as low as possible in order not to discourage less prosperous residents from supporting the Trust; but it has often been suggested that we should increase subscriptions to boost our funds. In fact the majority of members actually pay more than the specified minimum sub.

The Trustees are, however, very concerned for the future of the Trust and the church, as the demographic of the village has changed. Increasing property values have made it attractive for families who came here in the 1970s to sell up and move on, at the same time making it virtually impossible for younger local families to afford to live here. The prices, however, are no deterrent to purchasers from London, for example; and nine of the fourteen dwellings in the centre of the village are now second homes – several very rarely visited. The average age of the membership of the Trust is steadily increasing, and it is difficult to find people prepared to make the commitment to raising funds that the preservation of the church requires.

We often wonder how much longer we will be able to carry on.

Fig. 1 (top): St John's, Fernham, Oxfordshire, from the south. Built in 1861 by J. W. Hugallas. (John Ward, September 2005)

Fig. 2 (bottom): Watching the Royal Wedding in Fernham Village Hall (i.e. St John's), 29 June 2011. The small size of the church and chancel are obvious. The photograph is taken from the new west-end mezzanine floor. (Neil Sutherland)

Fernham Village Trust, Oxfordshire

Becky Payne

Becky Payne is a freelance consultant on sustaining historic places of worship. She is Hon. Secretary of the Ecclesiological Society and Development Director of the Historic Religious Buildings Alliance.

Editor's introduction: Fernham church is one of two examples in this book where a village trust maintains a church building, and rents the space back to the PCC for church services. (The other example is Yarpole.) By kind permission of the publishers, this article largely reproduces a chapter in Becky Payne's book, Churches for Communities: Adapting Oxfordshire's Churches for Wider Use, *published in 2014 by the Oxfordshire Historic Churches Trust.*

FERNHAM IS A SMALL VILLAGE with a population of about 250, two miles south of Faringdon in the Vale of White Horse district in Oxfordshire. The small Grade II listed church of St John, on an elevated site at the centre of the village (Fig. 1), was built in 1861 in thirteenth-century style by the Gothic Revival architect J. W. Hugallas as a chapel of ease for the neighbouring village of Longcor.

Summary of the project

A major reordering and refurbishment project, undertaken between 2005 and 2010, created a space that doubles as place of worship and village hall. The pews were removed and replaced by wooden chairs and additional stacking chairs. The font was moved into the chancel. Underfloor heating and a new oak floor were installed. A fully accessible toilet and a well-equipped kitchen were put in at the west end, cleverly concealed behind oak doors. A mezzanine level with a glass-fronted rail was inserted, used for storage and for ringing the church bell. An audio-visual system and built-in projector screen were added (Figs 2 & 3).

Following these changes, the building is now managed – under a 30-year repairing lease from the diocese – by the Fernham Village Trust, which thus has responsibility for routine maintenance and insurance. The Parochial Church Council (PCC) hires the church from the Trust for Sunday services.

Background

After the village hall was damaged by fire and collapsed in 1955, the villagers used a large barn attached to the pub. When this was converted into a restaurant, they lost their only community space. At the same time regular church services were attracting a small, elderly congregation of about half a dozen and the PCC was increasingly concerned about rising maintenance and heating costs and future usage of the church. The heating system was practically non-existent, and lighting was provided by single bulbs dangling from fabric-covered wires. The roof was beginning to

Description

Victorian church maintained by village Trust, which rents the space back to the PCC for Sunday services and other church activities.

Trust founded
2008

Location
Two miles south of Faringdon, Oxfordshire (Vale of White Horse district).

Website (shared with village)
www.fernham.info

leak and the building was cold and damp. It could not be used for much beyond services, concerts and film nights, as the seventeen 'very hard' pews were all facing forward.

In 2002 the churchwarden, Charles Wickham, circulated a survey stating that the current congregation would be unable to sustain the church as it was. People were asked what they would like to do with the space and whether there would be objections to adapting it to meet modern needs. From the eighty-eight houses in the village, Mr Wickham achieved forty responses, almost all in favour of adapting the building as a combined church and village hall.

At this time the developer of a disused farm on the edge of the village was obliged, as part of the development agreement, to give the Parish Meeting (a smaller version of a Parish Council) a Section 106 disbursement worth £20,000, which could provide seed-corn funding for any project. The villagers agreed that the priority was for a village hall and initially serious consideration was given to putting up a brand new building. There was concern about the expense of maintaining and heating an old building with a high roof. They were aware of what had been done in nearby Little Coxwell: instead of refurbishing their listed church they had commissioned a new, brick-built, eco-friendly building.

Fig. 3: The interior in July 2013, looking west. A kitchen and toilets have been inserted, and above them a mezzanine floor, shielded from view by rails with frosted glass panelling. Folding chairs can just be seen against the wall to the left, and solid wooden chairs to the right. (Becky Payne)

However, it was finally recognised that refurbishing Fernham church to provide a village space would solve two problems at once and that, for a small village, it was better to preserve an old building at its heart rather than commission a new one on the edge of it. The Parish Meeting came on board and granted all the Section 106 money to the project as a measure of village support.

The project

In November 2004 Neil Sutherland, the St John's Treasurer and a chartered civil engineer, was asked to gather together a group of people with the necessary skills in finance and business, fundraising, and running village events. While some were churchgoers, people were approached for their skills rather than their links to the church. Charles Wickham and the incumbent, the Revd Richard Hancock, were included in an *ex officio* capacity.

The team understood the need to obtain a faculty for the scheme. However, they found the process lengthy and quite bureaucratic. Extra challenges arose when co-ordinating the seeking of permissions with fund-raising, as many major grant-funding bodies attach tight deadlines to their offers. A particular challenge for the project was that the team felt that the Victorian Society failed to appreciate that this was basically a 'rescue' project. Negotiations with the Victorian Society held up the project for a year and, at one point, there was a danger that the Big Lottery Fund grant of nearly £100,000 would be lost. In the end, however, both parties made compromises: the font was moved to the chancel, but the low walls dividing the nave from the chancel were retained, which has prevented the use of the chancel as a stage for plays.

The costs were £220,000 for the roof repairs, which included a complete new set of Cotswold stone tiles, and £184,000 for the conversion.

In a remarkable feat of solo fund-raising and project management, the churchwarden took charge of sourcing money for the roof repairs. The majority came from English Heritage and other church-supporting charities, among them the Oxfordshire Historic Churches Trust. Project Inspire concentrated on raising the funds for the community part of the project. In November 2007 it won a grant of £94,000 through the Big Lottery Fund and ITV's public voting competition, 'The People's Millions', which brought publicity and increased confidence. Additional funds came from other Trusts, local benefactors and fund-raising events such as film nights and talks, which helped to keep people engaged with the project.

Responsibility for the building

After long and careful negotiations with the diocese, an agreement was reached on the management of the building post-conversion. Project Inspire took on the repairing lease from the Diocese and responsibility for the routine maintenance of the building with an expectation, written into the lease, that if there are major works, Project Inspire will pay 60%, while the church community and PCC will contribute 40%, a ratio of 60:40 reflecting the split between chancel and nave areas. Negotiating this lease was a further major challenge to the project.

In a later development, at a meeting of villagers in May 2012, it was agreed that Project Inspire and another group, the Fernham Events Committee, should join forces to become the Fernham Village Trust. This charitable trust was set up as a company limited by guarantee to limit the liability of the Trustees and to meet funding criteria; it runs village events and now manages the use of St John's and Fernham Village Hall (that is, the church building) by the community and the church, and covers the running costs of the building, including insurance. The management committee is elected every year at the Trust's AGM and members serve a year.

Versatile venue and place of worship

The converted church, with its brand new roof, was opened in June 2010 by the Earl of Wessex. It has proved to be a versatile venue for everything from dance classes to lectures and meetings, from birthday parties to craft fairs and concerts, and can seat up to 100 people comfortably.

It continues to be a place of worship and the chancel has remained unchanged, although the font was relocated to within the chancel area. As Neil Sutherland says, 'We are getting very used to the building being both a community space and a place of worship. We can have our Burns Night celebrations on a Saturday night and yet by 9 a.m. next morning everything is 'facing front' ready for morning worship'.

The PCC pays the Village Trust to hire the building for its services and other church activities, such as weddings and funerals. It also raises funds for its annual parish share, which goes towards clergy costs, and helps to cover the mission and outreach of the church. There is a service every week, with a typical congregation of about eight, rising into double figures in the summer months, much larger than this for special services. Devolving the cost of maintenance, insurance and heating to the Village Trust has reduced the financial burden on the PCC considerably, so it easier for the PCC to afford its annual parish share and remain as a viable local congregation. The PCC feel that this arrangement is sustainable in the longer term, despite the relatively small size of the worshipping community. A new house-for duty priest has recently been appointed, and it is hoped that this new leadership will strengthen the congregation.

Neil Sutherland explains that 'we are now four years into our 30-year lease agreement with the Diocese and it is working well. The Trust and the church work well together and set up many joint events such as the village fete, where the church organises the refreshments, which raises funds for them. Other events such as the fireworks are put on solely by the Trust and help to generate funds, some of which pay for the building insurance'.

The aim is to keep the hall hire as cheap as is cost-effective. Currently it can be hired for £15 per hour (including car park use), with a reduced rate of £7.50 per hour for Fernham villagers. A heating surcharge of £1.50 an hour is added between November and March.

Funds brought to the Trust by the Events Committee and Project Inspire, plus some grants, have enabled the completion of a car park. This is adjacent to the south-east corner of the churchyard, on glebe land given by the Diocese. It has improved disabled access across the churchyard to the south entrance and has made the hall more marketable to outside groups. The building can also be hired for private events. Space is planned to be created in the churchyard for a large marquee, by obtaining permission to clear some headstones, and this will be available for hire from the Trust along with tables and chairs, in which wedding breakfasts or buffet meals can be provided.

Impact

Neil Sutherland says the project has brought the community together. 'It is still a delightful little village church and when there is a service, the only visible change is that the font has moved and that there are now slightly more comfortable chairs than the previous pews. Now, it has been given a new lease of life.

'Prior to the conversion it was half a story as it was just a church with the ability to run one or two minor village events; now it has developed to become a focus of the community. We have not only provided a building for the community, which needed one, but provided a mechanism by which the church building, which remains a place of worship, is managed and supported by the community, and that is a really significant development'.

Fig. 1 (above): St Mary's, Fordham, Norfolk, from the south-east. The author's car and lawnmower can be seen to the right of the picture.

Fig. 2 (right): The interior of the church, a photograph not intended for publication, but which gives some idea of the simplicity and quiet holiness of the interior.

The sometimes unhappy story of Fordham St Mary, Norfolk

Robert Walker

Robert Walker has recently retired from the role of Building Conservation Officer in Herefordshire.

I VISITED THE CHURCH IN 1994 in the role of Ely Diocesan Bells Advisor to see the important medieval bell which had been removed without permission from the west gable bell cote. The church had been declared redundant and despite being listed grade II★ (i.e. in the top 8% of listed buildings), it was not considered good enough to be vested in the Churches Conservation Trust. It seemed that it was heading for an alternative use; and in a depressed but pleasantly rural area that would have inevitably meant residential use and all the loss of character associated with 'conversion'. To add to the gloom of that occasion I was told of the intention to sell off everything inside the church, including the parquet flooring.

The simple historic holiness of the church and its beautiful, peaceful location between Breckland and the Fens spoke strongly for action (Figs 1 & 2). The long decline of the building, its lost tower and lost aisle, its condition, the desolate, uncared-for atmosphere about the place, the community turning its back and the lack of interest on the part of established conservation bodies were seemingly quieter voices that should, with hindsight, have been more carefully heeded. But I was confident; I had experience of fund raising and conservation projects as a founder of the Cambridgeshire Historic Churches Trust and the Cambridgeshire Building Preservation Trust, and could see a challenge rather than a lost cause. I put a detailed proposal to the Diocesan Redundant Churches Uses Committee and the church was subsequently conveyed, with all of its surviving furnishings and fittings, including the bell and a fine fourteenth-century grave slab, to The Fordham St Mary Preservation Trust and its three Trustees.

We were able to raise funds to carry out all of the works identified in the last quinquennial inspection report, including re-slating the nave and quite extensive masonry repairs and repointing. This was achieved by personal approaches, by sharing the proceeds of the Cambridgeshire Historic Churches Trust annual conference and by a very generous English Heritage grant. A begging letter in the mailings of other conservation societies was also worthwhile. None of that money was raised locally. Two years into our stewardship the building had been put into better condition, and we had also got to grips with the churchyard, including the part retained by the group of local parishes because it contained recent burials.

We held a number of musical events in the church, principally to introduce the Trust to the locals. There is no electricity so these

Description
A church in Norfolk, until recently owned by a single-building Trust, now transferred to the Friends of Friendless churches.

Trust founded
1994

Location
Two miles south of Downham Market, Norfolk.

Access
By arrangement.

Website
www.friendsoffriendless churches.org.uk

events were candle-lit, partly using a number of iron candelabra which were made by Randle Feilden. When the Trust was being established the local villages' Trust and the local churches seemed almost wholly preoccupied with possible competition in fund raising, or that we mighty establish a holiday let which would spoil business for one of their own projects. Our aim was however simply preservation of a 'prayer in stone' and that seemed to get, if not support, then sceptical acceptance. I have to say that we did not meet all of our objectives in terms of the use of the building, and events were few, nor did we monitor visitor numbers or produce a guide book.

Our neighbours, the Wadsley brothers, whose forebears were buried in the grave yard, were kindly and helpful. They kept a key to admit visitors, trimmed the hedge and appreciated our care of the churchyard as a whole. One of my fellow Trustees, Chris Clare, spent many days cleaning the interior and working on the graveyard – work that she continues to do out of sincere love of the place.

I knew that the three Trustees could not be involved forever, and that a small group with one church, could not be sustained, for the very same reasons that the local parishioners could not sustain the building, but I firmly believed that we had given the little church a second chance, a reprieve from 'grand designs', and at least the possibility of a sacred future.

Challenge

The challenge to our fragile organisation came five years later when I felt compelled to answer a call to work for the Iona Community at their Hebridean island centre. We had, however, in that time, made local contacts and the Trust was taken over by a number of local people. I went to Scotland feeling that the job was done, the little church was once more in the care of local people and, encouragingly, they had begun positively by restoring the bell to its cote.

Three years later, I received a call from the local team minister saying that the Trust was seeking to dispose of the little church. The cares and responsibilities, the annual chore of raising money for the insurance premium, and a feeling that it was time for a new use had caused a change of mind. By an odd stroke of luck, we found that when we acquired the church it was the three original Trustees who owned it, not the Trust (an arrangement favoured by the Church Commissioners but one we probably would not have accepted had it been made clear initially). This eventually led to the church and the Trust coming back to us, after long discussions involving the very patient, and quite justifiably exasperated, attention of the Commissioners' redundant churches officers.

It was impossible for me to look after the building from a distance and a local solution also now seemed impossible, so I approached the Friends of Friendless Churches and the Norfolk Historic Churches Trust; two established and permanent organisations, both of which had expanded their portfolios of redundant buildings in the years since we acquired the little church. Matthew Saunders of the Friends asked that the Norfolk Trust be given first refusal, which it did after nearly two years of deliberation, and the Friends subsequently acquired the church from the three Trustees.

Implications

Not long ago I was involved, in the role of Building Conservation Officer, with a group considering the acquisition of the ruined (only the tower and some chancel masonry standing) church at Avenbury in Herefordshire. The church had been conveyed to an absentee private individual some years before and he had subsequently lost interest without carrying out any of the required consolidation work. It was a different situation to Fordham's, but not entirely so, and it made me think of our experience. It is obvious that church buildings that are not converted to new uses, and which cannot therefore earn their living, can only be sustained by an enduring owner. That would, ideally, be a national or county trust, but it could be a deep pocketed individual, for example in the case of an estate church, or a local secular group in a thriving village or town. I don't think there is any dogmatic rule – each situation will be different – but it is the remote rural buildings, of which greater numbers will become redundant, that will always be the most difficult to sustain, particularly if they cannot meet the requirements of the principal grant-giving bodies who are less interested in the repair of historic fabric for its own sake.

In our case, it is quite obvious that without the saving intervention of the Friends, a new use would have had to be found and the 'prayer in stone' would have reached its 'amen'.

Fig. 1: St Mary's, Ickworth, Suffolk, the interior from the chancel steps, looking north, a photo taken after the restoration of the building.

Ickworth Church Conservation Trust

IN JUNE 2013 there was a service of blessing at St Mary's, Ickworth, Suffolk to mark – and celebrate – its re-opening after a major restoration project. This followed nearly three decades of neglect. The church had been boarded up to protect the vandalised stained glass, the tower had caved in, fabric was being lost to the elements, and the building was surrounded by undergrowth and becoming dangerous to approach. The six-year programme of restoration was spearheaded by the owners of the church, the Ickworth Church Conservation Trust, which was set up in 2006, and is one of the youngest Trusts described in this book. Following the restoration, the church is now open to the public almost every day, and used for special services and occasional concerts.

Background

Ickworth church lies deep inside the grounds of Ickworth house, in an 1800 acre park designed by Capability Brown. The house and park are owned by the National Trust, and part of the house is open to visitors, the rest being used as a hotel and conference centre. The church has been described as having 'exceptional' landscape value, featuring in several sight lines, and is (in the words of English Heritage) 'a classic estate church demonstrating the social hierarchy of the period', where the owners of the house and many of their long-standing staff have been buried for hundreds of years.

At its core the church, which is listed Grade II★, is medieval. There was a thorough restoration in 1833, when the south aisle was built, containing the family pew and new burial vault – architecturally the aisle is notable for the use of factory made concrete blocks, extremely unusual in ecclesiastical architecture of the time. In 1910–11 the church was re-ordered by Blomfield, who introduced stained glass in the east window. During these works a fourteenth-century wall painting of the Angel of the Annunciation was uncovered. The church has some sixteenth-century Flemish roundels, and a three-decker pulpit. It is set in a graveyard with many memorials, dating from 1725.

For many years this has been a church with few if any parishioners, for between 1700 and 1731, John Hervey, the first Earl of Bristol, improved the appearance of his park by rehousing his tenants at nearby Horringer, which had its own church. So Ickworth church lost most of its parishioners; but the household still worshipped there, and the church and churchyard continued to be used for burials. Indeed, the Herveys have been buried in the building since 1467, and there are some 35 monuments to the family in the church and churchyard.

Fig. 2 (: Window, showing damage before restoration. The undamaged roundel at top right is sixteenth-century Flemish.

By the 1950s there were perhaps only half a dozen services a year, but the church was kept in good condition. In 1956, following the death some years earlier of the fourth Marquess of Bristol, the house and its grounds were handed over to the National Trust, but the church remained as a parish church of the Church of England, with a right of way over the grounds. In 1984 the church was declared redundant, and two years later the Church Commissioners sold the church and its graveyard to the seventh Marquess, John Hervey. A maximum of six church services per year were allowed in the building, and future burial rights were restricted (the Hervey family can still be buried in the vault). Unfortunately the church was not maintained, and fell into the very poor state described earlier (Figs 2–4), and in 1998 was placed on the English Heritage Buildings at Risk register.

The Trust

When the seventh Marquess died in 1999, ownership of the dilapidated church was at first unresolved, but in 2005 it eventually passed to the eighth Marquess, Frederick Hervey. He was determined to see the building restored, and in 2006 he set up the Ickworth Church Conservation Trust, and transferred ownership of the church to the Trust. Its aims include providing 'public benefit', particularly for local people and visitors to Ickworth House, and enabling 'public and private worship and religious ceremonies to be held in the [church] building together with other community events, concerts, drama and the like'.

The letter of wishes to the Trustees when the church was handed over expanded on this. The Marquess wanted the church to be run by a local Trust, not a national one, to stay in touch with the local community. He was not expecting the building to be kept in a time-warp, and anticipated that it might adapt with the

Fig. 3 (left): The family pew in the south gallery, before restoration.

Fig. 4 (right): The south wall of the chancel, before restoration.

times, but such adaptation should 'be in keeping with the past'. He was wary of too much commercialisation, whilst recognising that the building had to pay its way: in particular, he valued the idea of it being used for 'quiet contemplation'. He thought it important that it should be open and accessible, especially to local people.

The Trust was carefully structured to be focused, entrepreneurial and light on its feet; to be sustainable over the longer term; and to allow the historic interest of the Bristol family in the building to be appropriately maintained. Thus there are three Trustees, all of whom are appointed by virtue of their office: the Dean of St Edmundsbury, and the incumbent of neighbouring Horringer church (the Rector had always also been the Rector of Ickworth Church), both of whom may appoint substitutes; and the Marquess of Bristol, who as chairman has two votes. All decisions require three votes. One reason for having two clerics as Trustees is that the Marquess wanted the building to be as similar as possible to a normal working church, to the point where he hoped people would not notice it was different from other churches, unless they looked at its ownership structure.

From 2006 onwards the Trust undertook active and sustained fund raising to repair and restore the church (Fig. 5). In the first few years money was obtained from a variety of sources, many of them local, and something of the order of £100k was spent on the building to make it wind and watertight, and to prepare a detailed specification of what needed doing. An initial application to the

Fig. 5: The church today from the south.

Heritage Lottery Fund (HLF) was rejected, but a second was successful, with a grant of £767k, with additional funding of £325k from English Heritage. With further support from a wide mix of other donors, the total cost of restoration was about £1.2m. The HLF grant included funds for writing a business plan for the church, and for interpretative material (guidebooks, website, apps, signage, discovery boxes), and also for supporting the initial costs of administering activities in the church. Disabled access was provided.

Moving forward

Ickworth is a popular National Trust property, and has some 160,000 visitors each year, and these provide a ready-made visitor base for the church. The church is unlocked every day by a National Trust volunteer, and although the building is some distance from the house, a good number of people make their way to it (the National Trust provides a buggy for those with mobility problems).

As well as a conservation management plan, the Church Trust has commissioned a costed annual maintenance action plan, much of which can be carried out by volunteers, and has set up a sinking fund for longer-term repair cycles. Although many visitors make donations (a gift of two pounds is suggested), more is needed to maintain the building over the long term, and a mix of activities are held, both to raise money and to give the building a continuing vitality and purpose. There are paid tours, some of which include a visit to the Hervey vault, musical concerts (seven this year between April and September, one of them a harmonium concert) and occasional services – one recent service, for example, was the christening of the grandson of someone who has helped hugely with the restoration project.

The early nineteenth-century gallery and pews (Fig. 6) are still in the church, including a family pew, and the Trust has no intention of removing these, feeling that they are important for the building's character. There are no toilets in the church, no heating, and no mains lighting; the church has six lights which run off a rechargeable battery and provide as much light as a wall lamp at home, however these are typically only used during events, and sometimes the church is lit by candlelight. These factors all limit what can be done in the building, but not to the extent that the Trust feels unduly constrained.

The Trust is now moving away from the challenges of financing and driving forward a major project to the very different issues involved in sustaining the building in the longer term. There was considerable local voluntary support for restoring the building, and in the congregation at the re-opening service were many who had given considerable time and energy to this six-year

Fig. 6: The interior today, looking east from the west gallery. The family pew is the raised area just visible to the right. The medieval wall painting can perhaps be glimpsed on the east wall to the south of the altar.

project. Although life has now become quieter and more routine, the continued enthusiasm of volunteers to keep the building alive and well is essential, whilst at the same time the Trust is determined that administration and decision-making will be efficient and professional, and based on local needs. At the moment the development of activities in the church, and overall operational decisions, are the responsibility of a single energetic individual, not a Trustee, who is paid a small retainer (but works much longer hours than he is paid), whilst other volunteers provide crucial practical or technical support. This is working well: but in the longer term, it is recognised that the Trust may need to consider other structures, such as a group of committed individuals answering to the Trustees, perhaps employing a clerk to take matters forward between meetings.

At the re-opening service the Marquess said he had completed his job, and felt he had created a platform which would enable local people to enjoy and make use of the space, as well as help with its ongoing sustainability and upkeep. The Marquess mentioned that he felt his job had now shifted from Captain to rudder as now what was needed by him was general steering with a lighter touch. All the Trustees hope that the church will continue to be available for public benefit and enjoyment for many generations to come.

Advice and learning

Asked what advice he would give to others thinking of doing something similar, the Marquess said:

"We worked to a number of principles, which might or might not be appropriate in other situations.

"First we never cut any corners on the quality of professionals or the work done. We preferred to wait longer, even for a few years, until we had everything lined up to do the best job possible rather than do a 'good enough' job that would last just ten to fifteen years. We wanted a restoration so good that none of us would be alive the next time a major renewal was needed. And it is worth choosing a good architect even if they are a little more expensive – not least, the right architect can also in effect act as a project manager.

"Secondly, think hard about your organisation. Having a small number of decision-makers for the restoration project makes it more flexible, especially as mid project you need to make quick executive decisions on site. Find people who will have an emotional vested interested in the project to be part of the team. And delegate, even with budgets. We broke our budget into smaller chunks and told the appointed people how much money they had for their jobs, and they had to make sure their parts of the work came in on budget.

"When choosing Trustees think long term. Once those first appointed die or retire, what is the process for new appointments? – you need a detailed process in place. If you get this wrong the whole thing will collapse in the future. You may find that the large grant makers try and change your decision making process or structure, but if you have a good reason for not wanting to change, then resist the pressure and explain why. After all, neither of you wants to end up in a position where you cannot efficiently use the grant you have been given – this is ultimately bad for everyone.

"As for fundraising, if you apply to HLF, then try and get any matched funding in first, as unless you raise what you said, you will not be able to start the project. Start with fundraising from smaller local trusts before going regional and national, as generally the smaller they are the quicker they can give you an answer (and hopefully a cheque), and this gives a head start which encourages everyone and impresses other grant givers. You must try and be realistic about the money you need. We were, but even so, it left very little slack, and with hindsight we should have included more contingency for unforeseen costs. In the end, we were on budget, but luck had something to do with that.

"The project took so long (2006–2013) mainly because getting our money took so long. This was I think down to our inexperience of who to approach and how to approach them. In fact, from our experience, it can be very helpful if you either have contacts or can strike up personal relationships with the smaller grant-giving bodies, so that you can communicate what you are trying to do. Furthermore, we lost about three years with our first failed HLF grant application, and from our experience I would strongly advise anyone seeking a large HLF grant to get someone on the team from the beginning who has detailed experience of their application and decision-making processes.

"Finally, we are now trying to set up activities and events which we can 'cut and paste' on an annual basis, as opposed to trying to create new ones each year from scratch, which can be very time consuming."

Fig. 1 (above): The old church of St Andrew ('Melton Old Church'), Melton, Suffolk. Most of the church is medieval. The chancel was taken down and replaced with a stuccoed apsidal east end when the church was converted to a mortuary chapel in the mid nineteenth century. (Charmian Berry)

Fig. 2 (left): A few of the World War I crosses to be found in the church. (Charmian Berry)

The Melton Old Church Society

THE MELTON OLD CHURCH SOCIETY was founded on 26 April 1982, making it one of the oldest single-church trusts in this book. It was set up by people in Melton, Suffolk (population 3,700 in 2001) who were not happy with the Church Commissioners plans to sell the old church of St Andrew (listed Grade II★) for conversion into a hostel.

The church

The old church, essentially a medieval building, is a little way away from the centre of Melton, down by the river and surrounded by trees. The coming of the railway and new roads in the mid nineteenth century meant that the old church was replaced in 1868 by a newer building nearer the centre of the village. But the new church had no graveyard, and the old church, although reduced in size in late Victorian times, continued to be used by the parish for funerals and as an occasional chapel of ease, and was much loved (Fig. 1). But in 1977 it was declared redundant.

Five years later, in 1982, the Melton Old Church Society purchased the old church from the Church Commissioners, and the Society, in the person of its Trustees, now holds the church in perpetuity, for the purposes of Christian, community and educational use. The church is deconsecrated, so no sacramental services can be held there, but until recently burials took place in the graveyard (maintained by the parochial church council). Cremated remains are still interred there.

There are a number of items drawing visitors to the building – family history, a fifteenth-century brass to a priest and what may be his parents, an unusual collection of eleven WWI crosses (Fig. 2), and the monument to an important geologist, Searles Valentine Wood, together of course with the tranquillity of the medieval church and churchyard. The church is not routinely open for visitors, though in practice it is often unlocked as events are often happening in the building, and at other times the key can be provided when required. There are plans for better signs to explain how to obtain the key.

Using the building

The building has no pews, which were removed some time before the Society took over, which creates a flexible space, with stackable chairs when needed. Some twenty or so years ago the Society (farsighted for its time) realised that toilets were essential if the building were to fulfil its potential, and carried out fund raising to provide these, the heating was also replaced by the Committee. A kitchen has also been introduced.

Description
Medieval building, looked after by single-church trust since 1982.

Founded
1982

Location
About half a mile NE of Melton.

Access
By keyholder.

Fig. 3: A social event taking place in the Victorian apse. (Simon Knott)

As a result, the building is used for something like a dozen events per year, and these raise funds for its upkeep (Fig. 3). They are the sort of events one would expect – occasional services, talks, exhibitions, musical concerts and so forth – and the Society has also built up an enviable (and profitable) reputation for providing excellent teas, which can be eaten in the beautiful surroundings of the churchyard. Some of these events are organised by the Society, and others by local folk who pay rent for the use of the building. In each case, tea often follows!

Although there is a village hall, and the parish church is active, it appears the village is lively enough, and the old church special enough, for these venues to survive alongside each other. The present incumbent of the parish church is a supporter of the old church. Although in the earlier days of the Society there might have been a sense of separation between the parish church and the old church, particular efforts have been made more recently to ensure that good relations are maintained.

As well as fund-raising events, the Society raises money through its membership scheme, which has of the order of 200 members, each paying seven pounds per year. They receive an annual newsletter, listing the events for the year ahead. With subscriptions and continual fundraising, the Society has always managed to stay in the black, despite considerable expenditure (averaging about £5k per annum over the last five years), and despite the lack of any significant endowment. It has kept the church in good repair: at the time of writing, work was being done to deal with beetle infestation, and the hatchments are going to be cleaned and restored.

The future

The Society is independent, and has no backing either from statutory bodies or other Trusts. It is run by a committee, the Trustees not being members of the committee. As in many committees, there have in the past thirty years been periods of tension, and these have had to be dealt with without the opportunity of falling back to a supervening body for advice or support, or to provide guaranteed continuity. But the committee has continued to function, and to find new members when required. Indeed, so long as the committee can continue to renew itself, and people wish to attend events, and assuming no unexpectedly large repair bills, it is felt that the Society is in a strong position to continue its role of maintaining the Old Church as a benefit for the people of Melton and the general public.

Fig. 1: The church of St Andrew, Mickfield, Suffolk, seen from the west. The tower-porch is fourteenth-century. The church was closed and ruinous for many years, but has been both rescued as a building and given new life as a local inter-denominational Christian centre. The base of the tower-porch now houses a kitchen. (James Banks; www.flickr.com/photos/banksfam/)

VIEWPOINT: St Andrew's, Mickfield, Suffolk

Editor's note: Our VIEWPOINT pieces allow individual views to be vigorously expressed, so long as they are well-founded on personal experience or evidence. The story of Mickfield church certainly falls within this category, told here in an abbreviated and updated version of a short booklet written by the author in 2007. The full version can be obtained from the author, whose details are given at the end of the piece. It explores the wider context of the closure of rural churches.

Mark Wright

Mark Wright is a Lay Reader in the Church of England.

THE MICKFIELD STORY IN 2007
The closure of Mickfield church

MICKFIELD, IN MID-SUFFOLK, had been established as a parish at least by the close of the tenth century and a church built around that time, dedicated to St Andrew. The tower was added in 1310 and the present church built around the Saxon church, which was then demolished (Fig. 1). Some of the windows were enlarged in the perpendicular period but the church remains essentially the same today. Even the Victorians did little other than replace the tracery in the east window. We still have the foundations of the Saxon church in place and part of its south doorway. The church is listed Grade I.

The Mickfield school closed in 1955, followed by the forge, the pub, the Post Office and the village shop. There were previously a dozen small farms in the parish; now only one survives (run by an 80 year old on his own), the rest being amalgamated into two large landholdings based at Mickfield Hall and a farm outside the parish. On the other hand, the influx of people to occupy new houses the 1980s, which led to the population rising to more than 200, was instrumental in the building of a Village Centre for social purposes and the adjoining Parish Meadow now provides a playground with swings and football posts for the children.

In 1928 the then squire living in Mickfield Hall died; he had been churchwarden for 52 years. Five years later the new Rector was told he would have to take on a second parish; he finished up with four, and all of them closed after his death. The last Rector died in office in 1969. Thereafter things went down fast; Mickfield Ecclesiastical (but not Civil) Parish was amalgamated with Stonham Aspal in 1972, with St Andrew's briefly remaining open as a chapel of ease with a fortnightly Evensong. Cracks appeared in the tower and the church was closed in September 1975 and declared officially 'redundant' two years later.

As an aside, those who know me know how I feel about the rural benefice system and the damage it has done. Parishes have become grouped together with one priest given the job of caring

Description

A Trust which took over and refurbished a previously ruined redundant church and uses it as a non-denominational Christian centre offering public worship, retreats and quiet days, especially for local people.

Trust established
2002

Location

Mickfield, Suffolk, about five miles north-east of Stowmarket.

Access
The church is normally open.

for up to a dozen communities. Obviously, to know everyone in all their parishes is quite impossible, as is the daily saying of Morning and Evening Prayer in every church. Each type of Sunday service has its supporters so when parishes are grouped the single service in each church is set at different times, if at all, on different Sundays of the month according to the form it takes. Having services at different times makes routine attendance difficult. On some Sundays all churches except one are closed and their congregations invited to attend a 'Benefice Service'; in practice, most of them do not. Clergy who have been rushing around on Sunday mornings are loath to hold evening services, which have died. Essentially all this happened because the reduced number of clergy were not prepared (or even allowed, never mind encouraged, by their dioceses) to delegate. Yet, there is an army of ten thousand Lay Readers who since Victorian times have been plugging the holes in clergy rotas; and church wardens continue to be appointed in most parishes, but their leadership was lost. None of this needed to happen.

To return to Mickfield. There was a parish petition for the re-opening of the church in 1980 but there was no positive response from the Diocese. By this time a programme of house building in the village was underway which was to increase the housing stock by the end of the century by almost a half. The church however simply stood unused; over thirty portable items were removed in the 1980s – the altar to Crowfield Church, the one remaining usable bell to Boulge and the rest of the items to Stonham Aspal.

Finally St Andrew's was sold for housing in 1989. The new owner stripped and sold the remaining church furnishings (including the valuable choir stalls) and installed eight foundation points designed apparently to enable the church to be split horizontally to create an upper floor throughout. This enabled the planning permission to be extended indefinitely.

The new owner then emigrated and the church was extensively vandalized with every window and most memorials broken; some lead was stolen from the roof and the local children used it as an unofficial adventure playground. Had the local District Council not intervened St Andrew's would have been a ruin by the Millennium. However the Council had two splendid Conservation Officers who supervised temporary repairs to the roof, boarded up the windows and finally took the owner to court in 2002. In this uncontested action, the court authorised the sale of the church to the Suffolk Architectural Heritage Trust (SAHT) with the intention of the restoration of the building.

Arriving in Mickfield
My wife and I first arrived in Mickfield in April 2001. We found

St Andrew's and fought our way through the undergrowth (some of which was taller than the church) to the priest's door which, amazingly, was unlocked. We then had to wait over a year for the court case and nearly another two years before work even started. We then exchanged contracts with SAHT for the purchase of St Andrew's once the shell of the historic structure had been repaired by them. English Heritage paid for half the cost of this work and we paid the other half as purchase price. Upon acquiring St Andrew's we immediately leased it to the Anglia Church Trust (which we had set up for the purpose of running St Andrew's and, potentially, other churches) at a peppercorn rent.

Work started on 1 March 2004 and finished on St Andrew's Day at the end of November. Full refurbishment meant putting in a permanent nave floor with underfloor heating, adding a west-end gallery with facilities below and multi-purpose use above, installing electricity and oil-fired central heating, the addition of toilets and a kitchen and a bedroom in the tower! A rood 'screen' (in the form of a curtain) was put back (after 500 years) to divide the exclusively worship chancel from the multi-purpose nave, in accordance with the original layout of the church (Figs. 2 & 3).

Then there was the matter of furnishing; we asked the Stonham Aspal and Crowfield PCCs if we could borrow back the items they had removed for safe keeping in the 1980s and they agreed but the Diocese did not. Two years later a third of the items were sent for auction and we bought them back but the rest remain at Stonham and the altar at Crowfield. And so we approached the Chelmsford Diocese and bought a number of items from them. We also did some detective work and found two of Mickfield's ancient choir stalls in an antique shop in Norwich and the Cottam Will Trust kindly paid for their return to us (Fig. 4). A service to celebrate the refurbishment was held on 10 July 2005.

Developing the life of St Andrew's

When we arrived at Mickfield two people were going regularly to church in Stonham Aspal (technically the parish church) and a few more attended the Gospel Hall on the parish boundary. One or two others worshipped elsewhere – the rest (if they had any thoughts on the matter at all) felt that the Church had abandoned them. Five years later (without poaching anyone from another church) there is a congregation at St Andrew's of between 40 and 50 'regulars' (defined as attending at least once a month) and a similar number of 'occasionals' who we see less often. Around half of each group live in Mickfield.

We think that this (and indeed other secular gatherings and events) prove that residential communities still do wish to be

Fig. 2: The meeting area, located in the nave of the church. This is used for general meetings, and when the 'rood screen' curtains are drawn back, can extend the area used for worship. At the west end of the meeting room, not shown because above the photographer's head, is a gallery with seating area. (Jean McCreanor; www.flickr.com/photos/52219527@N00/)

communities. With the closure of many if not all the other community facilities in many of our villages, the church is often the only feature left. This makes it the more important that the church should return to being the focus of the village. It should be open every day. There is a huge case for taking pews out and substituting chairs which can be variously configured for different purposes. It follows that the church should not stand out as the only public buildings today not to have toilets. Kitchens too should be added to enable refreshments to be offered after services every Sunday and through the week. Some may even like to go further and establish a bedroom which can offer overnight accommodation to pilgrims or a home for a pastor or caretaker.

Inside, the church needs to be welcoming; ideally someone there to welcome visitors between services as well as at service times is good. An office where welcomers can get on with other things between visitors can help make this practicable. But there also needs to be information, toys and activities for children and perhaps a cup of tea. There is a lot to be said for *not* making a charge for tea or indeed anything else.

Fig. 3: The sanctuary, at the east end of the chancel. The chancel is used for services of worship, divided from the meeting area by a curtain. (Jean McCreanor; www.flickr.com/photos/52219527@N00/)

Communication is also vital; at the most basic there is the notice board. But word processors now make it within almost anyone's ability to devise a presentable village news-sheet which can be up to date and which should go out to all houses with news about the community as a whole but with the church as the centre. A flag always flying from the tower or steeple gives the message that the church is in business and can be seen from a distance.

Graveyards are still very important to people in the community, sometimes more so than the churches. But a distinction can be made between the part that is open and has had recent burials and the part that is only of historical interest. Monastic gardens have something to teach us here.

At St Andrew's, we have tried to act on most of these principles, and the reaction of parishioners and visitors alike is usually very positive. True, there are a few people who attended the church before closure who don't like the changes; one objected when someone in the village offered a couple of armchairs which are now at the back of the nave. Our services,

Fig. 4: One of the medieval bench ends now in the chancel. The tail of the chained animal would suggest he or she was a lion. Through the generosity of the Cottam Will Trust this was recovered from an antique shop after disposal by the previous owner. (Jean McCreanor; www.flickr.com/ photos/52219527@N00/)

many of which struggle to attract a double-figures congregation, are mainly held in the chancel but the atmosphere is quite cosy with the chancel arch curtained where the rood screen once was. We use the nave for larger congregations, for informal services, meetings and parties while the west-end gallery has toilets and an office below and a social area above. The tower now has a kitchen on the ground floor and a bedroom above.

We avoid splitting our congregation on Sunday mornings by having BCP Matins or Eucharist (at which our Chaplain presides) sung for half an hour, breaking for refreshments and then continuing with an informal service based on family worship for another half an hour. In this way we accommodate all tastes but unite everyone over refreshments half way. Some come to the BCP service and leave after the coffee; others come for refreshment and say on for informal worship; a few stay for the whole time.

Services are at the same times each day with Morning Prayer at 9 a.m. and Evening Prayer at 6 p.m. Sunday to Saturday. We lay on 'special' services as often as we can get away with it – which usually means monthly. Total church attendance (including me!) for our second full year was around 3250, up by around a third on the previous twelve months.

We also welcome visitors (Fig. 5). Some come for the architecture others for some event or for quiet space; for the latter we have developed the old churchyard (closed in 1922) around the church with arbours and a hermitage (for when it is wet) where people can sit, a herb garden and a hospitality garden to grow things to feed visitors and a meeting area surrounded by a cloister walk. The east end has a traditional semi-circular rose garden. Those wishing to come for a longer retreat can be accommodated in the tower.

In the second year of being up-and-running we welcomed nearly 600 such visitors plus another 250 who came for the first wedding at St Andrew's for 36 years and an earlier wedding anniversary celebration. We always offer hospitality and we never charge or hold fund-raising events as such. We make no charge for anything, not for any use of the building (even weddings), not for hospitality, nor any items to take away. We hold events but whether they are religious or social we never make a charge. All our income comes from donations through which we comfortably pay our way, with an annual budget of around £7000.

Fig. 5: The Trust sets out to make the visitor welcome. (Simon Knott, www.suffolkchurches.co.uk)

Postscript

This is by way of a postscript. My wife and I moved out of Mickfield in 2010, and now live in north Norfolk. This was primarily because of work and family commitments, but also because we felt the need to start the process of disengagement at St Andrew's. I have been coming back for a couple of weekends a month but otherwise it has been down to the community to take on the mantle – a challenge to which it has responded admirably. With a Worship Team of some sixteen people set up when we left, virtually all the 60 services a month were covered, and life at St Andrew's has continued and developed.

Looking back, the most important achievement has been our miniscule contribution to Church unity . . .

And how about our aspiration to share what we have discovered and to pool it with the parallel achievements of others? In this we have to admit failure thus far.

St Andrew's welcomes those who wish to share in its life. For further details, the church office may be contacted at 01449 711640 or by contacting the author at markwright.act@gmail.com.

Fig. 1 (top): The small church of St Mary's, No Mans Heath, Warwickshire, built by G. E. Street in 1863. (Larissa)

Fig. 2 (bottom): The interior of the church looking east on the opening day after restoration and refurbishment by the Friends.

St Mary's, No Mans Heath, Warwickshire

Editor's note: No Mans Heath once had a reputation for being outside the law. It is probably coincidence, but this is the only Trust in this book which had its origins in an act of Civil Protest.

Anne Barney

Anne Barney is a Trustee of the Friends of St Mary's on the Heath

Lawlessness

As suggested by its name, No Mans Heath in the county of Staffordshire once belonged to no man. It was situated in an area of about 15 acres of heathland, outside the manorial system, and lying on the junction of four counties – Derbyshire, Leicestershire, Warwickshire and Staffordshire – and in the early 1800s not under the authority of any of them. Furthermore, it was extra-parochial, that is, outside the Church of England's parish system, forming a small patch of land between three neighbouring parishes. Over time, a hamlet of squatters grew up, the squatters paying no local taxes and subject to no local jurisdiction.

Not surprisingly, it was a place where activities on the fringes of the law, such as bare knuckled prize fighting, could be held fairly safely with audiences of up to 15,000 people attending.

During the mid nineteenth century steps were taken to regularise the situation. The boundaries of Warwickshire were moved to include the hamlet, and in 1873 the ecclesiastical parish of No Mans Heath was created, with a population of 122. Ten years before then, it was decided that the inhabitants required spiritual guidance and so in 1863, the little church of St Mary the Virgin was opened, optimistically planned to seat 100 people (Fig. 1). It was designed by G. E. Street, and was paid for by public subscription, costing a little under £350. Stained glass was separately donated by a local vicar.

It is a pretty church, in an attractive churchyard. The small size of the building and of its potential congregation can be gauged by the fact that just fifty people celebrated communion when it was opened by the Bishop.

Civil Protest

This little church and churchyard served the community for more than a hundred years until declining congregations led to its closure towards the end of the twentieth century. Even today there are only 55 houses in the village, many occupied by commuters or the elderly, so closure may have been inevitable.

What galvanised the village into action was the discovery in 1998 that the diocese intended to sell the building for development and, in particular, that it intended to move some of the graves in the churchyard to be interred elsewhere – we were told, into a mass grave. Which graves were involved was never

Description
Trust preserving a small village church.

Founded
2002

Location
No Mans Heath, Warwickshire (about six miles north-east of Tamworth, Staffordshire).

Access
For events and by arrangement.

made clear. Many of those living in the village had relatives buried in the churchyard, and there was considerable disquiet.

The diocese was not forthcoming about the details of the proposed sale. A meeting was held in the village hall and the hall was packed with villagers past and present and a great number of sympathisers who felt indignant at the turn of events. From this a committee was formed, 'The Friends of St. Mary's on the Heath'.

Then news leaked out of a confidential meeting at the church between the diocese and potential purchasers. The committee and villagers hastily organised a protest outside the building where the meeting was being held – well-behaved, quiet and polite, but with placards vigorously complaining about the plan to move some of the burials ('RIP but not in No Man's Heath', and amongst others, 'Took your money off the plate, now they want you out the gate'). It had been arranged that the Press and BBC television were there to film it, and the protest made the television news that evening.

The next move was to apply for spot listing; this resulted in a Grade II listing for the church to prevent it being knocked down.

There was then was a lengthy period of negotiation between a committee of villagers and the diocese. These discussions did not run entirely smoothly. Questions were asked in the House; the estimated cost of repairs became a matter of significant disagreement (the church had not been maintained); the villagers wanted the already-dispersed church furnishings to be brought back; and the diocese (as is usual) wanted a business plan.

During this time those living in the village were systematically collecting money and getting themselves organised. One very successful fund-raising approach set up at about this time, and still continuing, was to set up a Lottery Bonus Ball group of 49 people who choose to pay £1 per week. If their chosen number comes up as the bonus ball on the National Lottery they win £25 and of course £24 goes into the fund, with the opportunity to play twice a week. To give some context to this, the cost of insuring the building is around £1200 per year.

Legal agreement and repairs

Eventually agreement was reached. The Friends were set up in 2002 as a charitable Trust, and took over the church and church-yard for a peppercorn rent about a year later. Burials are allowed in the churchyard which is managed by the local Parish Council, but as normal, there are restrictions on the use of the building for services. It is now licensed under the Licensing Act 2003.

Repairs and alterations began not long after, much of the work being carried out by local tradesmen at favourable rates or donating their time. The building was put in good order and decorated, with decent heating and lighting, with all health and safety issues covered. The pews are still in the building, and other items which had been removed by the diocese were returned (Fig. 2). The church itself has no car parking, but parking is possible by arrangement not far away. Toilets are in the village hall nearby.

There was a grand opening ceremony. Everyone who had been involved in any way was invited including the solicitor who worked on behalf of the Friends and the Euro MP Mike O'Brien who acted as mediator. Once again, it was covered by the Press.

Use of the building

There is a village hall nearby, so the church does not need to operate as a general purpose hall. Indeed, this was never the intention, the primary motivation being to preserve the graveyard untouched and keep the church as a public space open to the villagers.

A number of events are held in the building each year – for example, it is used by a history group – though the number has declined over the years since the Friends took over. In particular, each year the church is decorated for Christmas, and this attracts visitors (and donations). A carol service is organised, candlelit as it would have been when the church was first built 100 years ago, serving mince pies and mulled wine on Christmas Eve. During this period, the decorated and candlelit church gives the opportunity for villagers to sit quietly in the candlelight and reflect, especially helpful to those who have recently lost loved ones, and is proving increasingly popular.

Finances are in good shape from ongoing donations, with several years operating costs in the bank, and no major repairs required. There is no membership structure, but people are kept in touch with forthcoming events. There are many attendees who come from outside the village to the events.

Most of the organising committee also live outside the village. As finances are not an issue, there is a worry that the major threat to the long-term sustainability of the work of the Friends is finding others who will follow and carry on the good work.

When asked for advice to others, one long-standing Trustee said: 'Opposing the hierarchy may be daunting, but it can be done – and if necessary, include a genteel Civil Protest'.

A book on the village, A Potted History of No Mans Heath – 'The Village on the Ridge', *is available for sale for £10.00 including postage and packing from, Anne Barney, 40 Main Road, Sheepy Magna, Atherstone, CV9 3QR. Proceeds are split between the church and the Village Hall.*

Fig. 1: The interior of St John the Baptist, Plumpton, Northamptonshire, looking west. The box pews date from the major works carried out in 1822.

Plumpton, Northamptonshire

THE NIGHT BEFORE EASTER SUNDAY at St John the Baptist, in the tiny hamlet of Plumpton in Northamptonshire, and the ancient box pews filled with people. Some families crowd into the larger pews at the front while individuals take a seat at the back. The church is lit only by candlelight and as music from the organ plays there is quiet chatter. There's louder talking from some pews. But then it is eleven o'clock at night, it's after dinner and it's a Saturday night.

This service is unique. As indeed are all the services. Because rarely is there the same vicar or organist and sometimes members of the congregation travel a long distance to be here.

St John the Baptist (listed Grade II), is hidden away in rural Northamptonshire in the tiny settlement of Plumpton. It has a 700-year history, with the list of rectors for the church dating back to 1229.

Inside, it still has the box pews and commandment boards from its refitting of 1822 (Figs. 1 & 2). There is a marble wall monument to Ann Moore who died in 1683, with swags and a cherub's head; and a tomb to the Aris family, whose descendent Michael Aris was the late husband of Burmese opposition leader Aung San Suu Kyi. And there is also a grave that bears the name William Shakespeare. Whether he wrote poems one cannot verify but he lived in the early nineteenth century!

But were it not for group of local friends this ancient church would no longer hold services; it would be yet another defunct church sold off for development.

Declared redundant in the early 1990s and with just one service a year held in its damp and dusty confines, it was after such a service in 1996 that Northamptonshire resident Sir John Greenaway made a remark to Mike Sakkali, who lived in Rectory Farm, the adjoining property. 'Why don't we get together and buy and restore it,' he said before driving off home.

He took a call later that evening from Mike who asked if he was serious. 'Well I couldn't say no,' recalls Sir John some 12 years on. And so they recruited some other neighbours including PR consultant and fundraiser Francis Sitwell and art expert James Miller.

After a good year of wrangling, in which they set up a charity and endured protracted negotiations with the diocese, they bought the church and graveyard for the princely sum of £2,500 (Fig. 3).

With an agreement to maintain the church for religious services and to hold those services at times agreed by the

William Sitwell

William Sitwell is Chairman of the St John The Baptist, Plumpton Heritage Trust.

Description
The Trust cares for St John the Baptist, Plumpton, which is used for services on special occasions.

Founded
1995

Location
Plumpton, Northamptonshire (about seven miles west of Towcester).

Access
By keyholder.

Twitter
@PlumptonChurch

Fig. 2: The interior looking east. The font may be seventeenth-century. The east window is of the fourteenth century. The monument to Anne Moore (d.1683) is on the south side of the chancel arch.

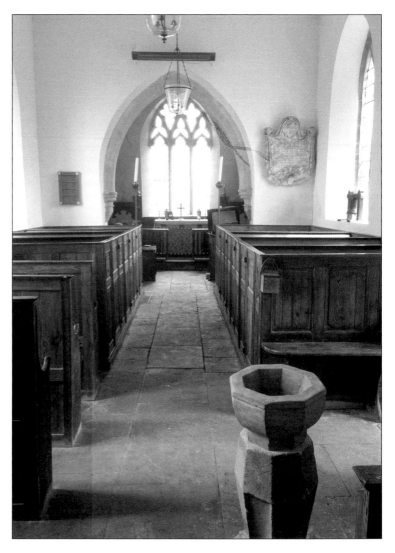

incumbent of the benefice, the Trustees gave the church a new lease of life. They restored it, purchased an organ and ensured the building was safe and sound.

Today there are up to a dozen services held each year and they include Christmas carols, a Patronal Festival and a number of Evensongs.

And now the Trustees have a new chairman. Perhaps the role came with the house because my family moved into Rectory Farm in 2010 and I was soon elected to the position.

We meet as Trustees at least once a year and organise who will take services. It means finding a vicar and an organist and publicising services. But there can be few places in England that hold the charm of Plumpton, with its combination of Gothic windows, box pews and wooden panelling. Acoustics are good and the Trustees can fill the church with their singing if numbers are rather small for some services.

I'm looking forward to the first of our services this year and it'll be one of my favourite, the Easter vigil on 19 April. Let's hope we can find a vicar…

For more information on St John the Baptist, follow @PlumptonChurch on Twitter.

Fig. 3: The exterior, from the south. The plaque over the porch says the church was rebuilt in 1822, but it is clear some medieval work was retained. The priest's door is of the fourteenth century.

Fig. 1: St Mary's, Rokeby, Co. Durham, from the west. Built in the 1750s to the initial design of Sir Thomas Robinson (who later built Glynde, Sussex); unfinished when Robinson sold the estate in 1769 and finished by John Carr. Consecrated as the parish church in 1776 (some sources say 1778). The liturgical west end in fact faces south.

St Mary's, Rokeby, Co. Durham

Introduction

THIS CHURCH WAS BUILT to the design of Sir Thomas Robinson Bt from about 1755 in order to replace the parish church of Rokeby built at the intersection of the rivers Tees and Greta and within the park he wished to enclose. Unusually, it is built on a north/south axis (Fig. 1). He sold the estate, including the incomplete church to my great-great-great-grandfather in 1769. Though he, Sir Thomas, agreed to complete it he failed to do so. It was completed by my family and consecrated as the parish church in 1776. The church was extended in the mid-nineteenth century but was otherwise hardly altered (Figs 2 &3).

But if the church was not altered the congregation it was built to serve did. There is no village: the only centres of occupation were and are the farmsteads and Rokeby Park. At Rokeby, as elsewhere, the rural population was decimated in the latter half of the twentieth century. Accordingly, by 2000, the congregation had died and not been replaced. Redundancy was inevitable. Attempts to find some charitable Trust or organisation to take it on were unsuccessful. It was clear that the Church Commissioners were determined to rid themselves of the responsibility for its maintenance as a Grade II★ building building at any price – provided that it did not involve them paying the purchaser! In the event the church was declared to be redundant in 2006. I bought the church and graveyard in the name of a family Trust for £1.

Subsequent use and challenges

We maintain the church and churchyard at our expense. There are occasional services in connection with burials, usually in the churchyard, and once a year we hold a carol concert for the benefit of local charities. There are good solid oak pews, heating, lighting and a small car park accessed only from the A66. There are no other facilities

The major problems are, and for at least the last 50 years have been, the A66 and security. The A66 is a major east/west thoroughfare. At the point where it passes the church it is single carriageway; the cars and lorries are doing more than 60mph. It is a considerable hazard for anyone seeking to drive to the church and was, in my belief, a major reason for the redundancy. Whether or not a consequence of the road, the church has been broken into at least twice in the last 25 years. There have also been at least three external thefts of lead and the antique bell. The insurance did not cover their replacement.

Obviously there is a limit to the amount of time and money my family can spend on caring for the church. The future depends

Sir Andrew Morritt

Sir Andrew Morritt, CVO, is a former Chancellor of the High Court of England and Wales.

Description
Parish church which, following redundancy, was acquired by a family Trust.

Location
Rokeby, Co. Durham.

Access
Private

Fig. 2: St Mary's, chancel and organ chamber, added in 1877. There is an 'undercroft' underneath. The nineteenth-century parts of the building are in hybrid classical/Romanesque style.

on the Department of Transport completing the dualling of the A66. It is absurd that the stretch opposite the church is still single carriageway and without speed limit. The necessary road widening has obvious problems and consequences for the Rectory and the churchyard to the south of the church. The Department would have to construct an alternative access to the church from the minor road to the north. If a sound barrier of some sort were constructed between the church and the A66 and a proper alternative access was built the church could be converted to some alternative, and profitable, use. It could make a first class house or collection of flats; it might well have other uses, for example a rehearsal hall for orchestras or producers of entertainments. It occupies a superb position; the problem was and is the A66 and the traffic it carries.

Advice to those considering similar arrangements

My advice would be twofold. Make sure that you have sufficiently recognised your long term liabilities; and do not expect any help from HM Revenue & Customs (HMRC). It is no exaggeration to say that the long term problems for St Mary's depend on the Department of Transport. They are exacerbated by HMRC's refusal to allow the costs of maintenance and repair to be set against gross income from other sources. Unless and until these problems are dealt with, St Mary's will remain a burden on the estate.

Fig. 3: The interior of St Mary's looking east. The nave contains monuments by Nollekens and Westmacott.

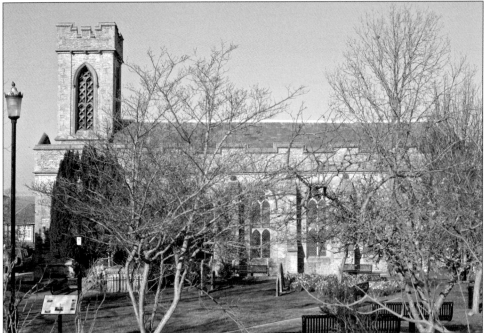

Fig. 1 (top) :St Thomas's, Ryde, from the south-west. The church was built in 1827 by Thomas Player. The building has important townscape value.

Fig. 2 (bottom): The church from the south, looking over one of the graveyards. The two-storey windows provide light for the galleries. (Carl Rosenberg)

St Thomas's church, Ryde, Isle of Wight: the story so far

ST THOMAS'S is a redundant proprietary chapel, closed in the 1950s, restored from dereliction at considerable expense by an independent Trust in the late 1980s and 1990s, then acquired by the Isle of Wight Council.

So far so good. Unfortunately – despite being an important local landmark, and in a fair state of repair – it has no obvious use and is not paying its way.

Closure, dereliction and repair

The church was built as a proprietary chapel, a chapel of ease to the parish of Newchurch. The current building was constructed in 1827 by George Player, to the designs of James Sanderson of Cork Street, London. It is listed Grade II, the listing description describing it as being built of stone in 'rudimentary gothic', with tall Perpendicular windows, a castellated parapet, and a small square west tower with bells, also castellated. The tower had a wooden spire until 1947, when it became unsafe and was taken down. The interior has a U-shaped gallery, and the gallery retains its pewing; the nave is largely clear of pews, though there is a bank of box pews remaining at one side of the nave under the gallery. There are a large number of monuments, and some interesting stained glass, a copy of an Italian triptych.

The church remained in the possession of the Brigstocke family until 1956 when the last family member died, and services in the church were discontinued in June 1959. Subsequently the church was not maintained, and there was some vandalism, and the church moved towards dereliction. Those attending the Isle of Wight Festival in the 1960s apparently have fond memories of dossing down in the building, accompanied by pigeons. By 1969 there was the threat of demolition.

In 1972, a group called The Friends of St Thomas was formed with the aim of restoring the church and seven years later the St Thomas's Trust was formed. The Trust's intention was to lease the building from the Portsmouth Diocese, and then restore the church, but it took until 1985 to sign the lease, and it was only in January 1987 that repair work started. In the late 1990s a Heritage Lottery Fund Grant of more than £400k was awarded to restore the building, including roof repairs, and repairs to the windows and the west front. At this time the organ was removed from the church, and the pulpit taken out; the latter is now in storage within the church.

In the meantime, in 1982 Medina Borough Council had taken over the churchyard. The southern graveyard was laid out as a garden of rest, the memorials being moved to the walls.

Fig. 3: Two mobile-phone snapshots of an event in the church. Notice the galleries, stained glass, monuments and commandment boards.

Fortunately the northern graveyard (the "sea captains' graveyard"), which contains some locally significant memorials, has not been altered.

Acquisition by the Isle of Wight Council

In November 2004, after considerable discussion, the freehold of the church was acquired by the Isle of Wight Council (not to be confused with the Ryde Town Council). The building has been deconsecrated (a legal change, not a religious rite), and is now known as the St Thomas's Heritage Centre.

The Council's intention was to use the building as a heritage museum and exhibition centre. However there are a number of difficulties, and the plan has not been pursued. The building lies on a hill, and the nearest parking is about one hundred and fifty yards away – parking has not been possible in front of the building as this is a burial ground. Access is poor for those with mobility difficulties. There is no heating in the building, though there is enough power for lighting and for refreshments. There are some safety risks from grates missing from the floor and the gallery is now out of bounds as the gallery rails are not high enough for modern health and safety requirements.

Most importantly, the building does not have two fire escapes, so no more than sixty people can use it at any one time. Any building work on the site would be complicated by the presence of the graveyards, and the nature of the subsoil may cause difficulties.

The future

So the idea of a heritage museum has not come to fruition. The building is used for the Ryde Arts Festival and for occasional events, and is hired out from time to time at a relatively low cost (one hundred pounds per day). At one stage a local firm had its offices there. Yet for most of the time it is unused, and it does not cover its costs. A significant capital injection will be required to return the building to full public use, or indeed any full-time use. But what would that use be?

As yet, no formal market interest in the building has been sought by the Council, but this may change in the coming year.

There are no immediate threats to the building, but the future is uncertain. Everyone seems to want something to be done about St Thomas's, but no-one is sure what. For a building of such importance to the history and townscape of Ryde, this is unfortunate.

Acknowledgements
The earlier material in this article relies heavily on the website of the Ryde Social Heritage Group, at www.rydecemetery.org.uk/StThomasChurch Graveyard.asp, where a fuller account may be found. The views expressed here are the editor's own, and any errors are his responsibility.

Fig. 1: St Peter's, Sibton, Suffolk, looking east. The pews have been removed, and new flooring installed which respects the original subdivision of the space. In the far corner some chairs are stacked. The chancel is largely untouched. This is a large and flexible space, well looked after.

The Friends of St Peter's, Sibton, Suffolk

The beginning

SIBTON IS A SMALL GROUPING of houses along the busy A1120, just east of Peasenhall in Suffolk. St Peter's church has Norman doorways and much medieval fabric, with a hammerbeam roof, and a font carved with Wild Men, and other furnishings of interest, including some good monuments. It is listed at Grade I.

But fewer than 200 people live in Sibton, and by 1986, there had been a significant decline in church membership. The church was declared a Chapel of Ease to the neighbouring village of Peasenhall, with a joint Parochial Church Council (PCC). From this time, although occasional services were held, the building was virtually abandoned and the church went into serious disrepair. By the early 1990s the joint PCC felt there was no alternative but to recommend redundancy.

There had been no consultation, so this is when the Sibton residents first became aware of the crisis. A simple survey was conducted to gather views, the results of which demonstrated that a good percentage of the residents wanted the church to be retained. There were statutory public meetings with the Archdeacon, and some considerable rancour.

Eventually, three options were put forward. The church could be closed and the building put into the care of the diocese, with its future completely uncertain. Or the church could be closed, and the building could be bought by people in the parish for one pound. Or, thirdly, those in the parish could be given one year to raise sufficient funds to put the building in a sound condition and show the need for the church to stay open in the parish. This was the preferred option, and out of this the Friends were born.

The Friends and their 'objects'

The Friends attracted an excellent team. At the head was an experienced chairman filled with enthusiasm and determination to succeed. Looking back, it was clearly an important factor in the team's subsequent success that members established their precise purpose as a team, and recorded this and kept it firmly in mind. Business meetings were held on a very regular basis, and recorded fully, and steps were taken to communicate with and involve those outside the central team.

The first newsletter, of December 1997, announced that within the year, funds raised amounted to £7500. By then the Friends 'objects' had been agreed (summarised as the 'repair, maintenance and improvement of St Peter's church, Sibton, for the use of the local community'), the Constitution formulated

Description
A Friends group which persuaded a diocese to keep a church open and return it to full parochial status. The Friends have an agreement for use of the building.

Friends established
1997

Location
About a mile east of Peasenhall, Suffolk.

Access
The church is normally open.

Fig. 2: St Peter's from the south-east. The dark wooden building containing the toilets can be glimpsed hiding amongst the trees to the left. The churchyard is being managed for wildlife.

under the guidance of a professional Stewardship Advisor, and registration with the Charity Commission had been finalised. The creation of an Appeal Brochure followed, circulated to grant-making bodies, companies and private individuals. As one committee member recalls, 'We worked jolly hard in this first year, raising over £25,000'.

The Friends' aims have guided its activities from the beginning. They include saving St Peter's Church (and its graveyard) both as a place of worship and also as a centre for the local community for future generations. The Friends are to raise funds for insurance, for fabric repairs, and for re-ordering and improvements to make the building more comfortable and convenient, including for future community and fund-raising events. They are to make St Peter's self-financing, to preserve its future.

In 1997, near the beginning, a document called *Suggested Major Project Works* was produced which outlined proposals for improvement, re-ordering and restoration and proposed how to obtain grants. Since then, this document has guided the Friends' programme of works, working in close consultation with the architect.

Amongst other things, the north aisle roof has been repaired, and the north aisle cleared of fixed seating to deal with problems of damp. Later a new floor and new heating were installed in the church and as part of this project the nave was cleared of fixed seating, making a very large clear space which can be used for many different activities (Fig. 1). The shorter pews are preserved around the wall, and negotiations with the diocese continue regarding the possible sale of the longer ones, now stored behind the organ. The church heating is now effective and efficient.

A 'kitchenette in a chest' has been introduced together with outside toilets using a natural disposal system, and thought is being given to making better use of the space under the tower, and this would also help with draughts (Figs 2 & 3). Further work will be needed on the lighting, and elsewhere on the fabric. Underneath the whitewash, particularly in the chancel, Victorian stencilled wall decorations have survived, but there have not been the funds to restore these. The chancel was not allowed to be reordered due to the quality of its Victorian furnishings; it is used for normal Sunday services.

The church is normally open, and attracts a good number of visitors, with the remains of the ruined abbey opposite generating some tourist traffic. Parking is limited, but for special occasions a neighbouring field can be used. The churchyard is managed on the principles suggested by the Suffolk Wildlife Trust.

The Fundraising role, so clear in the Constitution, has been an agenda item for each meeting of the committee, and in the early days was headed by a particular officer. For example a note from the early period records: three coffee mornings; a plant sale, with open gardens and strawberry teas; a concert of words and music; an organ recital; an illustrated talk; two variety shows; and, on the local farm, a heavy horse working day and the Sibton Horse Show. Membership subscriptions and donations have always been appreciated, but membership has never been particularly large and is now quite low (about thirty people) and planned fundraising continues to be central to the financial success of the project and continues to this day.

In the current year there are about eight events organised by the Friends (concerts, exhibitions and so forth), and some twenty-five events diarised by the PCC (such as visits by a cyclists group, or the University of the Third Age). Friends events seem largely to be supported by those outside the village.

Becoming a parish again

From the early days a primary concern of the Friends was the ultimate goal of self-sufficiency for the church and its use for church worship. The role of the PCC was fully recognised, and church representation on the Friends committee has included the Churchwardens, and *ex officio* the Vicar and/or a PCC member. No significant conflict has arisen from the differing roles of the two organisations.

As a result of this close working, on 1 January 2004 St Peter's Church regained its status as a parish church, in the new ecclesiastical parish of Sibton. In addition, the relationship of trust achieved between Friends and PCC led to an Agreement authorised by Faculty of the Consistory Court of the diocese in

May that year. The Agreement, which refers to the objects of the Friends, is for a thirty year period, and enables the Friends the use of the nave for events, in consultation with the PCC.

In 2007, ten years after the Foundation of the Friends, there was a special service to celebrate the achievements of Friends and PCC, attended by Bishop Clive Young.

Looking forward

The Friends activities have been characterised by a 'snakes and ladder' existence, up followed by down, some good progress followed by planned work being dashed through some unforeseen complication. From the point of view of the Friends, the negotiation of proposals with church officials has sometimes been found to be difficult and on occasion personally upsetting. The Friends have learnt to accept that there will be both pitfalls and pain on the way. There have been times, too, over the past seventeen or so years, when the committee itself has not worked entirely smoothly together.

But a huge amount has been achieved, and in general terms the future of the building looks good, with the Friends and PCC working together to keep the building alive and valued. At present, however, the committee of the Friends is significantly short of members and attempting to recruit new and younger ones, as well as find a new Chairman and Secretary; and the PCC is similarly dependent on a very small number of committed individuals to handle its activities. Furthermore not many people worship at St Peter's now. Although there are two benefice services in the church each year, which do attract good attendances, the rest of the time there are just two evening services per month, attracting congregations in middling single figures. It may be that a new pattern of services will emerge, for example services in summer only.

A further issue is that the character of the village is undoubtedly changing, with more home-workers, more people renting rather than owning their property so tending to stay a shorter time and planting fewer roots, and a general reduction in community feeling – all these factors make it harder to maintain contact with those in the village, and this tends to reduce the level of support for activities in the church.

Looking back to 1996, those involved in the Friends find it hard to remember that the church of St Peter was unexpectedly going to be made redundant and no longer available for use by the village. Yet, despite the subsequent years of commitment and work by the Friends, the extensive repairs, the re-ordering and opening up of the space, the re-establishment of the parish and reintroduction of regular services, and the considerable use made of the building, this threat may still be in the background, hanging over the building simply through lack of people to continue the good work. But Sibton has no other village hall: the meeting space provided by the church is surely needed for the foreseeable future.

Fig. 1: St Margaret's, Southolt, Suffolk, from the south-west.

St Margaret's Chapel of Ease Trust, Southolt, Suffolk

SOUTHOLT, SUFFOLK IS A VERY SMALL PLACE, with only 28 dwellings and about 50 adults living in the village. St Margaret's church was a Chapel of Ease attached to another larger parish, at one point Bedingfield, but historically with Worlingworth. It was declared redundant in 1979 and the altar table and altar rails were given to other churches and both the floor brass of Margaret Armiger dated 1585 and the Royal Arms of George III are now in Mendlesham Church.

After redundancy, the Church of England attempted to sell the building but was not successful. In the 1990's a group of residents, led by the Chair of the Parish Meeting, began the long process of taking over control of the church in order to preserve it for the village, rather than see it converted to some commercial or other use. The Church of England finally leased the church to Southolt for 99 years at a peppercorn rent and a Trust was set up to take charge of the church's affairs in 1996. The Trust is required to keep the church wind- and weather-proof and undertake the repairs necessary for this, and to insure the building. It remains consecrated.

The church building is small, just a medieval nave with bellcote and a chancel (Fig. 1) (the latter brick of 1907). It has a notable porch with checker-board flushwork. There are two stained glass windows: one is a memorial to a one-time vicar and the other is the west window dedicated to our patron saint, displaying St Margaret and the dragon. The font is fifteenth-century and depicts saints and 'wild men' (Fig. 2). Most of the Victorian pews were removed before the Trust took over, which makes the space more flexible for uses other than services, but the pulpit, choir stalls and lectern are still in place. There is a Victorian school-room attached to the north side of the nave, still retaining some of its original furnishings, which is used as the vestry.

The Trust and its activities

The Trust consists of eight Trustees who elect their Chair, Secretary and Treasurer at the Spring AGM and meet regularly throughout the year to plan events, services and restoration work. The church holds two or three services each year as well as weddings, funerals and christenings. The Christmas candle-lit Carol Service is a very popular service and the church is always full, usually about 100 attending. The services are taken by a retired local vicar who has been very supportive of St Margaret's since the Trust has been responsible. The Trustees, together with a small number of other residents, work hard at arranging the

Carolyn Evans

Carolyn Evans is Chair of the Southolt Chapel of Ease Trust.

Description
A small church in a hamlet, run by a Trust that holds a mixture of religious services and fund raising events.

Trust established
1996

Location
About eight miles north-west of Framlingham, Suffolk.

Access
Keyholder in village.

services, caring for the churchyard and organising fund-raising events for restoration or maintenance work on the building.

The church can be used for other purposes, for instance a Macmillan Coffee Morning one year, but is limited by its lack of facilities (Fig. 3). There is no electricity supply to the church and no water. The Trust relies on local houses for toilet facilities, if required. There is adequate parking for normal visitors. For a big event such as the Carol Service or a fund raiser we use residents' parking areas – the villagers have always been happy to open up their drives etc for the big events. We can use the village green itself, in front of the church, but it has been a problem in the winter because cars have got stuck.

The aim of the Trust is to ensure the continued existence of the church as the historic heart of this tiny community. For some people it is of religious significance but for others it is important as a social and historic building at the village centre. The churchyard was mapped and all grave inscriptions recorded by two residents in 2001 and the information has been useful to

Fig. 3: The interior, looking east. The nave is clear, and stackable chairs can be put out when needed. There is no electricity, which is brought in by temporary cable when necessary. The hangings are dried flowers from a wedding held a year or two back.

occasional visitors on genealogical quests. Local families have their particular areas of the graveyard and funerals and burials are still taking place at St Margaret's. It is an attractive and well-tended churchyard, far removed from the overgrown state it was in when first taken over.

Over the last fifteen years the church has again become very much the heart of the village. The variety of uses for the building has been interesting. At the millennium, eighteen residents chose to see in the new century in the church with candles, readings, a radio for hearing Big Ben's chimes and champagne to celebrate. When a local couple retook their wedding vows to celebrate forty years of marriage, they organised a fund-raising Baroque Concert to entertain their guests. Other concerts have followed: young performers in need of an audience have entertained in the church on several occasions and an old friend of local residents gave a musical performance and brought in funds for restoration. St Margaret's was a theatre venue for one performance as part of a local drama festival. The church has also occasionally provided a meeting place for parish business, displaying and discussing local building applications.

The Trust was fortunate in receiving help and support from the Society for the Protection of Ancient Buildings and benefitted from practical work on the church by volunteers on summer workshops over a period of three years. Local residents housed and fed the SPAB team for two weeks in July and learned from their expertise. The experience was mutually beneficial and great fun!

The Trust has accomplished a great deal in restoring the church building and in addition to funds raised by events, has benefitted from the generosity of local families. So far it has not been necessary to apply for any grants for repair work. Fundamental to all the efforts is the good fortune to receive a regular small income from the village Townlands Trust which underpins the financial maintenance of the church. Our overall income is typically a few thousand pounds per year. The external flint work has been repaired and re-pointed, the nave roof has been redone, the broken windows in the porch and nave have been re-glazed, the protective mesh-work on the two stained glass windows and the outer porch gates has been renewed, the bell-gable has been repaired so that the single bell can be safely rung, repairs have been made to the ancient church door which still retains its sanctuary ring, the interior walls have been lime-washed and the building is now in good repair generally. The next project is the chancel roof which requires attention.

In addition, one Trustee is an accomplished embroiderer and has designed and created an altar frontal in glorious colours and is currently working on a lectern 'fall'. When prepared for a service or event, the tiny church looks wonderful. A local amateur historian has researched some of the church's history which the Trust has published as a guide with illustrations by our resident architect and a cover illustration by our local artist.

Reflections

The success of Southolt events lies in the variety and the breadth of appeal. The usual services are Easter Holy Communion, Summer Service, Harvest Festival and Christmas Carol Service, although not all happen every year. They are all, though, social events as well, and this is important to their success. The Easter Service is always followed by coffee and biscuits and the Carol Service is rounded off with mulled wine and mince pies and a warm atmosphere in the church. The Harvest gives an opportunity for a fund-raising Harvest Supper which usually draws about sixty people. The Summer Service is written by Trustees and is full of music, hymns and poetry to celebrate summer and the natural world. Tickets are sold to the 'Strawberries and wine on the Green' event which takes place afterwards on the common beside the churchyard. All our services are on Saturdays in order not to compete with regular church services and usually start at 6.30pm. They draw in friends and residents from local villages and are well attended.

It all sounds easy and in a way it was. We were lucky that we had a good mix of skills and experiences amongst the interested villagers. We had a number of recently retired people who had the time to take the project on, and a real determination to keep the church at the heart of the village as it was in the past.

In the future, the main concern will be to sustain this level of involvement and commitment. It is a priority to encourage younger people to participate in events and appreciate the role the church building plays as a community focus. So far finding Trustees has not been a problem, but our age-profile is decidedly silver! We would like some youngsters on board but there are very few in the village, and this may be an issue in future.

Fig. 1 (right): The church of St James, Warter, East Riding of Yorkshire. This was built in 1861 by Habershon and Pite, and closed for worship in 1976. The story of how a Trust restored it to life some twenty years later is told in this article.

Fig. 2 (below): One side of an explanatory leaflet produced in 2011 when two stained glass lunettes by Robert Anning Bell, originally in a mausoleum in the churchyard, were restored and placed in the church.

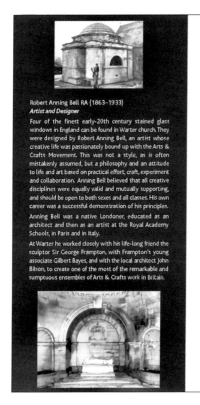

Robert Anning Bell RA (1863–1933)
Artist and Designer

Four of the finest early-20th century stained glass windows in England can be found in Warter church. They were designed by Robert Anning Bell, an artist whose creative life was passionately bound up with the Arts & Crafts Movement. This was not a style, as is often mistakenly assumed, but a philosophy and an attitude to life and art based on practical effort, craft, experiment and collaboration. Anning Bell believed that all creative disciplines were equally valid and mutually supporting, and should be open to both sexes and all classes. His own career was a successful demonstration of his principles.

Anning Bell was a native Londoner, educated as an architect and then as an artist at the Royal Academy Schools, in Paris and in Italy.

At Warter he worked closely with his life-long friend the sculptor Sir George Frampton, with Frampton's young associate Gilbert Bayes, and with the local architect John Bilson, to create one of the most of the remarkable and sumptuous ensembles of Arts & Crafts work in Britain.

St James' Heritage Preservation Trust

Registered Charity 1058064

The church of St James Warter was declared redundant in 1990 and later threatened with demolition. It was saved by the St James Warter Preservation Trust which now owns the church and the greater part of the churchyard.

With substantial grants from the Heritage Lottery Fund and LEADER +, the building was restored in 2006 and adapted for use as a cultural educational and heritage centre for the Yorkshire Wolds.

The newly returned stained lunettes from the demolished mausoleum were restored to their glorious best by Keith Barley Studios, Dunnington, nr York with funding from LEADER in 2011.

We are in need of donations to help keep this fine building open and in use. The church is available for use for concerts, conferences, meetings, exhibitions and open in the summer months—on specific dates for teas and cakes too.

Contact: Rose Horspool 01377 219135
roseandrobin@vistaarts.co.uk
The Old Chapel, North Dalton, nr. Driffield, East Yorkshire, YO25 9XA

ST JAMES' HERITAGE PRESERVATION TRUST

Stained Glass Lunettes at St James' Warter

St James's church, Warter, Yorkshire

I AM TOLD IT ALL BEGAN with a champagne picnic in the graveyard at Warter, one summer's day in the 1990s.

Warter is a tiny estate village of about one hundred people, and the church at Warter is large for such a small village, built in 1861 by Habershon and Pite and listed Grade II (Fig. 1). It had been closed for worship in 1976, some twenty years before the picnic, and been up for sale ever since, but no one had wanted it. Now there was talk of demolishing it and taking away its important Arts & Crafts work – including sculptures by Sir George Frampton and glass by Robert Anning Bell, and in the churchyard two bronze sculptures by Gilbert Bayes.

A group of interested people met at the church to discuss possibilities, and had a picnic afterwards. By the time the food – and the champagne – were finished, the picnickers had decided that they would buy the building to save it from demolition and keep the contents in the village. And that was the start of the then Yorkshire Wolds Buildings Preservation Trust (now St James Warter Preservation Trust).

The Trust committee had eight people, including some with professional experience in Heritage Management and the production of marketing and interpretative materials. It is this mix of skills which make this case rather different from many others in this book. It was the explicit intention of the Trust to develop the future of the building as heritage-based, but forward- and outward-looking and providing a service to local people.

Using the building

After amicable negotiations, the Trust paid the diocese £1 for the church. This lump sum included the graveyard, which is closed and now being managed for wildlife.

The first task, a huge one, was to bring the building up to scratch and make it ready for a new use. This was done with the aid of a grant from the European LEADER fund (about £100k) and the Heritage Lottery Fund (about £500k). This project took several years of everyone's life, but was seen as absolutely necessary to give the building a sustainable future: as well as major repairs, and the updating of the electrics, a small kitchen and toilets were inserted. This work was completed in 2006.

Display stands were acquired for exhibitions, and interpretation panels were produced to explain the building and its history. Leaflets were put on display for local tourist trails and suchlike. Although most of the pews were left in place, a few were taken out to increase the space, and this gave enough room for activities.

Description
The Trust uses St James, Warter as a heritage centre for a range of activities.

Founded
1996

Location
Warter, East Riding of Yorkshire.

Access
Open daily.

The Trust renamed the building the Yorkshire Heritage Centre, and the Trust itself now operates under the name 'St James Warter Preservation Trust'.

The building is available for hire, and the Trust itself arranges some fifteen or twenty activities a year in the building (Figs 3 & 4). These include concerts, lectures, exhibitions, stained glass workshops and – unusually – art workshops for children from difficult backgrounds through 'Children's University Hull' and a drop-in café on summer Sunday afternoons. There are also a small number of services, at Harvest Festival for instance. Parking is available nearby and is not an issue.

The Trust continues to develop the building. In 2011, with further funding from LEADER, two stained glass lunettes by Robert Anning Bell were restored and placed in the church (Fig. 2). They had been in store since the mid 1960s, when the mausoleum in the churchyard in which they were originally installed had been pulled down.

For the last eight years, the church has never been locked, something of which the Trust is particularly proud (though the decision was not taken lightly). This is clearly appreciated by visitors, both local and those from further afield.

Fig. 3: The Pocklington Swing Band performing in the church. There is ample room for activities of various types.

The Trust does not have a subscribing membership. Income is generated from donations and events. Running costs vary, but are typically a few thousand pounds per year. As elsewhere, the main running costs are heating and insurance. Time and materials for upkeep of the graveyard are donated.

Looking back, looking forward

The Trust was fortunate (or wise) in including on its committee people with some very specialist skills relating to the management, marketing and interpretation of heritage, and the committee have not found it hard to devise new uses for the building whilst maintaining its essential integrity. Since its foundation there have been a couple of new Trustees and a new Chair, and the average age of the Trustees is probably hovering around the sixty mark, so there are no immediate issues of succession or continuity.

It is noticeable, though, that only the Treasurer actually lives in Warter. There is room for greater engagement with people living in the village, though its population being so small and its being an estate village probably do not make this easy. Some people in the village act as 'Associate Trustees' for particular events, and once a year there is a joint fund-raising event (a strawberry tea) with the village, so there are reasonable ties into the local community.

The Trust recently discussed its medium-term future. There is money in the bank and the building is financially self-sustaining. Trust members are committed and energetic. There is a history of new Trustees becoming involved, and there has been one smooth change of Chair. The use of the building is not dependent on nostalgia, or a small group of regulars. So the major medium-term risks are probably a sudden crisis, or the unexpected attrition of the committee through illness or people moving away.

Advice to others

Asked for advice to others thinking of taking over a church building, one of the original Trustees made four points:

"First, it will take a lot of time at the beginning, but don't give up. Secondly when applying for grants, be prepared to record everything, putting a fair value on the time spent by committee members and other volunteers, as this can sometimes count towards matched funding. Thirdly, make sure the building has a use which benefits people, to generate support and make it possible to apply to major grant-givers.

"Finally, from the very beginning take photographs and keep records of everything you do – this helps in telling your story and gaining support in many different situations."

Sadly, there are no photographs of the champagne picnic.

Fig. 4: An exhibition in the church, using the chancel and the area in front of the pews

Fig. 1: The church of St Nicholas, Wattisham, Suffolk, from the south-east. The west tower is faced with cement. (Brokentaco, under CC licence)

St Nicholas's, Wattisham, Suffolk

ST NICHOLAS'S CHURCH IN WATTISHAM was made redundant in 1968. It is a relatively small medieval building, with tower, nave and chancel of the fourteenth and fifteenth century. Inside there is the dado of a medieval screen, and some poppy-headed bench ends. There are dormer windows each side of the nave, to light the screen. The building is listed Grade II★.

The Trust

Wattisham is a fairly remote place. After redundancy, the church stood on its own, quietly decaying for nearly 20 years. In 1988 the building was offered to the Parish Council at a price of £2000 and the parish took over the building, but could not afford to insure it, let alone start the necessary repairs.

In 1990 a few of the more wealthy retired residents took over the building. They formed a charitable Trust – 'The St Nicholas Trust (Wattisham)'– raised money and put a lot of time into repairing the building. The Trust called on local builders and tradesmen for advice, and begged and borrowed tools and materials to make the building safe and watertight. A good deal of money was put in by the original Trustees themselves, and money was also raised through fund raising events such as fetes, dog shows and musical events. The roof was fixed, the interior plastered and a new floor laid.

The original intention of the Trustees was to use the building as a musical centre. However this did not work out as planned, due to the location of the village, so the church started to be used for a more mixed programme of musical and village events, and exhibitions, as it has been ever since. There are about fifteen or twenty events per year, the majority organised by the Trust, some being private hire. The interior is open, with no pews, and chairs can be laid out as needed. The money raised is ploughed back into the building.

The original Trustees are no longer involved, and the building has in effect been passed over to the hamlet as a community centre. New Trustees tend to be drawn from those who show an interest in the activities

What we have learnt

We have learnt a good deal.

First, anybody wishing to take over a redundant church needs to have a full plan of what the building is to be used for, and to research if there is a desire for it in the local community. Our church is in a hamlet of less than 100 people and I would say you

David Cooper

David Cooper is a farmer working near Wattisham, and a Trustee of the Trust looking after the church.

Description
A Trust which restored and looks after a medieval church for the local community after taking it over from the Parish Council.

Founded
1990

Location
Wattisham, Suffolk (about five miles south of Stowmarket).

Access
Named keyholder.

Fig. 2: (top): The interior of St Nicholas, looking east.

Fig. 3 (bottom): The interior of St Nicholas, looking west.

need at least 40% of them to be interested in the activities which are going to be put on.

Secondly, be aware that even if a church building has been redundant for decades there will still be those in the community that will think that anything other than religious activities in the building are not acceptable.

Thirdly, when in discussions with the Church Commissioners make sure they are clear what you want to use the building for. Cover all the options e.g. food, alcohol, music and even dancing in the building. Make sure that the graveyard is fully discussed.

Our graveyard is still open and owned by the Church Commissioners, but the Trust is responsible for the upkeep, which can be expensive.

Fourthly look into insurance for the building. If the building is to be hired out you will probably need particular insurance to cover this. The Church Commissioners required insurance that covered rebuilding costs, which now stand at £1,600,000 for a small church that has a fire-safety restriction of 80 people in the building at any one time. Our insurance bill for 2014/15 is over £2250.

Finally, under no circumstances take on a redundant church until you are sure there is access to the public. This may seem strange but our church at the moment has none. All our church has is a 'churchway', which only allows residents of the village and the vicar legal right over it, not others. We rely on our friendly farmer neighbour for car parking; without his support we would struggle both with parking and access to the building. So the future for our church is not clear. We are hoping to divert a footpath through the graveyard to give us full public access, and this will help us to apply for Lottery grants.

At the moment we are ticking along quite nicely, raising about seven thousand pounds per year, but the insurance costs (our biggest expense) are going up more than inflation, and until we can apply for Lottery grants we cannot put any capital into developing the building.

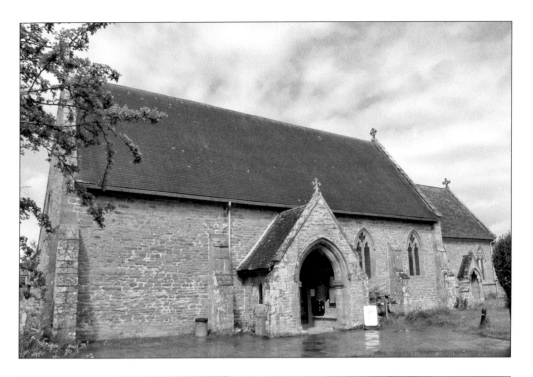

Fig. 1 (top): St Leonard's, Yarpole, Herefordshire, photographed on a wet day in 2014. The church is of the fourteenth century, restored and altered by G. G. Scott in 1864. (Tewkes)

Fig. 2 (bottom): The interior looking west, photographed from the chancel arch in 2010. The hand-rail to the pulpit can be seen at bottom left. At the west end is the shop (closed when the photograph was taken), with the café above. In the north aisle are toilets and a vestry.

Yarpole Community Project, within St Leonard's, Yarpole, Herefordshire

YARPOLE IS ONE OF JUST TWO CASES in this book where a community group has taken full responsibility for looking after a still-open church, and the congregation make a financial contribution for use of the space for worship. (The other is Fernham.) This arrangement was not made in a vacuum, but was one outcome – perhaps the natural outcome – of a major community project not only to reorganise the interior of the church building, but also to put the village shop and a café in the west end.

Yarpole itself is a quite a remote place, with a population of about 700. The church building, dedicated to St Leonard, is of average size (Fig. 1). It has a medieval aisle and nave, much restored by   G. G. Scott in 1864, and a detached thirteenth-century bell tower to the south, which is listed Grade I, while the church itself is listed Grade II★.

Community shop and community centre

In 2004 the Parish Plan highlighted the fact that the parish was losing its shop, and also identified the under-use of the church building as an issue.

As a result the community set up its own shop in 2005, housed temporarily in a portacabin. They then set out to find a permanent site for the shop, and one of the possibilities they identified was the back of the church, together with a cafe and post office.

For the Parochial Church Council (PCC), this came at a time when it was actively considering how to reconnect with the wider community, and make more use of the church building. There was no immediate threat. The congregation was a reasonable size, and the church building in quite good condition, although many of the facilities needed upgrading and the pews were not especially comfortable. But the PCC was keen to find ways to make the church a useful asset to the community, and to manage their cost burdens, and they encouraged the introduction of the shop into the church.

This was agreed, and plans were drawn up in 2006 to gut and refurbish the nave, and work was completed in 2009, at a total cost of £240k (Fig. 2). Those who have been through a similar process will appreciate just how much blood, sweat and tears will have been involved in driving the project through: but that is outside the scope of this piece.

Description
Community group providing various services inside a church building, for which they are responsible; PCC makes financial contribution for use of building..

Location
Yarpole, Herefordshire.

Access
Open daily.

Website
www.yarpole.com

Fig. 3: The café (photographed in 2010). The kitchen area is through the arch. The stair up from the nave is to the right.

As part of the project, the nave of the church was cleared and given a new floor and underfloor heating, and the roof was insulated. There were lengthy discussions about the possibility of a screen between chancel and nave, but this was not introduced and is now thought unnecessary. In fact, the chancel was not included in these changes, and is more or less untouched. So the chancel area is a somewhat heavy Victorian outpost in an otherwise elegant and modern interior, though there are plans to extend the underfloor heating into the chancel area and re-order it.

Thus in Autumn 2009 Yarpole Community Shop began operating in purpose-built rooms at the west end of the church building. It was the first full-time shop to operate in a church, and won several awards. Above the shop is a gallery with a café (the Gallery Café; see Figures 3 & 4), and in the aisle of the building are the toilets and a vestry.

The shop opens every day and employs two part-time members of staff, one of whom is also the postmaster (Fig. 5). The rest of those working in the shop and café are volunteers. There

are about forty of them, either working front of house to a rota, or doing administration at home in their spare time. This opportunity for volunteering and working with others is a very positive social spin-off from the project.

Fig. 4: The café (photographed in 2010), looking east over the nave towards the chancel.

The shop is set up not as a charity, but as a registered Industrial and Provident Society, a legal vehicle which offers the benefit of limited liability but without all the Companies Act requirements. More than three hundred people in the village have purchased non-redeemable £10 shares in the shop.

The use of volunteers reduces the cost base of the shop and allows it to compete head to head with the supermarket chains on price and convenience: indeed, there are explicit price comparisons on the community website, to encourage people to use the shop. Turnover is now more than £100k per year, and a small surplus is made (typically several thousand pounds). After putting money into reserves, and making loan repayments to Co-operative and Community Finance which provided initial working capital, any dividend is ploughed back into village life. When the loan has been repaid in a year or two, careful

Fig. 5: The shop and post office (photographed in 2010).

consideration will be given to the possibility of the shop contributing to the costs of maintaining the building.

The rest of the church building is available for hire. There is a combined booking system with the village hall, as one of the objectives of the project was not to put the hall at risk. The latter tends to have more regular engagements, whilst the church building tends to be available on a more flexible basis. Although parking at the church is a significant problem, discussions are under way about opening up another space as a mixed parking and recreational area.

One regular user of the church building is the PCC, which makes an annual contribution towards overall costs, and uses of the space on Sunday and for other services.

Long term management of the building

The entire building, and the graveyard, is now the responsibility of the St Leonard's Management Group, which is the inclusive management committee which represents all the users of the building. The Parish Council has been consistently supportive and given grants for various purposes, and the Parish Clerk has recently become a member of the management committee. At present St Leonard's Management is not a legally independent body (it answers to the PCC), though it could become one in future, a step that is broadly supported by the diocese.

In essence, then, the PCC has handed over responsibility for the care of the church and churchyard to another body, St Leonard's Management, in return for an annual contribution. Thus the PCC has reduced the uncertainty of its cost base, and has reduced its time burden looking after the building, and the building itself is much more attractive and practical. A building which was looked after by the PCC and not used for most of the time, is now looked after by another group and is being used much more frequently, and the PCC can still use it when it needs to.

How sustainable is this arrangement?

One question about sustainability is the long-term willingness of people to serve as active committee members. Here the need for key individuals to step down and hand over has already been publicly acknowledged and discussed; and turnout at the AGM is still good, implying continuing interest and commitment from members. In the end, of course, only time will tell; but there are none of the warning signs one has seen elsewhere.

As for the shop as a business, its sustainability will depend on the continued availability of volunteers, and the ability to attract custom. Ten years in, and the signs are good for both these. An explanatory note about the arrangements is available to everyone moving into the village, so that people understand that the future of the shop depends on them, both as customers and as volunteers. In general, the continued availability of the church building will help promote the sustainability of the shop.

What of the sustainability of the church building? The PCC contributes towards the cost of maintaining the building and its graveyard, and although the shop does not currently contribute it may well do so in future. A further income stream is already present, from hiring the space out.

There is no way of knowing how the income from rents will work over the longer term, though, again, the signs are good. A deliberate effort is being made to market the building as a modern facility to those outside the area, to bring in new money; it now has wifi and a hidden hanging system for exhibitions. And the possibility of a weekly GP's surgery is being discussed. It seems probable that if the worshipping community ever fell away and decided it no longer had a need for the building, then the other income streams would continue to cover the cost of maintenance and ongoing repairs.

It is unlikely that capital injections to improve the building will ever be met entirely from income. The porch has now been glazed to allow the doors to stand open without draughts, and a lift to the gallery is shortly to be introduced. Capital intensive schemes such as these will probably always need more donations and more grants – and more volunteer time spent in fund-raising.

Over the longer term, one significant advantage of the new arrangements for the future of the church building is that many more people in the village now feel they have a stake in the building: that they 'own' it. If the building ever needed major repairs, not only is the organisational infrastructure in place to see things through, but there would probably be widespread support for saving what is now seen as a community asset.

Acknowledgements
The editor is grateful for those who helped with information about the work at Yarpole. The views expressed here are his own, and any errors are his responsibility.

Part 3

IDEAS, DEVELOPMENTS, STATEMENTS

Church Trusts and the Cathedral and Church Buildings Division of the Church of England

We are grateful to the Cathedral and Church Buildings Division of the Church of England for giving their views on Trusts, in the wider context both of keeping churches open and the considerations which apply when a church closes.

Gabriel Byng

Gabriel Byng is Secretary to the Statutory Advisory Committee on Closed and Closing Churches (a committee of the Church Buildings Council of the Church of England).

THE CLOSURE OF ANY CHURCH is a great sadness, and one which the Church of England works hard to avoid. Before closing, churches go through a lengthy process to ensure that there really is no other option, trying first to adapt them to alternative uses, find new fundraising structures, and encourage local participation.

Keeping churches open and serving their community

Farmers' markets, shops, post offices, activity centres, social groups, coffee mornings, bands, Citizens Advice Bureaux, food banks, night shelters, and, more recently, credit unions have all taken their place in church naves and halls. This is more than a last ditch attempt to keep churches open. At its core is a belief that church buildings are at the heart of the Church's mission and a vital community resource. In villages these are often the only public building in which these activities could take place, and, whatever the urban or rural environment, they offer a way for churches to look outwards into their community and to offer a service to their parishioners. Churches, just like their congregations, must be servants to their neighbours.

Keeping churches open and useful for their local communities has always been part of the Church's duty. Naves, which have been the responsibility of the parishioners (rather than the clergy) since the thirteenth century, have always been multipurpose structures. Their use for activities we might recognise as secular was indistinguishable from their wider, 'religious' purpose in the community. Protecting livestock in a storm and providing a space for worship are both Christian activities, different sides of the same coin. Often their most important function is just to be open, providing a quiet space for those seeking comfort and contemplation.

The Church of England's Cathedral and Church Buildings Division (CCB) has been involved in encouraging churches to find 'complementary uses' for many years, most recently through the 'Open and Sustainable' initiative. Alongside expanding its advice on developing other uses and providing case studies, the

CCB has identified five legal options open to parishes according to the number of services and the extent of the other activities that take place (see appendix). These range from allowing some other functions under licence to 'rebooting' the church as a 'footprint parish'. (Examples of 'reboots' include St James's, Toxteth, 'rebooted' as an extra-parochial place of worship after 30 years vested in the Churches Conservation Trust, and St Paul's, Hammersmith, taken on as an extra-parochial place of worship by the congregation at Holy Trinity, Brompton.) The CCB has also been involved in setting up local Friends Groups and similar bodies to increase the resources, in terms of both finance and expertise, available to parish churches. There is further information on www.ChurchCare.co.uk/open-sustainable.

When a church closes

However, declining congregations, increasing repair costs, and other financial pressures mean that some churches cannot remain open. This difficult judgement is one that the Parochial Church Council must make for itself, before it is approved by the diocesan Mission and Pastoral Committee. The case is then referred to the Church Commissioners who ask for advice on the aesthetic and historical significance of the church building and its contents from the Statutory Advisory Committee (SAC), a sub-committee of the CCB.

The SAC is concerned to ensure that both buildings and contents are used appropriately during and after their closure. An exceptional few, of the highest architectural significance, (around two a year of roughly twenty closures in total) are taken over by The Churches Conservation Trust (CCT) and will remain open to the public and well looked after. This is not an easy option, however, as the CCT's funding is being cut by as much as 20 per cent a year while the number of churches it is responsible for increases. In these cases, although the church can often still be used for occasional services, it ceases to be the parish church and can no longer carry out many parochial functions.

Churches for whom no use can be found, and which remain unoccupied, may, eventually, be considered for demolition. However, between these two extremes are a whole range of alternatives. Some become private houses or offices and disappear into private ownership, but others can be preserved as village halls, rehearsal spaces, or for other community uses.

The SAC has often recommended the latter option, particularly if the building is of some architectural interest but not important enough to be vested in the CCT. However, the alternatives can be heavily restricted by the nature of church buildings, which are not often of dimensions that lend themselves easily to other functions, or by the exceptional significance of the fabric (which is often protected by secular legislation as a listed building). Relocating furniture, window glass, and fonts is often difficult but these objects can be of exceptional artistic, spiritual, and historical importance. Some alternative uses are, of course, much less desirable than others, both because of the damaging effect they have on the fabric of the building and its significance, or as they reduce or end public access.

Trusts

A small number of parishes, keen to preserve their church for community and/or religious use, but unable to maintain it as an open parish church, opt to set up a Trust to look after the fabric after closure. The total number of these Trusts is small, as many parishes choose to set up Trusts (or other similar bodies, such as Friends' Groups) in order to keep the church open rather than after they have closed. From the perspective of the SAC there are many advantages to the creation of a Trust to own a closed church. The fabric can usually be retained unchanged, or almost unchanged. It removes the demand for new floors, rooms, or walls, disturbing the lofty dimensions of the church, and the need to remove fixtures or fittings that have a long historic and aesthetic association with the building, as is often the case when churches become houses or businesses.

Most importantly, the church remains open to the public and can often be used for some Christian services, usually no more than six each year. In many parts of the country, the church is the only communal building and a wonderful resource for the area, as well as the only religious building, and can be kept as such by a Trust. One excellent example can be found at St John, Toller Whelme, Dorset, which continues to be used for occasional services. As communities are increasingly encouraged to provide secular activities for themselves, structures like parish churches (as well as the social capital they can help to concentrate) will be important to keep open.

Appendix: Legal options for complementary use of church buildings (extract)

This is an extract from the above document, published in 2013. The full document explores the legal and financial/funding issues for each option.

Option 1

Almost wholly a place of worship with facilities to support this function, limited other use under licence.

Option 2

Primarily a place of worship, some of the building used for other (complementary) purposes under lease, using Section 68 of the Mission and Pastoral Measure 2011 (MPM)

Option 3

Mostly used for other purposes under lease but part still used as a regular place of worship, using MPM.

Option 4

Primarily used for other purposes and closed for regular worship under MPM, but part used under licence for occasional services. Church building under secular jurisdiction.

Option 5: 'Reboot'

This is a church closed using MPM and 'rebooted' as a footprint parish or extra-parochial place of worship. Then Pathway 1–3.

The full document may be found at http://tinyurl.com/fivelegaloptions or at www.churchcare.co.uk/images/Legal_options_chart_-_updated_05.pdf A readable guide to that part of the MPM dealing with the wider use of part of a church building will be found at http://tinyurl.com/wideruse or at www.churchofengland.org/media/1500116/pamguide.doc.

Pilgrim churches: a possibility for the Church in Wales

This article is based on a paper discussed by the Representative Body of the Church in Wales. The concept of Pilgrim churches is now being taken forward on an exploratory basis, as explained in the final paragraph.

Alex Glanville

Alex Glanville is the Head of Property Services of the Church in Wales.

The issue

THE CHURCH IN WALES possesses a large number of small, remote churches and chapels in rural places. These serve a tiny congregation and have few members. They are largely unviable and cannot meet their parish share commitments.

If declared redundant, sale is possible but often at a low value and the after use does little for the mission and ministry of the Church. The large-scale redundancy of these buildings will impact very negatively on the mission and ministry of the Church in terms of reputation and public perception.

The concept

These small places could be kept as monuments or shrines; as simple places where walkers/pilgrims/tourists can visit for quiet contemplation and prayer. The approach would be that of basic care and maintenance, such as gutter clearance and minor holding repairs for safety. The buildings would be left in a 'basic state' with no heating or electrics.

A local person or group would need to be responsible for cleaning and 'keeping an eye' on the building from time to time. There would be no formal services but occasional worship activities could take place if the wider parish wished them to happen. Some funds would need to be raised annually to carry our basic maintenance and cover public liability insurance (perhaps £1000–£2000). The idea is that Community Council, Representative Body of the Church in Wales (RB), Diocese and other local parties might contribute into a joint fund.

How does it work in detail?

Pilgrim churches are redundant churches which the Church in Wales has decided to retain as simple, wayside places for visitors. Retaining such buildings costs money (insurance, repairs etc) and these costs will be covered by joint cooperation between province, diocese and local people.

To be a Pilgrim church, a building should meet the following criteria:

- Small in size – generally single cell, simple buildings
- Generally in reasonable condition – minor works only

- Heritage value is not a major criteria but generally listed buildings will fall into this scheme
- Located in a visitor area e.g. on walking or cycling routes
- A bedrock of local support including from the PCC
- Not obviously re-developable for significant value
- Supported by the bishop of the Diocese

The management arrangements for such buildings will be as follows.

1. Use

The Pilgrim church will be open every day for visitors. A local person will agree to open and lock up as necessary (or potentially a timed lock could be installed).

The local PCC should agree to hold around six public services each year in the building. The form and content of these services will be agreed with the Diocesan bishop.

It is possible for the PCC to use the church for funeral services, baptisms and wedding blessings. Marriages could only be held under Archbishop of Canterbury's special licence. Fees for such services would be apportioned between PCC and the church's fund appropriately.

Local people and groups will be encouraged to install displays, leaflets, and information about the church, community and local area.

Wider publicity for the church will be arranged as necessary e.g. local road signage, websites, tourist publicity etc.

2. Insurance

The RB will arrange and pay for appropriate insurance cover for the building.

3. Repairs etc

Local people will need to be identified to act as caretaker for the building ensuring regular inspections and arranging minor maintenance as necessary.

The Diocese will continue to include the building within its Quinquennial Inspection scheme (though surveyors should be clear that a 'minimum necessary' approach is to be taken). Action to address identified issues will be agreed between the parties.

Funding of such repairs will be addressed as necessary between the Diocese and RB.

Generally, it is anticipated that electricity and gas supplies will be cut off to minimise costs. However, a decision will be made in each case depending on the likely running costs and the condition of the electrical installation.

Grants may be applied for from external bodies if deemed necessary.

4. Funding

Any funds held by the PCC specifically for the church at redundancy will be held in a special fund for the church.

- Collections raised at services in the church will be passed by the PCC to this fund.
- Donations for the church may be accepted for inclusion in the fund.
- Fees for special services (baptisms, funeral services etc) would be apportioned between PCC and the church's fund on a 50-50 basis.
- Expenditure (electricity, maintenance, repairs etc) will be paid from the church's fund held by the Diocese. Any shortfall will be met by the RB and/or the Diocese.
- All expenditure will be agreed in advance by the RB and the Diocese.

5. Caretaker

A local person will be identified as the caretaker. This person will work as a volunteer for the Representative Body and will perform the following duties:

- To arrange regular inspections of the church to check for security, need for repair or maintenance and to keep the building interior reasonably clean
- To identify and manage other local people who wish to volunteer to help care for the church
- To report any building problems to the nominated RB/Diocesan contact to agree action
- To arrange for minor maintenance tasks to be undertaken either personally or with a local volunteer (for simple low level tasks such as cleaning or gully clearance) or via a local contractor as agreed with the RB/Diocesan contact
- To arrange to open and unlock the building each day or other timetable as agreed. This can be done personally or with the help of other local volunteers the caretaker might organise.
- To set up a hospitality table for visitors with simple refreshments such as bottled water and fair-trade products (to be funded from an honesty box)
- To liaise with the PCC over the arrangements for special services to be held in the church and organise accordingly
- If possible, to organise displays and information relating to the building to inform visitors and arrange special open days etc. This work might be undertaken by other local volunteers the caretaker might identify.

The caretaker and all volunteers will be covered by the RB's insurance arrangements for public liability.

Fig. 1: St Garmon's, Llanarmon Mynydd Mawr. The final service in the church as a parish church was held in February 2014, and the parish was amalgamated with a neighbouring parish. However the church has not closed, and six services are being organised for the current year. (Crown Copyright: Royal Commission on the Ancient and Historical Monuments of Wales)

An example

The first Pilgrim church is being developed at St Garmon's, Llanarmon Mynydd Mawr (Fig. 1). This church sits on the southern end of the Berwyn Mountain range to the west of Oswestry.

The PCC do not feel able to continue their ministry from this church, but there are a number of local people who want to see the church retained. Its small size, good condition and great location make it an ideal Pilgrim church. The surrounding graveyard is owned by the Community Council.

At the time of writing (July 2014) the following weblink gave details of service times at St Garmon's: http://stasaph.churchinwales.org.uk/news/2014/01/new-era-for-st-garmons-church/

Diocesan Trust Churches: an innovative scheme from the Diocese of Norwich

In July 2014 it was announced that the Diocese of Norwich would be setting up a new scheme, known as Diocesan Church Trusts. The following is an abbreviated version of that announcement, reproduced by kind permission from the ChurchCare website. The web address for the full version is given at the end of the article.

LATER THIS YEAR (2014) the Diocese of Norwich, which has a magnificent heritage of over 600 church buildings, most of which are listed as Grade I or II★, will launch an innovative scheme known as 'Diocesan Trust Churches'. This will allow churches that would otherwise face redundancy because they are in depopulated or isolated communities to remain open to the local community for occasional services, while some of their normal activities will cease. This Trust, which will be legally separate from the Board of Finance and funded other than through the Parish Share, will take on a basic level of insurance and preventative maintenance but crucially without formally closing the building or making it redundant.

It is envisaged that this will be a way of enabling church buildings to rest for a while before, hopefully, resurrecting to new life. There are many examples within the Diocese of Norwich, and elsewhere, of how just a couple of people can reinvigorate the life of a church, or where an open building has generated a worshipping community even in depopulated areas. The Rt Revd Graham James, Bishop of Norwich, said: "The legacy of our medieval church buildings is a glorious one but a headache in tiny settlements. We hope this scheme will avoid the pitfalls of redundancy, release local Christians from being simply custodians of the nation's heritage, while ensuring these buildings still have a witness as houses of God".

The Venerable Steven Betts, Archdeacon of Norfolk, said: "The Church of England is working hard to maintain a vital part of the nation's heritage but this is a growing challenge when there are so few people available to assist. This is not through any failure of mission and ministry, but a natural result of a decreasing population in small villages and hamlets, often with other nearby churches in the benefice. The Diocesan Trust Churches model will allow resources to be devoted to mission and ministry while ancient buildings, which form an integral part of Britain's Christian history, are looked after for generations to come".

The Church Buildings Council believes that this creative idea from the Diocese of Norwich has a huge amount to commend it, and may prove an attractive model for other dioceses to follow. Anne Sloman, Chair of the Church Buildings Council said: "The Council understands all too well the pressures on rural churches in depopulated areas and the Diocesan Trust Churches model has the advantage of enabling churches to stay open, welcome visitors, and provide essential community space. Moreover, by continuing to hold occasional services including weddings and funerals, these beautiful buildings will still be eligible for a whole range of outside grants to maintain their structure and contents".

Issued by the Church Buildings Council, July 2014

The full version may be accessed at http://tinyurl.com/diocesantrust churches or at www.churchcare.co.uk/churches/open-sustainable/friends-and-trusts/diocesan-trust-churches

Festival churches: a step towards sustainable rural ministry into the future

This article is based on a blog the author wrote in December 2013 at http://alwaysperhaps.wordpress.com. It is published here by kind permission.

Anna Norman-Walker

Canon Anna Norman-Walker is the Diocesan Missioner in Exeter Diocese.

Context

IN DEVON we have large numbers of rural churches. Some of our churches are facing significant challenges, in deeply rural settings where there is an average Sunday attendance of under ten people, and where the local church goers are aging, finances are strained and the maintenance of church buildings has become an unsustainable task.

Ordained and licensed ministry is becoming increasingly thin on the ground with fewer clergy having oversight for more and more parishes; expectations on them inevitably set them up for failure. This creates a vicious circle of feeling undervalued and over-worked and seeing little or no fruit of their labours, whilst knowing that the locals think the church numbers have dropped off because they think you 'don't visit as much as your predecessor'. Morale among many rural clergy is at an all-time low.

The vast majority of our parishes have been part of benefice teams for many years and have become accustomed to sharing ordained ministry. But some of our larger rural and semi-rural parishes are experiencing this for the first time as they have engaged in the process of pastoral reorganisation through our 2003 strategic plan *Moving On in Mission & Ministry* (MOIMM).[1] Some parishes are now asking important questions about the future of their churches and for some of them the time is right to begin a new way of being the church 'local' within the larger 'Mission Community'. (The concept of 'Mission Community' is of a sustainable worshipping group of more than 150 people. It was introduced in MOIMM.)

The commitment of local people

The local church has tried for years to harness the commitment of local, non-regular-churchgoing, but supportive people to help finance the ongoing life of the local church. Some villages have active 'Friends' groups who are an enormous help, though they are few and far between.

---

1   This can be found at http://tinyurl.com/MOIMM.

Success has been mixed. However, if there is any suggestion that the local church is due for closure local people often react strongly and emotions run high at public meetings and letters to the local paper fly!

This of course is because local people understand the village church is 'their church' (even if they do not attend on Sundays). They also see the village church as an iconic local building which connects and unites people past, present and future (Granny is in the churchyard, etc). And they know, as visitors books tell us, that people use our church buildings as tourists or returners and are pleased to find it open.

Importantly, people do attend church consistently for weddings, funerals and baptisms (the so-called 'occasional offices') and 'Festival Services' namely Christmas (carols or midnight), Harvest, Remembrance, Mothering Sunday and Easter (less so). This list is *probably* in popularity order. There are also often local traditions and festivals which are part of the village's story which can have an act of worship as part of them and tend to attract non-regular churchgoers.

Festival churches

For those churches where regular attendance is negligible and where the regular Sunday worship is deemed no longer viable, rather than pursuing church 'closure' the suggestion is to invite the local community to make a bid to become a 'Festival church', to hold the sorts of services listed above.

This is to avoid church closure and it needs to be presented as such to the local community.

A Festival church would provide weddings, funerals and baptisms for those living in the parish (or with qualifying connection), and also a public act of worship on the major festivals listed above. Villages could opt in or out of whichever festivals were deemed locally appropriate. The building would be kept watertight and windproof, the churchyard maintained, and insurance provided. Arrangements could also be made locally regarding key holders and access to the building for visitors, or to open it on a Sunday for private prayer.

If a village felt they wanted their church to become a Festival church they could apply to the Diocese, who would provide them with all of the above at a locally determined cost per annum. This could be calculated on the basis of the various direct costs (such as insurance, upkeep of the churchyard, basic building maintenance and cleaning) and an assessment of past occasional office provision (with charges made direct to those for whom the offices are offered).

This would be the cost to the village of a Festival church and saving their church from 'closure'. The village could then determine how this cost might be met.

Worship and mission

This project could be deemed simply as a common sense way for managing decline but I believe that it could in fact be the catalyst in many rural communities for renewal and discipleship.

If the Diocesan vision set out in our strategy (MOIMM) is to become a reality there needs to be an opportunity for Christian worship and discipleship that extends to and is accessible to every community in Devon, so it is important that within each Mission Community there is a well-resourced weekly worship centre. Where there is weekly provision of quality worship and a commitment to mission both through evangelism and community engagement, along with a serious commitment to discipleship, all the evidence suggests that churches grow. In time a village with a Festival church may have a good number of people from that village as members of the Mission Community who would like to begin a fresh worshipping presence in the village itself. The building might then be restored to a weekly worship centre and fresh structures established, appropriately negotiated, such as a Church Plant or Bishop's Mission Order.

I believe that this will also relieve the church of some of the 'militant localism' that has held sway for many years in some places and makes itself known supremely in an unwillingness to travel out of the village to worship on a Sunday. Our Free Church and Roman Catholic friends have done so for years: what makes us Anglicans any different? Ironically, the place of greatest resistance to this sort of strategy will likely come from this group of people!

This is by no means a watertight proposal and it raises as many questions as solutions, not least theological questions about the 'church' and pastoral ministry. Then there are issues of building costs and what happens when the tower falls down! However these issues will present themselves regardless of whether or not the church is a Festival or a Parish church and at least with the Festival church model there is potentially a larger group of stakeholders from the local community who can address the challenge together.

Four imaginary case studies, set in the future

Trevor Cooper

THIS NOTE is a slightly abbreviated version of a piece I wrote for private circulation in 2005. It describes four imaginary case-studies, set ten years in the future (so 2015), and was intended to demonstrate the potential flexibility of church Trusts (though I see that I missed the opportunities provided by a Trust having a long-term lease rather than freehold ownership). Note that references to the '2012 Measure' and to the 'UK Churches Trust' are to entirely imaginary arrangements.

1. St Mary's, Smallton – a living church, its use widened by a Trust

St Mary's, Smallton is a large medieval parish church in a decayed market town, now closer to being a village. There is a small but stable congregation.

Since 2015, the freehold has been owned by the Smallton Church Trust (under the aegis of the UK Churches Trust). The Trust bears all the cost of repairs. The Parochial Church Council (PCC) pays an agreed rent.

The Trust is charged with maintaining a substantial part of the building as a centre for worship, whilst developing other uses. At the moment part of the building is screened off for office use (rented out to a local architect) and there is a pleasant open space at the back hired out for evening classes. The chancel and east end of the nave are largely unchanged.

The building falls under secular planning control. However, the Trustees are bound under the terms of the Trust to follow the guidance of the DAC and Chancellor, on the grounds that the building is in a similar position to a PCC wishing to lease part of the building. The management plan for the building agreed with the Local Authority recognises this arrangement. Before the Trust took over, a long term plan for modifications was agreed.

Should pastoral reorganisation ever lead to the parish being abolished as a separate entity, then the Trustees continue in ownership. They are bound to give first refusal for continued use by some other Christian group on a routine basis.

Key points

In many ways, the situation is much the same as it would be if the PCC created and managed long-term leases for part of the building. The difference is that the congregation are not burdened with this responsibility; instead, they pay rent. Furthermore, the building lies in the hands of the wider community who benefit from it, and are responsible for it.

Closure would be a relatively smooth process.

2. St Anselm's, Kilnley – a living church, preserved by a Trust

St Anselm's, Kilnley is a stunning high-Victorian church of international importance. Built in brick by a local industrialist in memory of his late mother, it is an enormous building, known (at least, so the guide books say) as the 'Cathedral of the Kilns'.

But it has never been full. Now, with demographic changes, it supports a steady congregation of about 30 people, rising to 50 or so for family services. They rattle around, but love their church.

Although the church is not closed, since 2015 the building has been owned by the Kilnley Church Conservation Trust under the 2012 Measure. A long-term, renewable agreement has been made with the parish, who pay the Trust a rent for the routine use of the building, but have no maintenance responsibility. The parish operates in the normal way, with PCC and churchwardens. The agreement also stipulates that the building will be available for educational and artistic ventures, and tourism, which the Trust itself looks after.

Recently the parish wished to reorder the sanctuary. They applied for a faculty in the normal way, but also needed the permission of the Trust – a rather more onerous requirement, as the Trustees lay very great weight on the historic fabric, and considerably less on liturgical taste, and made it quite clear that the low wall at the top of the sanctuary steps must be unaltered, and the relationship of the altar and reredos left untouched, despite its practical difficulties. Nor would they allow the sanctuary to be carpeted. This reduced the options open to the parish. But they understood this would be the case when they signed up.

Should pastoral reorganisation ever lead to the parish being abolished as a separate entity, then the Trustees are bound to search for some other Christian group to use the building.

Key points

The parish pay for use of the church. The Trust has shouldered responsibility for this very important building, but in return it restricts the changes which are allowed – the Trust's interest lies in *preservation*, whilst allowing use.

The Trust will continue to have responsibility even if the church is closed, making this process relatively smooth.

3. St Margaret's, Upperplace – a closed church, used by the community

St Margaret's, Upperplace is a medieval building listed Grade II. It lies in Upperplace, a village of some 300 hundred inhabitants.

The church was closed in 2014. The redundancy was handled under the 2012 Measure, which allowed a Community Trust first refusal of the building at no cost, provided that Anglican worship was allowed to continue on a routine basis. As a result, there was no waiting period, and the use of the building for worship continued without a break, avoiding any sense of a purposeless building or the risk of the dispersal of the congregation. The congregation is no longer parochial, and has no separate legal personality, but its continued existence has moral support (though no financial support) from the diocese.

The church is now owned by the Upperplace Community Trust (whose probity is assured by the UK Churches Trust). Amongst the Trustees are ex officio members of the Parish Council and other local stakeholders. In practice a couple of members of the congregation are also Trustees, though on a personal, not an ex officio basis.

The Trust is developing the building for a range of community uses. Changes to the building are governed by secular planning law. When the building was acquired by the Trust, a long-term management plan was agreed with the Local Authority, which included a variety of improvements and alterations. The Trust has now fitted the building out with a kitchen and toilets. They have created a large open area with flexible screening, currently used by a commercial nursery school in the day, and as rehearsal area for the local drama group in the evenings. A smaller area is set aside as offices, with broadband, rentable by the day, and used as a study centre for students during the evening. There is a pervading smell of coffee in the building.

Under the terms of the Trust, the chancel is reserved for worship. The congregation pay a rent. They have no responsibility for the building. Like anyone else they can propose changes to the building which the Trust will consider on their merits. But they have no special rights in this respect.

Should the congregation ever decide to stop using the building, or no longer be able to afford the (very reasonable) rent, then the Trust would be free to make whatever use it chose of the chancel area (subject to planning consent).

Key points
The church is closed and there is no PCC. The building is used by a regular congregation, which pays rent. There was a smooth transition to ownership by the Trust, without a lengthy waiting period during which the congregation might disperse and the building deteriorate. Any legal complexities over the routine use for worship of a redundant parish church have been resolved.

4. St Bridget's, Deepcombe – a closed church, preserved by a Trust
St Bridget's, Deepcombe is a small church, next to a farmyard a mile from the nearest centre of population. The fabric is largely

medieval but of no particular interest. What is special is an unspoilt interior of the late seventeenth and early eighteenth century. The naïve box pews and two-decker pulpit, the simple chancel arrangements, and the hanging oil-lamps, create a very special atmosphere. But they make it impossible to use the building for anything other than church services.

The church was closed in 2014. It was instantaneously transferred (under the terms of the 2012 Measure) to the Deepcombe Church Preservation Trust. The Trust maintains the building, encouraging local interest and support, and actively using it as an educational and tourist resource. The objective of the Trustees is to preserve the building in its current state, whilst encouraging appropriate use.

Importantly, there is no restriction on Anglican services being held there. Thus the neighbouring church at Littlecombe holds a 'quiet service' here once a month during Spring and Summer, paying the Trust a reasonable hire charge. The church is also finding increased use as centre for meditation during diocesan retreats – again, rental is paid for this use. (There is an arrangement with the local pub, which provides food, toilets and a meeting room for the retreats.) In addition, the church is popular for weddings, and for harvest festivals and carol services.

Careful trawling through the marriage and baptismal registers has allowed a Friends group to be set up of those who had some previous connection with the church. This group organises a bi-annual picnic and thanksgiving service and special services for the renewal of vows.

All this formed part of the business plan which was formally reviewed as part of the closure process.

Key points

To preserve its historical integrity, the church is only used for religious purposes, and there is no attempt to widen its use. In some respects, this is not unlike the way in which the Churches Conservation Trust (CCT) recognises that some of its buildings can realistically only be used for limited purposes.

But the arrangement is different from that of the CCT in two important respects. First there are routine religious services, without restriction. Secondly the Trust is local and a condition of moving to Trust status was a viable business plan. This removes the problem of free-loading (local use of a building being funded nationally).

This piece originally formed the appendix to my personal submission in July 2005 to the Review of Clergy Terms of Service, which at that time was considering questions of ownership of Church of England property.

Heritage Lottery Fund Grants for Places of Worship: eligibility of churches looked after by charitable Trusts

THE GRANTS FOR PLACES OF WORSHIP programme is one of many Heritage Lottery Fund (HLF) grant schemes. A list of all the HLF grant programmes can be found on our website at www.hlf.org.uk/HowToApply/programmes. Clicking through to 'Grants for Places of Worship' will bring up details of that scheme.

The Grants for Places of Worship programme is for projects that involve urgent structural repairs to public listed places of worship. As part of a repair project we can also fund work to encourage greater community use and engagement. Places of worship can apply for a grant from £10,000 to £250,000.

The assessment process is competitive and we cannot fund all of the good-quality applications that are received.

Our *Application Guidance* explains that, under this programme, we fund projects that repair listed places of worship that are currently used for worship at least six times a year.

However it has been pointed out that our *Application Guidance* also says that certain types of project are 'unlikely to win support under this programme', and these include projects that involve work to 'faith buildings that are no longer used for regular worship'.

The Ecclesiological Society has therefore asked us to clarify whether this grants programme is open to listed churches and chapels owned or otherwise cared for by charitable Trusts (the subject of this special edition of *Ecclesiology Today*); and if so, whether applications from such Trusts are considered on an equal footing with places of worship owned by a faith group, or whether the fact of being cared for by a charitable Trust of itself places these applications at a disadvantage.

The HLF considers each charitable Trust caring for a listed place of worship on a case by case basis, as each Trust is different. Amongst other considerations, there must be six public services or more per year held in the building, and these services must be open to the general public, rather than restricted to particular guests as is often the case with weddings and baptisms. We are pleased to confirm that appropriate charitable Trusts are already and will continue to be eligible for this grants programme, being treated on the same footing as other valid applications. Any charitable Trust caring for a listed church or chapel is invited to contact us for an exploratory discussion about the grant scheme.

Heritage Lottery Fund, August 2014

The Listed Places of Worship Grant Scheme

Since last year (2013), the Listed Places of Worship Grant Scheme has been opened up to some Trusts. The third paragraph gives the details. We are grateful to the Department for Culture, Media and Sport (DCMS) for this explanatory note.

THE LISTED PLACES OF WORSHIP GRANT SCHEME is run by the Government and makes grants in respect of the VAT paid on most repairs, maintenance and alterations to listed places of worship.

A listed place of worship may apply for grants towards eligible costs where the building's sole or main purpose is as a place of public religious worship and the cost of repairs and alterations is the responsibility of a local congregation or recognised faith group. Another criteria of the scheme is that the place of worship must be open to the general public for at least six religious services a year, and that these services are publicised and not by invitation only.

Certain specified organisations which look after redundant places of worship are exempt from the requirement to hold six services. DCMS will consider new applications from other religious or charitable groups caring for redundant places of worship and not able to meet the requirement of six services a year. In order to be eligible for the scheme, groups must be able to demonstrate that their principal or primary purpose is to conserve, repair and maintain redundant listed places of worship which are not in private ownership. Applications should be made in the first instance to the Listed Places of Worship Grant Scheme and should include the registered charity number, where applicable, along with any other supporting evidence to show how the criteria are met.

Further details of works which are eligible can be found on the scheme's website at www.lpwscheme.org.uk. You can also speak to an adviser on the local rate helpline number 0845 0136601.

DCMS, June 2014

OBITUARY: The Revd Dr Michael Peel (1931–2014)

The Society's Council was saddened to learn of the death at the age of eighty-two on the 20 May of the Revd Dr Michael Peel, a member of the Society for many years, a former Chairman of the Society's Council and a Vice-President of the Society.

After National Service in the RAF, Michael read French and German at Bristol University – graduating in 1955, before training for the ministry at Wycliffe Hall, Oxford. He was ordained in 1959 and served his title at St Matthew's, Stretford in the Diocese of Manchester. He was priested in September, 1960. Between 1961 and 1962 he served a second curacy in the Parish of Chorlton-upon-Medlock in Manchester and as one of two Anglican chaplains attached to the University, where he met his wife Daloni. Whilst in Manchester Michael also studied for his BD, awarded in 1965.

Michael served as Vicar of Chirbury and Curate-in-Charge of Marton-in-Chirbury in the Diocese of Hereford between 1965 and 1968; as Rector of Iver Heath in the Diocese of Oxford between 1968 and 1987; as Vicar of Linslade in the Diocese of St Alban's between 1987 and 1995; and Warden of The College of St Barnabas – a community of forty retired Anglican priests – in Lingfield, Surrey, between 1995 and 2000.

In 2000, Michael and his wife, Daloni retired to Glemsford near Sudbury, Suffolk; moving in 2003 to Thurston, just outside Bury St Edmund's, where he maintained permission to officiate.

Whilst fulfilling the duties and demands of a parish priest, Michael completed research on the life and work of Antoine Francois Prévost d'Exiles – Abbé Prévost, on whom he had first worked at the University of Bordeaux in the 1950s, for which he was awarded a Master of Letters degree from Bristol University in 1973; and on the London Episcopate of Archbishop Archibald Tait for which he was awarded his doctorate by King's College, University of London in 1988.

Michael was first elected to the Society's Council in May, 1981, and served as its Chairman between 1985 and 1992.

Michael succeeded Terence Blood as Chairman, and with Stephen Humphrey as Honorary Secretary and other existing and new members of the Council, led the Society through a challenging period of change and growth whilst ensuring the effective continuity and development of the Society's programme of talks and visits and the publication of its regular *Newsletter* and occasional *Monographs* and *Papers*. Michael took a particular interest in the organisation of the Society's Annual Service in various City and other churches, at which past members of the Society were commemorated, and initiated a series of convivial dinners for members of the Council and other members of the Society following meetings and visits. On his retirement, Michael and his wife were presented with Life Membership of the Society in recognition and appreciation of his significant contribution to the Society and Daloni's support for Michael in his role as Chairman.

Michael will be remembered with gratitude as a valued colleague on the Society's Council, for his friendship, for his effective leadership of the Society in the late 1980s and early 1990s, and for his continuing support for the Council and the Society over subsequent years. A priest of sound faith and considerable energy and integrity reflecting his firmly held values and principles, Michael delighted and flourished in his role as a parish priest. In a different age, Michael's service and ministry would have been more generously recognised by the Church.

Paul Velluet, Chairman of the Council, 1992–1999

Book reviews

Kirk Ambrose, *The Marvellous and the Monstrous in the Sculpture of Twelfth-Century Europe*. Boydell Press, 2013, 187 pp., 40 b&w pls, £50.00 hdbk, ISBN 978 1 84383 831 9

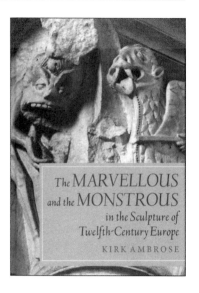

This is a short book which boldly deals with a big, diverse and elusive topic. Kirk Ambrose's subject is the plethora of monsters, defined as 'imaginary creatures,' which inhabit the surfaces of twelfth-century sculpture. Rather than dismiss them as simply representative of 'negative agendas', or as decorative space-fillers in an age when most surviving art demonstrates a *horror vacui*, he seeks to explore the possibilities of casting such creatures in a more positive light, harnessing the rich resources of modern critical and psycho-analytical theory to assist him in his task. Although the title refers to Europe, the book mostly uses French examples to examine the subject. Four chapters take as case studies the south tympanum from St Paul de Varax not far from the Lyonnais in Eastern France, a nave capital from the Cluniac abbey of Mozac in Auvergne, a capital from Moutiers- St- Jean now in the Fogg Museum at Harvard University, and a capital in the nave at Vézelay. A final chapter deals with a tympanum from the church of Rio Mau in Portugal dated to around the turn of the twelfth/thirteenth centuries. The approach is based on a close examination of these objects but little is said to justify the choice of examples except that each depicts a monster or monsters. It is remarkable that, given the wide choice of monstrous imagery available in Romanesque sculpture, Ambrose includes an example which is no longer in its original position so denying himself the possibility to discuss its location and context which presumably would give tighter parameters to the interpretational quest. Overall however such considerations are not given precedence in the argument, nor is there much comparison of the case studies with other Romanesque examples to give an indication whether the discussion is based on exceptional or typical features.

The book is a bibliographic treasure trove, especially of recent secondary literature, and Ambrose fully and generously acknowledges and builds on the contributions of many contemporary scholars, though the repeated reference to authors in the main text can be distracting and often obscures the thrust of his often complex lines of thought. Lack of clarity is exacerbated by a tendency to over-problematize issues, and through adopting a rich array of critical terms instead of a simpler and equally adequate vocabulary which would make the book more accessible to a wider audience. Interesting digressions are not always linked to the main theme. There are some fascinating passages, for instance about monastic views of figurative sculpture and the role of physical sight in the quest for spiritual insight, but it is hard to see how this specifically relates to depictions of the monstrous. It is a pity that the accompanying visual material is so small in scale and the quality of many of the pictures unworthy of the visually detailed points attached to them. It is impossible to see the nude figure in the Vézelay tympanum, Samson in the St Martin capital or the scaled belly on the Moutiers-St-Jean lion which is key to the argument.

This is a book which invites the reader to think ever more imaginatively about the process of looking at imagery, applying a number of theoretical approaches along the way which will stimulate further reflection for viewers of Romanesque art. Ambrose acknowledges that there are no definitive interpretations but nevertheless makes various journeys of enquiry within the text. If this reviewer was disappointed with the presentation of the book and the style of writing, there is no doubt that such intellectual journeys are worthwhile and valuable in broadening our thinking and understanding of our visual heritage.

Catherine Oakes, Kellogg College, University of Oxford

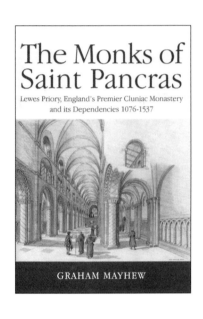

Graham Mayhew, *The Monks of Saint Pancras: Lewes Priory, England's Premier Cluniac Monastery and its Dependants 1076–1537*. Lewes History Press, 2014, 484 pp., many col. pls, 30 maps and plans, £45.00 hdbk, ISBN 978 0 99269 840 9

By January 1538, a month before he received the formal grant of the dissolved monastery of Lewes, Thomas Cromwell had employed Italian engineers to begin the demolition of the priory buildings. Just over three centuries later the Lewes to Brighton railway was planned to run across the south range, destroying anything that might remain of the chapter house and the east end of the Great Church. It must have seemed that the fortunes of the senior Cluniac monastery in England, and the second principal daughter house of Cluny, whose prior stood fourth in precedence within the Cluniac congregation, could not sink any lower. But there was a bright side to the onwards march of the railways. The preparation of the line revealed lead cists identified as those of Lewes's founders, William and Gundrada de Warenne (her tomb slab also survives). These discoveries stimulated excavation at the site, which has continued at various periods ever since, and led to a renewed interest in the history of the priory. In this book Graham Mayhew has produced a rich and detailed history not only of Lewes but of its dependencies, seven in England and two in Normandy, in the wider context of the congregation of Cluny. The author is realistic about the scant physical remains of Lewes, but is able to amass what may be to some a surprising amount of documentary evidence on which to base his account, including an incomplete cartulary of 1444, a thirteenth-century breviary/missal, and a number of account rolls. Mayhew begins with the foundation, growth, and consolidation of Lewes Priory, picking his way carefully through difficult sources such as the forged (or embellished) charters to demonstrate that the venture that brought monks from the heart of Cluniac monasticism to England was far from secure or destined to succeed. But succeed it did, through the patronage of its founders and their son, William II de Warenne, whose generosity earned him the title of second founder, and by 1135 Lewes had expanded to 200 monks housed in ten monasteries. The papal taxation of 1291 saw Lewes valued at £1014, which placed it eighth in the ranking of English monasteries. Mayhew never loses sight of the fact that Lewes was a place of prayer as well as a business corporation, and his second chapter puts the liturgy at the heart of the discussion, using the Lewes breviary/missal to discuss how a local monastery could adapt the Cluniac liturgy while at the same time retaining its identity within the congregation. One might think that the phrase 'the beauty of holiness' so often associated with Cluniac monasticism would be impossible to demonstrate at Lewes, given the poor survival of the physical setting in which worship took place. But Mayhew tackles the question – and very successfully too – by looking at the evidence from those parish churches of which Lewes was itself patron, the wall paintings, sculpture and stained glass, and placing it in the wider context of Cluniac art and architecture from France. If the twelfth and thirteenth centuries were a time of growth and success for Lewes, the period that followed was one of challenges and decline, and the contrast is well brought out in the discussion of Lewes's position as an alien priory (it received denizen status in 1351). Although not as rich in surviving archival sources as some English monasteries, enough survives from Lewes to throw light on its economic activities, and nine account rolls from between 1334 and 1399 from the reeve of West Walton illuminates this level of estate micromanagement, and towards the end of the life of the priory the larderer's accounts (from the 1530s) allow Mayhew to compare monastic consumption at Lewes with Westminster Abbey and the cathedral priory of Durham.

This is a rich and detailed monograph, based on original research, which illuminates the history of this important monastery. It is produced to a high standard, and enriched with colour photographs of manuscripts, stained glass sculpture, wall paintings, and reconstructions. My only quibble is that readers would be helped by a list of plates in the introductory matter, to accompany the list of maps and plans.

Janet Burton, University of Wales: Trinity St David

Toby Huitson, *Stairway to Heaven: The Functions of Medieval Upper Spaces*. Oxbow Books, 2014, xv + 264 pp., 130 ills, £35 pbk, ISBN 978 1 84217 861 4

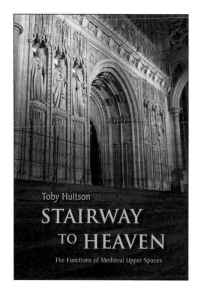

This book explores the significance and functions of 'upper spaces' in medieval ecclesiastical buildings and complexes of all kinds, focussed on England, but drawing in evidence from elsewhere in Europe. The idea behind the work is admirable: churches, particularly cathedrals and monasteries, have a large number of stairways, passages, tower rooms, rooms over porches, and spaces above the vaults, which are under-studied and unappreciated by visitors. Further, as the author points out, there is a good deal of mythology surrounding the purposes of some such spaces (such as the idea that towers were commonly for defence), and a good deal more which is debated (such as the purpose of triforium galleries or the use of upper rooms for anchorites). The topic is ripe for investigation.

The study draws on architectural evidence, which is critiqued at the start, and on a wealth of documentary and textual sources. The body of the work is divided into broad thematic chapters concerning devotional spaces (such as chapels), spaces used for enhancement of the liturgy in the body of the church (e.g., for choirs, lights, hangings), dramatic presentations, schooling and other educational activities, sleeping accommodation, maintenance, watching, and various kinds of storage including sacristies, treasuries and muniment rooms – the list of documented functions is enormous, and it is useful to have the evidence drawn together.

Understanding 'upper spaces' is not easy. Many uses did not require structural fixtures which might have survived, and uses could change without leaving any trace: even where written evidence exists for the use of a particular space in a particular way at a particular time it is relatively seldom possible to be certain that the documented function was the original or only one. This is fully acknowledged at several points in the text, and it is to the author's credit that he does not disguise the difficulties or attempt greater certainty than the evidence will allow – this is an admirably cautious book. The exploration proceeds from a presentation of evidence for a large number of uses of the kinds of space discussed, to a short discussion of how to assess the likelihood of various possibilities in particular buildings (paying attention to date, type of building (cathedral, parish church, etc.), location within the building, how widespread the functions were), and the application of the results to a small number of specific examples.

This is all eminently sensible; but there are problems with the execution. Part of the difficulty is the sheer diversity of spaces discussed. The book would have achieved greater focus had it concentrated only on spaces in church buildings, rather than including the upper floors of claustral ranges and even some agricultural buildings. The discussion of cloister and precinct buildings needs to be much more firmly set in the context of high-status secular accommodation than is either attempted or possible here; as it stands it is too short to say anything new, and the spaces concerned are mostly so different from those in the churches themselves it is a distraction. In addition, the six short case studies presented in chapter 7, while representing a good range of building contexts, are both too few in number and too short to carry the weight this part of the overall analysis should bear. One possibly promising line of enquiry is analysis of all the upper spaces – passages, chambers, roof walks – and of entry points to them in a number buildings, as this could provide some evidence for how accessible spaces were and who had access to them: the way is shown by three case studies in chapter 6, but they stand alone, apart from the text, as separate boxed features, and no attempt is made to analyse the implications of the data presented. Caution is expressed concerning how far inferences can be drawn from architectural analysis, but without a stronger admixture of it the functions envisaged by the builders risks not only being lost, but obscured by an often much later documentary record which may, as is acknowledged, reflect uses to which spaces have been put – the exploitation of accidentally created possibilities – rather than the original intent. As it stands, the overall conclusion, that the main functions in greater churches were related to music and liturgical drama, is not sufficiently strongly supported.

There are some infelicities in points of detail and in presentation. For example, chapter 7 contains a brief case study of the added chamber over the east end of Tynemouth Priory, but does not refer to

Richard Fawcett's discussion of it in *British Archaeological Association Conference Transactions*, 26 (2013), even though there is reference to that volume elsewhere in the text. The treadwheel (not, given the definition in chapter 7 n. 80, a windlass) and lifting boss in the crossing tower at Beverley Minster are treated as medieval, but the tower, wheel, vault and oculus are all early eighteenth-century; and three of the references to Beverley in the text (pp. 141, 145, 194) are missing from the index. There are several similarly minor slips in the referencing—e.g., different ways of citing Tolhurst's edition of *The Customary of Norwich* in chapter 3 nn. 1 and 30.

Overall, this is a book which addresses a significant and neglected topic. It is the result of considerable labour, and contains a useful compendium particularly of written evidence. That said, its method and presentation mean there is still much to be done in relation to the intended purposes of upper spaces in medieval churches.

P. S. Barnwell, Kellogg College, University of Oxford

Wim Vroom, *Financing Cathedral Building in the Middle Ages: The Generosity of the Faithful*. Amsterdam University Press, 2010, 734 pp., 93 col. ills, 14 graphs, 3 tables, £79.50 soft back, ISBN 978 90 8964 035 2

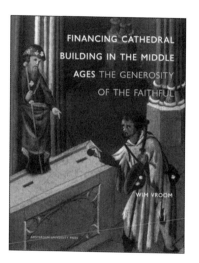

Financing Cathedral Building is the culmination of a lifetime's work and represents an expanded and revised English translation of a doctoral thesis first published in Dutch in 1981, and is based on detailed research in published and archival sources from across Europe. To describe it thus risks creating an impression of a dry, perhaps 'worthy', read, particularly as its subject is a branch of economic history, but while it is both heavy and heavy-weight, it is well-translated, a pleasure to read and beautifully crafted: a soft plasticised back makes it easy to handle, the voluminous notes are printed together at the end on slightly tinted paper for ease of reference, and two bookmarks facilitate reference between text and notes. The only quibbles with the presentation are that there are few direct references in the text to the illustrations, and that, while Latin primary sources are translated as well as given in the original, quotations from works in modern languages are not translated (except, oddly and sporadically for translations from Dutch), nor are medieval versions of the languages modernised: this editorial quirk should not, however, impede understanding by monoglot English-speakers.

The book is arranged in four large chapters. The first concerns the evolving institutional background of the administration of cathedral fabrics across Europe, focussing especially on the major and universal roles of the bishop and chapter, but also exploring the lesser and more variable responsibilities of local secular authorities and communities (particularly in Italy), and documents the widespread rise in the importance of the chapter at the expense of the bishop from the eleventh to the thirteenth century.

The remainder of the book concentrates on the thirteenth century onwards, the period from which the vast majority of documentation survives. The second, and largest, section analyses the sources of finance, drawing on a wide array of primary evidence. A great range of sources of income and fund-raising activity is outlined, from rents of land to various forms of gift, the sale of indulgences, and the borrowing and lending of money by means of annuities (which avoided the dangers of usury). The treatment is thematic, each potential kind of income treated in turn, though illustrated by reference to specific examples; some of the financial instruments and their management are complicated, but they are lucidly explained. The realities of fund-raising in relation to a specific cathedral are traced in the third chapter which takes as a detailed case-study Utrecht, for which exceptional documentation exists from the end of the fourteenth century until the later sixteenth. The balance of funding mechanisms used by each cathedral chapter varied with place, time and political circumstance, a fact which the shorter final chapter illustrates by giving summaries, necessarily somewhat impressionistic, of the mechanisms used by eight cathedrals spread across Europe, and St Peter's, Rome, in the sixteenth century.

Although the book contains its fair share of figures and quantitative analysis, including a useful appendix on the different currencies encountered, its main subject is not statistics. Rather, it is a history of fund-raising. As today, fund-raisers had to adapt their techniques to the circumstances in which they ran their campaigns, and the book is as much about *mentalités*, the financial culture of the middle ages in a religious context, as it is about economics. It is therefore very much about people, revealing the ingenuity of churchmen in finding ways of raising and managing money for what was accepted as a good cause, and the considerable lengths to which they went to work both with – and at times against – concurrent fund-raising campaigns for other religious institutions. Discussion of institutional history and administrative systems is illustrated throughout by carefully chosen examples involving actual cathedrals and their personnel, laying bare the whole range of human behaviour when dealing with money, from those who did their honest best to sharp-practice aimed at maximising donations or outwitting the opposition, and from generosity to miserliness.

The book is not, and does not claim to be, a history of the financing of any individual cathedral or building campaign, though it comes near to providing one in the case of Utrecht. Rather, it provides a clear and comprehensive guide to the resources available to fund-raisers and to the instruments and administrative systems evolved to support them. It is likely to become the standard point of reference for anyone interested in its subject. But it is much more than that, as it gives invaluable insights into the financial realities of some of Europe's major religious institutions, and opens a window on important aspects of medieval culture.

P. S. Barnwell, Kellogg College, University of Oxford

Ian Hinton, *The Alignment and Location of Medieval Rural Churches*. British Archaeological Reports, British Series, 560. Archaeopress, 2012, 168 pp., many figs and tables, £31 pbk, ISBN 978 1 4073 0973 6

A great deal has been written about the alignment of medieval churches, and many theories, practical and symbolic, plausible and fanciful, have been advanced concerning why the buildings were aligned precisely as they are. Now, for the first time, a large number of churches – some 2100 concentrated in sixteen English counties – has been analysed using rigorous statistical methods, enabling more robust conclusions to be drawn than has so far been possible. The science behind orientation is carefully explained, taking account of factors such as variations through time in the earth's magnetic field, and the effects of longitude, latitude, the height of the horizon and sloping sites. The methodology of the systematic survey of sites is described, and the results of the survey are presented. Comparison of the data with existing theories concerning the methods and seasons at which churches were set shows all the latter (including orientation at sunrise on Easter Day or the feast of the patronal saint) to be untenable. Patterns are sought in the survey data, and it is deduced that medieval churches were probably set out at sunrise on a day at the end of harvest – the season when agrarian communities might have time and energy to engage in building projects. The analysis is careful throughout; it is based on scientific and statistical principles and illustrated by numerous tables and graphs, but the text remains readable largely because much of the heavy-weight statistical presentation is placed a series of appendices. A further appendix contains discussion of the general lack of interest in orientation on the part of the early ecclesiologists and others in the nineteenth-century, and suggests, on the basis of examination of 400 churches, that church buildings were probably increasingly set out using a compass.

In a second, shorter, part of the book, the data gathered to understand the effects of topography on church alignment is also used to analyse the siting of churches in relation to other elements of the religious landscape and of settlements, with particular reference to Norfolk. The result is a questioning of the widely held view that manor houses and villages were built on new sites, and that churches and churchyards were either founded at the same time or later. Instead, it is proposed that the process may often have been the other way round: the burial-ground came first, and had a church inserted into it and the manor and settlement were built around it. This provocative idea needs testing elsewhere in the country: if the method and conclusions stand up to such scrutiny, the tentatively drawn conclusion presented here has the potential radically to alter our understanding of the process of local church foundation in the mid and late Anglo-Saxon period.

P. S. Barnwell, Kellogg College, University of Oxford

David Dymond and Clive Paine, *Five Centuries of an English Parish Church, 'The State of Melford Church', Suffolk*. EAH Press, Cambridge, 2012, 205 pp., 90 mainly col. pls, £15.00 plus £4.00 p&p, pbk, ISBN 978 0 9560384 6 3. (Copies from Clive Paine 01284 753411.)

This expanded version of a book first published in 1989 and again in a second edition of 1992 is a brightly written and multi textured history of one of England's most famous parish churches. As Diarmaid MacCulloch says in his foreword, the records of Long Melford are largely the product of the labours of four famous men of the parish – John Clopton, Roger Martin, Nathaniel Bisbie and William Parker – but their inspiration and the *raison d'être* of their work is their love of the building itself. As with the original, so this edition is essentially a collection of the

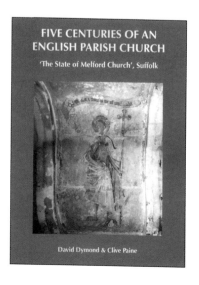

FIVE CENTURIES OF AN
ENGLISH PARISH CHURCH

'The State of Melford Church', Suffolk

David Dymond & Clive Paine

documents associated with them which are supplemented by church wardens' accounts, wills (the will of John Clopton is a church record in itself) and inventories of church goods. Many of these coalesce around the Reformation period and stand as telling witnesses to those turbulent times when goods were dispersed, sold, hidden away, restored and re-dispersed through the troubled decades of the mid sixteenth century; items exhaustively listed in the 1529 inventory, described as 'ould trashe' and destined for 'fyer wode' in the 1560s.

If the Reformation accounts have been well trawled by historians, the later history of the church, told here through equally valuable primary sources, is less well known. We are given the story of the re-fitting of the Lady Chapel as a school in the seventeenth century, the collapse and re-building of the tower in the eighteenth century and William Parker's notes on the nineteenth-century restoration; the latter largely explain the appearance of the church today. The Victorian sources in particular reveal the casualties of decision making, as one part of the history of the fabric is sacrificed to reveal another, or to give way to a reconstructed version of the medieval past. Through it all the voices of church wardens and local patrons can be heard as they devote themselves to preserving the building and its legacy for future generations. As Richard Almack, churchwarden in the 1830s, says in a passage describing the work he had done on the building: 'No person can conceive the work of labour I thus imposed upon myself'.

It is a multi-textured book not only because it combines scholarly commentary with primary source material, but because the text is accompanied by numerous plans and photographs, both old and contemporary, which are so helpful to the reader in explaining the complex history which is being told. There are reproductions too of some of the original documents and of the signatures of their authors. The introductory chapters reflect on the fabric and its medieval furnishings, notably the inscriptions in the masonry and the figured medieval glass, which supplement the documentary sources and further enhance our understanding of the mindset of the original patrons. Whilst the book is an indispensable resource for the professional historian, it is also perfectly accessible to the less informed reader with Latin texts translated into English, a glossary of specialist terms and short biographical notes on all the main protagonists involved in the church's history. No one can fail to be fascinated by Martin's account of the boy dressed up as a prophet charged with singing an antiphon from the top of a church turret on Palm Sunday or to wonder at the 2s 4d 'paid to Fyrmin the glasier for mending the windows that were broke at the scoole master's playe' in 1580.

This book is essentially a critical edition of the key documentary sources which record the history of the church. Those who are seeking an in depth examination of the architecture, the medieval glass or other fittings will need to look elsewhere. A careful reading of the documents themselves however, aided by the scholarly commentary provided, give the reader above all a story about a church community over five hundred years and about how its hopes and fears, worldly and spiritual, have shaped the building which visually expresses them.

Catherine Oakes, Kellogg College, University of Oxford

Natalie Mears and Alec Ryrie (eds), *Worship and the Parish Church in Early Modern Britain*. Ashgate, 2013, 250 pp., 4 b&w pls, £65.00 hdbk, ISBN 978 1 4094 2604 2

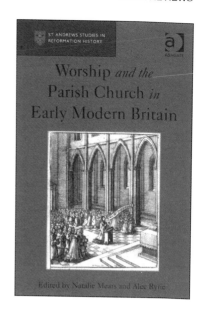

This is a lively collection of essays by ten experts in this field who push the boundaries of our understanding of what parish worship meant to congregations in early modern Britain. Rather than concentrating on the clergy, the godly or the practicalities of running a parish, these writers seek to inform us about many aspects of worship from prayer, preaching, appropriate body language in church, to music and ceremonial. It is a comment on how much work is being done in this enterprising interdisciplinary fashion, that fully to appreciate what is being offered, this volume should really be read alongside a companion volume on *Private and Domestic Devotion in Early Modern Britain*, edited by Jessica Martin and Alec Ryrie. There is quite a lot to take on board when the two books are read in tandem. This cultural history approach offers a rich vein that is well exploited by all the contributors to this collection. It eschews old top-down, institutional approaches and all the contributors are strong on probing and revealing tensions and complexities within their chosen stories. Hence, exposing differences between theory and practice is a theme that comes up in many of the articles. Hannah Cleugh and Natalie Mears, for example, illustrate how the Book of Common Prayer allowed greater latitude than many might have thought regarding services for burial and baptism, and supplementing gaps by provisions for state prayers. While at the close of the volume, Judith Maltby highlights that the Directory of Public Worship, that technically replaced the Prayer Book after 1645, was more a set of guidelines for clergy than a fully worked out liturgy. Problems of the nature of public prayer and the participation of the congregation are also well exposed throughout, most notably when John Craig probes exactly how people might have prayed, in what posture, with what gestures, and indeed, with what sounds. It is important to see these issues in full context, and Bryan Spinks draws links with earlier primers for devotion and discusses symptoms of an ambiguous settlement and elements of devotional weaning. Several articles provide excellent material on church music: Peter McCullough explores the musicality of the sermons of Lancelot Andrewes, highlighting the importance of the reign of James I in maintaining musical traditions in churches. Jonathan Willis has written at length about the survival of church music post Reformation, and in this volume he discusses the various discourses surrounding this subject and the role of music to edify, heal and elevate the spirit. Another great expert on church music, Christopher Marsh, then illustrates how bell ringing developed as a secular leisure activity, largely for young men, and yet still harked back to some elements of devotional usage. In contrast to the broader sweeps, Trevor Cooper provides an holistic study of worship at Little Gidding in the 1630s, paying particular attention to the architecture of worship, the altar, the pulpit, and the lectern, as well as the organ. One of the editors, Alec Ryrie discusses the fall and rise of fasting in the British Reformations, charting how this became secularised, privatised and occasionally public.

This is a wonderful collection of articles that all fulfil the task of exposing complexities, continuities, paradoxes, and tease out new ideas on what might seem at first sight a rather eclectic array of starting points. And there is the added benefit of a table of nationwide prayers from 1534–1641, provided by Natalie Mears, and a foretaste of more to come from a much larger project. Congratulations are due to the editors and their contributors on pulling this fascinating collection together   so well.

Andrew Foster, University of Kent

Richard Wheeler, *Oxfordshire's Best Churches*. Fircone Books, 2013, 270 pp., many col. pls, £25.00 hdbk, ISBN 978 1 907700 00 2

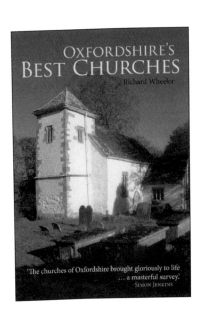

Oxfordshire, with the addition of the northern part of Berkshire in 1974, has over 500 churches of different denominations, the great majority being of medieval origin. From these Richard Wheeler has selected 116. The choice is admirable; it is hard to think of more than a handful whose claims might compete with any of those included. All are parish churches except for the private chantry chapel at Rycote and the Roman Catholic church of St Aloysius in Oxford. They range from large town churches, through the diversity of those in the villages which make up the greatest number in the county, to humble buildings isolated in fields or tucked behind farm buildings. While the selection is spread as evenly as possible across the county, it is striking that there are particularly numerous clusters in the ironstone country round Banbury, along the Windrush valley close to the limestone Taynton quarries, and again beneath the chalk scarp of the Berkshire Downs.

Following a substantial introduction which outlines the development of ecclesiastical architecture and fittings in the Oxfordshire context, the bulk of the book is devoted to extensive descriptions of fifty-one churches. These include not only the well-known stars like Iffley, Burford, Adderbury, Dorchester and St Mary's, Oxford, but also a number such as North Stoke and Somerton, Easington and Buckland which may be less familiar to many. Each church is placed in its setting and the exterior described, showing the development of the building, with the aid of ground plans for large or complex churches. Then follows a survey of the interior from west to east concentrating on the principal features and finishing with a summary of other points of interest. The accounts are clear and authoritative while at the same time delightfully vivid, individual and filled with infectious enthusiasm. Wheeler is professionally involved with historic buildings and is skilled at drawing attention to easily overlooked detail, whether it be the subtleties of the hood-moulds in the chancel at Langford or the songbirds round the headband of Elizabeth Wilcote's effigy at North Leigh. There is a generous helping of Wheeler's own excellent photographs. Each church has a full-page plate and a number of small marginal pictures. These are well integrated with the text and the only regret is the inevitable loss of detail in the occasional larger subject such as John Piper's Nativity window at Iffley.

A supplementary gazetteer contains a further sixty-five churches which are summarised briefly with an indication of the setting and of what is particularly notable in them. These are illustrated with a few full-page plates.

This is an attractively produced celebration of the pleasures available in a single county, designed to be used on site. Those who know these churches well will relish the stimulus of a fresh point of view and all will find Wheeler a perceptive and lively companion.

John Sims

Peter Stanford, *How to Read a Graveyard*. Bloomsbury Books, 2013, 263 pp., 31 b&w pls, £16.99 hdbk, ISBN 978 1 4411 7977 7

This highly selective journey through graveyard history in Western Europe is a short text, with much to commend it. For many it will be an easy and informative narrative. More specifically anyone who has sampled graveyard 'tourism', whether for architecture, landscape design, celebrity voyeurism or simple meditation reasons will certainly find something of interest.

Stanford enjoys his subject and communicates well. Sadly he is let down by poorly produced photographs and the lack of biographical references. As a counterbalance he concludes with an A–Z Chapter, helping us to view graveyards with some random, yet helpful, author's afterthoughts. As he makes no claim to be, in any way, comprehensive we are left to find value in his broad historical canvas and an all pervading panache.

If we want to know how previous generations faced up to death this is an excellent introductory guide. From Roman catacombs to Eco burials this is what Stanford calls 'journeys in the company of the dead'. The author clearly enjoys Italy's wealth of history and is pleased that poets of Byron's eminence provide valuable markers in his chronicle of burial habits. Throughout the text we are encouraged to find information and solace from monuments and settings often overlooked and, occasionally, misunderstood.

In addition some fascinating glimpses of selected city case studies in London, Liverpool and Edinburgh sit well alongside the rural idyllic settings in Norfolk, Buckinghamshire and Flanders. Ultimately the book is, perhaps, best viewed as a primer to a spectrum of more in-depth studies. Here I have in mind works such as that produced by Alan Butler in 2011: *How to Read Pre-Historic Monuments,* published by Watkins. Such reading should certainly conclude with David Meara and Lida Cardozo Kindersley's *Remembered Lives: Personal Memorials in Churches* (Cambridge University Press). Here we have a wonderful set of reminders on how a wider appreciation of the topic under discussion can be imaginatively and sensitively handled.

John Taylor, Higher Education International

Lawrence and Marjorie Lyle, *Canterbury and the Gothic Revival*. The History Press, 2013, 128 pp., 14 col. pls, 51 b&w pls, £14.95 pbk, ISBN 978 0 7524 6294 3

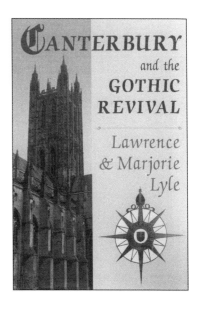

To say that this book ranges beyond its precise title would be a gross understatement. In 120 pages the authors consider the whole architectural history of Canterbury Cathedral, the history of the Church of England both in periods of 'gothic revival' and otherwise, the spread of Anglicanism to the colonies through missionary work, the various revolutions in Britain and Europe in the eighteenth and nineteenth centuries, the picturesque movement, the philosophy of Pugin, Willis' historical researches, the paintings of Thomas Sidney Cooper, and much else. Coverage is necessarily sketchy at times.

The central chapter, 'The Recovery of St Augustine's Abbey', describes A. J. Beresford Hope's purchase of the largely derelict abbey site with no particular purpose in mind, and the influences that led to the decision to set up a college for the training of missionaries, to use the St Augustine's site, and to commission the young Butterfield as architect. The result was the outstanding success with which readers of *Ecclesiology Today* are familiar, and which must have had a positive effect on Butterfield's career, although it may be doubted whether the building of All Saints', Margaret Street and the work of Sir G. G. Scott can properly be described as 'The Consequences of St Augustine's College'. The links described between Canterbury and Gothic Revival churches overseas are, if anything, even more tenuous.

The Lyles are enthusiasts for Canterbury and its cathedral, and write of it in a knowledgeable, engaging personal way ('when we visited Batalha we felt ourselves in the nave of Canterbury'). Outside the city their touch is less sure: Bishop Medley changes his see in the course of a day, and the Palace of Westminster changes its orientation; when they write 'first' they often mean first *in Canterbury*.

There are opportunities missed. I should have liked to know more about George Austin, the clerk of the works apparently responsible for the accurate Gothic in the rebuilding of the Cathedral's north-west tower, begun at the early date of 1832, and the romantic vision of the archbishop's throne. (Austin's *Builder* obituary – readily accessible at www.andrewclarkson.ca/6_ga.html – throws doubts on the Lyles' bland comments about Butterfield's pulpit in the Cathedral.) And I should have preferred to see photographs of Gothic Revival buildings in Canterbury, particularly the less accessible, rather than even beautiful ones of Strawberry Hill or All Saints' Margaret Street or thumbnail portraits of seventeenth-century divines. Willis' work on the Cathedral is identified as seminal but never properly explored. Nevertheless, there is valuable material here, particularly about St Augustine's College, and if the notion of the Gothic Revival spreading to the world from there is largely a fantasy, the book is certainly quite a good read.

Mark Ockelton

G.A. Bremner, *Imperial Gothic: Religious Architecture and High Anglican Culture in the British Empire c.1840–1870.* Yale University Press, 2013, 484 pp., 80 col. pls, 285 b&w pls, £50.00 hdbk, ISBN 978 0 300 18703 8

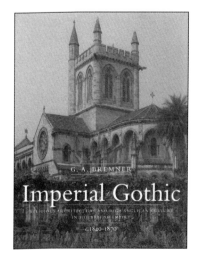

The Oxford Movement began to work its transformation of religious life in England at a time when English colonial settlement was increasing at an unprecedented rate. The colonies were beginning to look like an empire, and the empire required a Christian ministry. The men who spread out across the world in the 1830s and 1840s to represent the Church of England had been educated at Oxford and Cambridge, and most of them were animated by Tractarian principles. Since they represented the established Church, there was an understandable tendency among them to erect substantial temples of worship that would testify to the confidence and correctness of the new Anglicanism. The zealous spirit of the 1840s readily produced funds for colonial church-building, and the ecclesiological societies of Cambridge and Oxford were willing to provide plans and advice. Alex Bremner's remarkable book, so broad in scope, so amply documented, allows us to understand and admire the architectural consequences of the Tractarian Movement from Newfoundland to New Zealand, from Australia to Zanzibar.

At the centre of the imperial mission were the cathedrals. Church leaders and politicians came to realise that the Anglican role in newly-colonised lands needed to be more prominent than that of the Nonconformist churches, which had hitherto taken the lead by providing services for settlers and carrying out missionary work among the natives. The merits of episcopal rule had to be made evident. Settlers needed to be reminded that the Church of England was the established Church, so its buildings needed an air of authority and a style that would evoke memories of traditional England. Cathedrals helped to consolidate the identity of new towns, and integrate them into the system of colonial government. The Colonial Bishoprics' Fund, established in 1841 (and strongly supported by Gladstone), encouraged the growth of episcopal governance throughout the empire, and underwrote building costs. Colonial bishops often had forceful personalities and an ability to get things done fast, for the energy and commitment that drove them to take up appointments overseas caused them to be active directors of Church affairs once they had arrived.

The heroes of church-building in this grand survey include George Selwyn, first bishop of New Zealand, who had a strong sense of recapitulating history. Initially he was willing to operate out of a tent or tabernacle, like Moses in the wilderness, but he soon felt an analogy with St Augustine in Saxon Kent, a Christian among pagans, and approved the building of primitive wood or stone churches; then he advanced to small solid churches in the Norman style, defensive and durable. Eventually he moved confidently into Gothic, certain that the Church of England would prevail. In contrast, the energetic John Medley, bishop of Fredricton, New Brunswick, laid the foundation stone of his new cathedral within three months of arriving in his diocese in 1845. Amongst architects, Edmund Blacket, who had been a founding member of the Camden Society and who arrived in New South Wales in 1842, stands out for his many churches evocative of Old England.

Given the pervasive influence of the Cambridge Camden Society and its journal *The Ecclesiologist*, it is not surprising that Gothic – and 'Middle-Pointed' Gothic above all – was the preferred style for colonial cathedrals. Leading English architects offered their services, often gratis. G. G. Scott drew up plans for St John's Newfoundland in 1846, and for Christchurch New Zealand in 1862; Butterfield provided plans for Melbourne, Adelaide and Fredricton, Burges attended to Brisbane, and designed his masterpiece, St Fin Barre's cathedral at Cork, in England's closest colony. R. C. Carpenter was responsible for Colombo cathedral in Ceylon.

The great variations of climate across the empire gave rise to many modifications of Gothic as architects responded to the challenge of extreme conditions. There was Hyperborean Gothic adapted to the long freezing winters of Canada, and Tropical Gothic for India, the Far East and the West Indies. There were experiments with 'Speluncar' or cave-like designs that had massively thick walls for insulation, thought to be effective against extreme cold or extreme heat, and deeply recessed windows. In India, where some superb churches were built, usually by local architects, side aisles were sometimes altered into open verandahs for ventilation – and with the added advantage of allowing Indians to observe Christian services from a distance: a possible prelude to conversion.

Bremner's focus is on 'High Anglican culture' across the British Empire in mid-Victorian times because this culture illustrates the global outreach of the Oxford Movement and makes clear the ways in which it fortified the structures of governance in the colonies. His book impresses this reader for more reasons than a short review can accommodate. We are made aware of the challenges the different colonies posed to the Anglican ministry, we learn about the network of family connections among the leading colonial clergy, their background at Oxford or Cambridge, and their links to architectural advisors in England. There were many arguments over the style and materials appropriate to colonial churches, much discussion about the historical situation of the English Church in new lands, with backward glances to the spread of Christianity under the Roman Empire. This is a large and complex book, but it is clearly written, very well illustrated and vastly rewarding, for Alex Bremner proves to be an omniscient guide to an unfamiliar subject.

Graham Parry, University of York

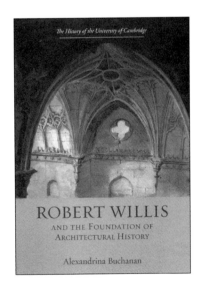

Alexandrina Buchanan, *Robert Willis and the Foundation of Architectural History*. Boydell Press, 2013, 452 pp., 82 b&w pls, £60.00 hdbk, ISBN 978 1 84383 800 5

This is an impressive work of scholarship about one of the superstars of the nineteenth-century architectural firmament who, while not as high-profile as Pugin, Ruskin or Scott, was held in huge regard in his day and by subsequent architectural historians. Willis's vast archive in Cambridge University Library was used by Pevsner when preparing the Slade Lectures of 1968-9 that reappeared in his splendid *Some Architectural Writers of the Nineteenth Century* (1972). He remarked: 'I cannot pretend to have read every page. There are thousands of them, and a student in search of a thesis would find them rewarding.' Alexandrina Buchanan took up the challenge, gaining her PhD on Willis in 1995, which forms the genesis of the present book. However, this is not, and cannot be a biography in the full sense as many details about Willis's life are unavailable and he was a person who, Buchanan points out, 'formed few intimate relationships': he left no personal reminiscences.

Willis achieved eminence in two broad areas of activity – first, engineering and mechanics, second, architectural scholarship. Crucially, the former informed the latter. By age 20 he was taking clocks apart, developing a new form of pedal for harps, and figuring out how a chess-playing machine was operated. He was also analysing buildings, understanding how *they* were put together and producing accurate and beautiful drawings of them. Willis went up to Cambridge in 1822, graduated in 1826 and secured fellowships at Gonville & Caius College. He pursued his interests as a 'scientist' (to use the term coined in 1834 by his friend and colleague, the great William Whewell), and in 1837 was appointed as Jacksonian Professor of Natural & Experimental Philosophy, a post that embraced a range of scientific subjects. But, beyond this day-job, it is for architectural history and structural analysis that he was most regarded in his lifetime and since. He published his first architectural work, *Remarks on the Architecture of the Middle Ages, especially of Italy* (1835) which introduced terms still in use today, such as dying mouldings, radiating chapels, tracery bars and compound piers. Without such a vocabulary it would be impossible to describe buildings: Buchanan notes Willis's influence on Ruskin whose diaries from 1846 began to incorporate his new terms.

Willis's method, more than any previous architectural writer, was based on the inductive, evidence-based principle, proceeding from observed fact, and, especially in his case, textual sources, to achieve a higher level of understanding. For ecclesiologists its crowning achievement was the great series of cathedral studies beginning in the mid-1840s with Canterbury and Winchester and which are masterpieces of clarity and insight. These mostly grew out of his visits for Archaeological Institute meetings when his inspirational lecturing was a star draw (his lectures to London artisans in the 1850s could have sold twice the 600 tickets available!): he often used models that he had designed and constructed. His greatest literary achievement was the three-volume *The Architectural History of the University of Cambridge* eventually published by his nephew in 1886 after extensive revision. Among other achievements were the publication of the ninth-century plan of Saint-Gall in Switzerland (1848) and the thirteenth-century album of Villard de Honnecourt (1859) for English readers, a reconstruction of the plan of the Church of the Holy Sepulchre in Jerusalem (*c*.1849), and advising on restorations and some new buildings (his only complete building was a (demolished) cemetery chapel at Wisbech designed in 1841 and as perfect a piece of ecclesiological propriety as anything erected at the time).

For most readers the name of Robert Willis is probably much less known than those of Pugin, Ruskin or the Cambridge Camden Society who are described by Buchanan as 'vehemently activist' (which they most certainly were). But the 'quieter' Willis helped underpin their work and his methods in structural archaeology remain in use today, as the book's Afterword explains. It is superbly researched and brings to the fore a major figure to whom all ecclesiologists and archaeologists have good reason to be grateful.

Geoff Brandwood

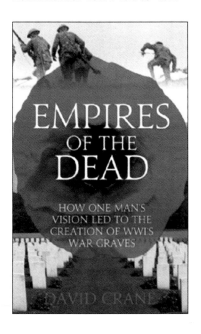

David Crane, *Empires of the Dead: How one man's vision led to the creation of WWI's War Graves*. William Collins, 2013, 289 pp., 27 b&w pls, £16.99 hdbk, ISBN 978 0 00 745665 9

This is a graphic account of how a traumatized society came to terms with the First World War's death, grief, pride and anger. The unprecedented scale of the carnage and the evolution of a coping strategy covering such horrendous loss is well outlined. David Crane's book singles out one man's role in coming to terms with the scale of the slaughter and the debt owed to thousands. Fabian Ware is seen as central to establishing the Graves Registration Commission. In time this became the Imperial, and then, the Commonwealth War Graves Commission.

Strangely it fell to Ware, as the former editor of the *Morning Post*, to pull together a diverse group of architects, politicians, soldiers and writers, amongst others, to remember the fallen, in a fitting and appropriate way. In essence, the book is a timely history of a visionary commemorative movement.

From 1905 onwards Ware's editorial hand built up numerous informal, world-wide networks. By recruiting people such as William Beveridge and, by being a shrewd executive, he demonstrated a unique range of organizational skills. These attributes were recognized in 1914 when he was appointed Commander of the Mobile Ambulance Unit. Ware developed this *ad hoc* role in caring for the missing, killed or buried well beyond that of a small scale amateur agency. His considerable tact, as well as very real administrative expertise was widely recognized and lead to the establishment of the Graves Registration Commission(GRC) with, needless to say, Ware at the helm. The GRC turned out to be a wonderfully Anglo-Saxon *ad hoc* hybrid. In many ways this was a semi-detached body with the Red Cross supplying men and vehicles alongside the Army covering the costs of crosses, rations and fuel. Eventually the Army absorbed the whole organization under Ware's leadership. Thanks, in large part to his considerable talents, many highly memorable and greatly acclaimed cemeteries were opened throughout the world.

What stands out is the simple fact that there is no such thing as a standard or typical 'Commission' cemetery. The leading roles of the likes of Baker, Blomfield and Lutyens, not to mention Stanley Spencer, all played a part in establishing a vast imaginative remembrance identity. The central, and often critical, role of Lutyens' work is thoroughly examined too. His temporary Whitehall Cenotaph not only guaranteed a permanent replacement but, in turn, generated a myriad of well appreciated variations. The miracle is that, despite vested interests, so much was achieved. Whatever the enormity of the task, the narrative conveys the monumental scale of marking such horrendous loss. In these circumstances it is remarkable that so many outstanding and highly distinctive places of pilgrimage were achieved, often with memorable architecture and landscaping of the highest sensitivity.

Above all this is a moving tribute to the legions who gave their lives, but also to the many agencies who sought to appropriately honour their memory. Sadly the text calls out for a really comprehensive set of relevant photographs as evocative as those provided by Skelton and Gliddon in their 2008 *Lutyens and the Great War*. This aside the book is profoundly moving account which is very much recommended.

John Taylor, Higher Education International

Becky Payne, *Churches for Communities: Adapting Oxfordshire's Churches for Wider Use*. Oxfordshire Historic Churches Trust, 2014, 135 pp., many col. pls, £15.00 pbk, ISBN 978 0 9927693 0 7

'Quietly, without, on the whole, a great deal of fuss, we are currently seeing the greatest alterations to the interiors of our churches since the late nineteenth century'. So writes the Rt Revd Colin Fletcher, Bishop of Dorchester, the originator of this well written and candid study of recent changes to a nicely balanced selection of (mainly) Church of England parish churches in Oxfordshire. It has been researched and written by Becky Payne whose career in English Heritage and the Church Buildings Council amply qualifies her for the task.

Twenty five examples are described and well illustrated though only three have plans. All but two are Church of England parish churches; eight are market town buildings, two are in Oxford itself, three are small, un-aisled village churches and ten follow the standard plan of west tower, aisled nave and chancel. Beyond the three Oxford examples, they are set in communities ranging from the 27,000 of Witney to the 100 of Elsfield. Most have concentrated on reorganising their naves by replacing pews and platforms with a flat floor (perhaps with underfloor heating) and stackable seating, adding a toilet and kitchen or servery. This process has become familiar across the country, thankfully replacing the late twentieth century fashion for curiously shaped extensions.

Each study briefly describes the building in its community and outlines the project, but devotes most space to the 'realisation' of the project, extensively quoting those most involved as client or user. It is the honesty of the contributors and the range of possibilities for change demonstrated in the case studies that make this book particularly valuable to any congregation wanting advice and inspiration to adapt their building. The architect's name is not always given and their views are rarely heard, which is a pity. Their comments might have formed a fourth concluding point, after the short end pieces 'Challenges, Lessons learned and Best piece of advice'. The common threads these produce are summarised by Becky Payne in her perceptive Introduction.

In my 2012 *Ecclesiology Today*, vol. 45 article I anticipated the Bishop of Dorchester's views but also outlined some of the pitfalls of working with the wider community. This is most often expressed in opposition to changes like the removal of pews (a recurring element in these case studies). It is frequently the change of internal character, rather than loss of significant fabric or fittings, that fuels opposition and statements of significance required for faculty applications often fail to distinguish between these two qualities. Pews will be dismissed as poor quality, catalogue work and whilst intrinsically true, their combined spatial value and contribution to the character of the church will only be mentioned in negative terms.

Becky Payne is right to suggest that more research is needed into 'whether or how we can measure what these projects are delivering'. It seems clear that whilst the community's engagement with the church building increases with use, that does not extend to an increase in church attendance. The meshing together of worship and social uses, originally accepted perhaps to raise funds, can also set up tensions beyond the mundane issues of who is responsible for what. The Witney vision of their church as 'The Venue' catering for weddings and conferences is a long way from the Hook Norton view that 'if we are not careful, all thoughts of it being a sacred place about God can easily be lost by people who just come in and use it as another venue'. Is Bishop Colin right to think these changes have emerged from 'fresh theological thinking' or are they simply pursued to avoid redundancy – 'the challenge is to use our churches or lose them' (Stratton Audley)? We shall see.

Richard Halsey, Chairman, Ely DAC

Short Notes

Lida Cardozo Kindersley and David Meara, Remembered *Lives: Personal Memorials in Churches*. Cambridge University Press, 2013, 84 pp., many col. pls, £12.00 pbk, ISBN 978 1 107 66448 7

In this engaging little book, the authors set out the case for a better understanding of personal memorials and the importance of maintaining this important tradition into the twenty-first century. The tradition flourished in Britain for over a thousand years, but it is of great concern to the authors – a prominent cleric and an eminent stone carver and letter cutter – that the future of this ancient art is by no means secure. 'The long tradition of personal commemoration is under threat from changing public attitudes and from a more hidden attitude in the Church of England, in turn making it increasingly difficult to maintain this tradition and the craft skills that go with it' writes Ms Kindersley. As well as examining a series of important historic examples, there is much emphasis on recent ones, and the book discusses in some detail the practical steps towards commissioning new memorials. In addition to the absorbing text, the book is an elegant model of modern book design and a pleasure to read.

Jon Cannon, *Medieval Church Architecture*. Shire Publications, 2014, 96 pp., many col. pls, £8.95 pbk, ISBN 978 0 74781 212 8

Thomas Rickman would be interested to know that the classification of English medieval architecture that he first proposed in 1817 remains alive and largely unchallenged. It forms the basis of this excellent architectural primer from Shire which, despite its compact form, clearly and comprehensively sets out the key aspects of the subject, and is richly illustrated throughout. It does not set out to break new ground, but it is, undoubtedly, the ideal starting point for a new generation of church visitors and has much to commend it.

The Ecclesiological Society

The Ecclesiological Society is for all those who love churches, and are interested in their fabric, furnishings and use. The Society was founded in 1879, as a successor to the Cambridge Camden Society of 1839. It has a lively programme, including various lectures, an annual conference, and visits to churches at a range of locations in the UK. Members receive the Society's periodical, *Ecclesiology Today*, twice a year.

Membership is open to all. For further details, see the Society's website at www.ecclsoc.org, or write to the Hon. Membership Secretary at the address given overleaf.

Contributions to *Ecclesiology Today*

The Editor is always pleased to receive articles for consideration for publication in *Ecclesiology Today*, or suggestions for proposed contributions, whether fully worked out or at an early stage in development. The Society wishes to encourage less-experienced authors, and the Editor is happy to provide informal support and guidance to those in this position.

In furtherance of the Society's aims, articles should promote 'the study of the arts, architecture and liturgy of the Christian Church'. They may be historical in nature, or reflect contemporary matters. They need not be restricted in time, place or denomination, and although in practice a significant number deal with Church of England churches, in recent years a wider range of material has been covered, a trend which it is wished to encourage. Articles dealing with individual buildings are welcome, although the Editor will expect the discussion to highlight matters of wider significance. The Society's interests cover a very wide field, and it is therefore important that articles should be written in a way which can be understood by anyone with a general interest in churches.

Most articles are objective and factual, but there is the opportunity for well-argued personal views on matters of general interest to be put forward in the occasional 'Viewpoint' series.

Prospective authors are invited to communicate with the Editor at the earliest possible stage. There is no formal process of refereeing, but articles will usually be sent to one or more readers for an independent opinion before acceptance for publication, and eventual publication may be dependent upon the author making such modifications as the Editor, in consultation with the readers, may recommend.

Proposed contributions should preferably be submitted by email. They should be prepared in accordance with the style guide, available on the Society's website or by application to the Editor. Authors are reminded that they are responsible for any fees and permissions required for the reproduction of illustrations.

Books for review should be sent to the Reviews Editor. Material for *Church Crawler* should be sent to the News Editor.